THE
BIONIC
BULLRIDER

MY LIFE STORY

BARRY BROWN

First Edition

ISBN #978 0 9790919 1 9

Dedicated to Lorayne, Ronnie, and my three grown children: Sandy Kaye, Barry Lee, and Dixie Ann, whom I dearly love. And to David Smith

Chapter One

Lord, help me! I called out, as I was being drug to death.

I thought about my daughter Sandy, who was in school not far from the field where I was about to meet my fate. I thought about my wife Margaret, who was working in town. I realized I was never going to see either of them again.

I rode rough stock, mainly bulls, for 28, years. I had wire holding my collar bone together. I nearly choked to death on my own tongue once, after being knocked out by a Brahma. I was named PRCA Comeback Cowboy of the Year in 1971. I had been an NFR qualifier. An article in the Orlando Sentinel dubbed me the Bionic Bull Rider, because of a history making operation I received to repair my sternum, which had been split in half by a bull. I continued to rodeo that way for more than two years, before undergoing the surgery.

After all of that, this was how it was going to end: being drug to death behind my saddle horse, Cruise Control.

Sandy Kaye, who was then six, had been after me to get a Christmas tree. December 8th. 1981, I dropped her off at Hooper Academy in Hope Hull, Alabama where she attended school. I returned home to saddle Cruise. He was a big bay horse, standing at 16.1 hands. After grabbing a handsaw we headed for the woods. What may have proven to be my final ride began down a blacktop road, about a half mile from the house, then crossing a large field putting me at least a mile from home. There was a 35, foot wide section cut out from the woods back to Interstate 65, which runs from Mobile thru Montgomery. It was there that I found the perfect Christmas tree.

Slipping one end of my six foot long rope over the saddle horn, I then tied the other end to the tree I had just cut down. Climbing back into the saddle, with the saw in my right hand while holding the reins in my left, I nudged the horse with my heels. After taking just a step or two, Cruise Control blew straight into the air, and wheeled around to the left. He did this so quickly, it left me standing way out on his left side, with my one foot still in the stirrup. My right leg was across the seat of the saddle, and I could feel the weight of the tree on the rope against it.

Quickly dropping the saw from my right hand, I grabbed the saddle horn. I was pulling leather. With my free hand, I grabbed the left rein close to the bit and pulled the horse's head around. With it tucked, he would be unable to run off. I was trying to slide back into the saddle, but Cruise kept leaping, and swung his hind quarters to the right, away from me, preventing me from being able to get back into the saddle. Falling to the ground, I landed on my back. My hand, which was still holding the rein, pulled Cruise over the top of me. This caused the 1,200 lb. horse to step on my chest. With both front legs standing squarely on the top of the chest, I turned the reins loose, and Cruise took off.

The rope, which was still tied to the Christmas tree and the saddle horn, had become wrapped around my right leg when I fell off. Cruise was dragging me, along with the tree; and he was running faster and faster.

Whoa Cruise! Whoa! I yelled. He was headed for home and was so spooked from the tree he responded by running harder, and faster. Thoughts were popping into my head about how once we reached the blacktop the hide would be peeled from my body. I managed to pull myself up far enough where I could grab hold of the rope with my right hand. I pulled the rope as hard as I could, trying to break it somehow, but it was useless. The rope was nylon and with the honda over the horn, there was no way it was going to break or come free. At times, the tree was spinning around with my body. Cruise was running really hard, and my back kept popping off the ground. I was pulling so hard on the rope that when I lost my grip my right arm flew back behind me. I had tried everything I could think of and now I was too weak to try anything else; I couldn't save myself.

Again, I thought about how I was going to be killed. After everything I had lived through I would die alone killed by a gentle saddle horse and a Christmas tree.

I shouted out, Lord, help me! As soon as I called out to the Lord, the rope broke. Cruise kept going, and ran home.

I could see my right arm stretched out beside me, my palm facing up. It was then that I noticed the end of my ring finger was gone, and there were pieces of skin sticking out where it used to be and covered with blood. I had been pulling so hard on the rope it pulled the end of my finger off. I turned my head away, afraid I may go into shock if I looked at my hand any longer.

I was in tremendous pain and unable to move. Knowing my ribs were broken from Cruise standing on my chest, I dared not try getting up; worrying that doing so may result in a punctured lung. Laying there in the clearing, moaning in pain, taking a breath became an effort, I began to think. Survival being instinct I thought about how nobody knew where I was or what had just happened. If I didn't force myself to get up and get some help, I would probably end up dying anyways. I managed to roll over and get to my feet. Being unable to stand up normally I began walking bent over holding my left side with my right hand, heading towards the blacktop.

I could barely walk; the muscles in my right leg were torn from the rope that had been wrapped around it. Looking across the field to see how much further I had to walk, I knew there was no way I could make it. Instinctively I was headed back towards the house. Then, I heard the traffic. Looking behind me I could see vehicles passing by on I-65. I thought I might be able to make it that far. Turning around very carefully, holding my side still having trouble breathing, I began to limp very slowly.

I kept saying, Lord, help me. Lord, help me. As I entered into the clearing, my eyes began to water profusely. My vision became so blurred; I was unable to see anything. The sun was shining into my eyes; I knew that the darkness on either side must be the woods. As long as I followed the light, I would be headed in the right direction.

I kept moving forward repeating, Lord, help me. My vision returned. I was almost at the interstate. Then, I came to a fence. How am I going to get over this fence? I asked myself. Reaching up taking hold of the top strand of wire I said again, Lord help me. Pulling myself up onto the fence I climbed over it very slowly.

I reached the pavement, still doubled over, and was on the northbound side of the Interstate. There wasn't any traffic coming on my side. Standing bent over, stretching my hand out in front of me, I began waving to the traffic across the wide grassy median. I was hoping someone would notice the blood all over my hand. I could see the southbound truckers looking, as they passed by. I kept waving my hand saying, help me help me, but no one stopped. I didn't blame them though, as I knew I looked a sight, probably looking more like I was drunk than injured.

Finally, there was traffic coming on my side. Still bent over I began waving my right hand saying, help me. Help me. No one would stop. By now, I was so weak, I dropped to my knees. I kept waving my arm, while holding my side. No one stopped. Growing weaker, and weaker, I fell over onto my back, unable to get up. With my elbow on the pavement, and my right hand still in the air, I continued waving my hand, hoping to get someone's attention.

At last, I could hear a car slowing down, as it passed me by. I listened, and then heard a car door close. A man's voice asked what's wrong? Looking over my shoulder, I saw him standing at his car. What's the matter? He asked.

With great effort, I managed to roll over and get to my feet. Taking one step I fell over. Then the Good Samaritan walked back to where I was laying. When I saw him standing over me, I asked him to call an ambulance.

He left right then, so I thought he was going to the next exit to call for help. Instead, he returned to lay his jacket over me. Then, he said, don't worry I won't leave you.

He stood beside me, trying to get someone to stop. I kept thinking to myself, go ahead, leave me, get some help. I don't mind being left alone, but I was unable to tell him, because I could hardly breathe.

After a little while, a car stopped and I listened to the man telling the driver to call an ambulance. The driver left, and sometime later, two state troopers arrived. They asked if there was anyone I wanted them to call, I managed to tell them my wife's name and where she worked.

There just happened to be an empty ambulance passing by on its way to Montgomery. The ambulance stopped, and I listened as the driver asked if the troopers needed any help. No, we have an ambulance on the way. One of them said.

The driver told the troopers, if they didn't need them, they were going to leave. Again, the troopers said, no... We have one coming. Ok, then, they said as they drove away.

Wait! Don't leave me here! I was thinking to myself. Without enough air in me to speak, the ambulance drove away. I couldn't believe it. I just kept thinking, don't leave me! Don't leave me! I reckon, since I was unable to tell those troopers just how bad a shape I was in, they didn't realize how bad off I really was.

When my ambulance arrived, the medical personnel bandaged my finger, and then began wrapping my neck. I wanted to tell them, there wasn't anything wrong with the neck, just get me to the hospital. Finally, they strapped me onto a flat, hard board, which made my ribs hurt even more.

Upon arrival at Jackson Hospital in Montgomery, I was unloaded from the ambulance. Margaret came running out of the emergency room screaming, you're alive! You're alive!

As I was rolled into the hospital, a doctor began removing the bandage from my hand. I looked up at Margaret and told her she had better leave, as she wouldn't want to see my finger.

I can take anything now, knowing you're not dead. she said. The call she had received only said that I had been in an accident with my horse, on the Interstate. She hadn't been told whether I was alive or dead. Margaret presumed I must have been hit by a semi truck.

When the doctor pulled the bandage from my hand, revealing what was left of the finger, Margaret gave out a big sigh as her knees buckled. The doctor caught her before she hit the floor. Then, he helped her out to a chair in the hall. He returned and began working on my finger again. By now, it was throbbing and hurting worse than the ribs.

I spent two days in the hospital, and then went home. Besides the partially missing finger, I had five broken ribs, and a collapsed lung, which had to be tapped. Plus, when the horse stepped on me, it broke one of the wires inside my chest.

A neighbor came to visit me at the hospital, telling me he seen the horse running on the road. He followed the horse back to the barn, where he unsaddled him, and put him up. My neighbor said he thought perhaps I was hurt, when he saw the horse running with an empty saddle, but had no way of knowing where to look for me. Had he seen the horse before it crossed the field, he would have found me.

Margaret brought the tree home, but she couldn't find the piece of finger. We had a lot to be thankful for that Christmas. Every year since then, I take the truck to get a tree.

Two years later, I went to the barn to feed the horses, and found Cruise dead. He had coliced in the night. Cruise Control was a good horse. Margaret qualified for the Southeast Circuit Finals, among the top fifteen barrel racers, competing on him.

Chapter Two

No one knows in this life who, when, where, or how certain things might influence their future...

Born and raised in the small town of Owosso, Michigan, the likelihood of becoming a professional rodeo cowboy; wasn't likely. My parents were Walter and Alice Brown; they had ten head of children. There were seven boys and three girls. Five of the boys rode bulls and became rodeo cowboys. Besides me, they are Ronnie, Lyle, Curt, and Dallas. Our youngest brother Darrell, the last born, became a jockey riding Thoroughbred racehorses.

My oldest brother Walter Arnold Junior, (aka) Arnold, quit high school after our grandpa Brown died when he was sixteen. He loved the farm life, and moved to the country to live with Grandma Brown, and worked for our Uncle Martin on the farm. Arnold married and bought his own farm in Shiawassee County when I was twelve. He now has a four thousand acre spread in Little River County, Arkansas, where he runs cattle on another five hundred acres. Lorayne was the only one of the three girls to become a cowgirl, she was the cause of all us boys getting into rodeo.

Lorayne's first love, from an early age, was flying. She began by joining the civil air patrol as a teenager; she scored 100% on her meteorology test resulting in a free first flying lesson. Soon she became a pilot, soloing at the young age of 16, before she could even drive a car. One weekend she heard of a rodeo in town and decided to go. Little did she know this simple decision would change her life, and impact so many more.

Lorayne was intrigued by the girls trick riding, wishing she could do something like that for a living. She just knew she would love it, everything about it fit in with her; she was a farm girl and could actually work (if you call something you love work) outside. She made her way around to talk to the girls who had been trick riding. Shirley Adams Biron told her to follow her dreams. Lorayne was referred to George Adams ranch near Indianapolis. Come spring, she had quit her job at Douglas Trucking Lines as assistant office manager and followed her dreams to the George Adams ranch. While there she learned ranch work and horseback riding.

She began her rodeo career when the Cherokee Hammond Wild West Show came to Indianapolis. She mounted her first saddle bronc at the very first show. Then Ed Davis taught Lorayne all the handholds men used for their trick and fancy riding. He also taught his wife to ride and she won competitions in Madison Square Garden's in New York.

Lorayne 1953

Lorayne

In 1957, she was found to have TB, and was put in a private TB, hospital for six months, taking four more years to totally get well it ended her rodeo riding, but never her desire to do it again. She then went back to her first love, flying, and became a Commercial Pilot with a flight instructor rating. Her son, Frank, named after Frank Biron, also rode bulls by the time he was 14. One time a bull tossed its head back catching Frank in the mouth, knocking out his front tooth. Raised in the rodeo, Lorayne says Frank cut his teeth on a saddle horn.

If it were not for rodeo, I would have more than likely ended up on an automobile assembly line, somewhere in Michigan for most of my life. There is no doubt, becoming a rodeo cowboy is the best thing that ever happened to me.

Chapter Three

When I was seven years old my mother moved us to St. Johns, Michigan. The stockyard was only two blocks from our home. When we walked to town, my brothers Lyle and Curt would cut through the stockyards to make the trip to town a little closer. We enjoyed looking at the livestock in all the pens, where there would be cattle, sheep, and hogs.

The sale was on Fridays and would last late into the night. Every Saturday morning Lyle, Curt, and I would go to the stockyards where several of the pens would be full of sheep. We would climb into those pens, and grab a sheep then hop on its back to ride it. The sheep would run like crazy with us on their back, then they would make a quick turn and we would fall off, rolling as we hit the ground. We would be laughing as it was so much fun. Then we would grab another sheep to ride.

When we tired of the sheep we would make our way to the sale ring where there usually were a few huge sows left in the ring from the night before. After climbing into the ring we would hop on one of the sows to ride em' but the sows wouldn't move. I don't remember which one of us came up with the idea, but we went to the store and bought the largest safety pin they had. Then we returned to the sale ring, and after getting on one of the sows, we would stick it in the butt with the pin. The sow would take off, running and squealing all the way. Riding those animals at the stockyards was so much fun.

Little did we know at the time, we would end up becoming rodeo cowboys.

At the age of nine I witnessed my first rodeo during summer vacation. My sister Lorayne, took Lyle and me with her to a Wild West show in Iron Mountain, Michigan which is in the Upper Peninsula. The Mackinaw Bridge wasn't built yet, so we took a huge freighter ship to get from Lower Michigan to the Upper Peninsula. From what I remember, it took several hours to cross the lake. As I was watching dozens of railroad cars and automobiles being loaded into the ship, including my sister's old pickup truck, horse, and trailer. I began thinking there was no way this huge boat could float, and I would drown as it sank half way across.

I believe Cliff Gatewood was the owner and stock contractor of this Wild West show. One of the cowboys working for him was Duke Jenson, who had a nine year old daughter by the name of Julie, and I had a big crush on her. One day Julie and I and a couple other rodeo kids were playing when a boy around my age who lived in Iron Mountain, came out to the rodeo grounds and was flirting with Julie. We ended up in a fist fight and I whooped him good. This would be the only time I got to go to a Gatewood Wild West show, and I never saw Julie again.

A year later brother Ronnie who was sixteen, wanted Lorayne to take him with her.

Our parents divorced, and Ronnie was living with our father in a small apartment above a bar in Owosso. Lorayne wanted Ronnie to stay home and finish high school first. Ronnie told her he was quitting school anyways and convinced her to let him go for the summer. He really enjoyed the Wild West shows and decided he would like to be a rodeo cowboy. Ronnie began riding bareback broncs, saddle broncs, bulls, and bull dogging/steer wrestling at the Wild West shows.

Three years later he began entering rodeos competing for prize money. I was twelve years old now, and Ronnie would take me with him sometimes. Arriving at the rodeo grounds in the middle of the night, we would sleep in the car or on the ground. When we would awake, there would be an aroma of coffee in the air. Several cowboys who had their families with them would have a camp fire with the coffee pot on. They would also cook up bacon and eggs. We were always invited to join them. I really enjoyed going to the rodeos, and began thinking about how one day I was going to be a rodeo cowboy.

The Wild West shows were a good place for a young cowboy to learn how to ride. There weren't any rodeo schools in those days. Wild West shows were seven days a week and many times there would be two performances a day. The same horses and bulls were bucked every performance, so most of them didn't buck very well. They were somewhat like a traveling carnival, as the cowboys had to do all the work, such as putting up the arena fence, then setting up the bucking chutes and livestock pens. They also fed and watered the rough stock and rode them. Of course they were supposed to get paid, but when a show didn't make any money the cowboys weren't paid. Many a time, the cowboy had to go hungry, but never considered quitting. There were many days I went hungry and never once did I ever think of quitting, as you will find out later in this book.

Photo by Jerry Gustofasan

Chapter Four

When I was fifteen, my mother and her sister took me to a Wild West show in Saginaw, Michigan to watch my brother Ronnie ride. Arriving at the rodeo grounds, my mother was attempting to drive through the entrance where Ronnie told her to go, when a cop stopped her. He told her only rodeo contestants could enter through the gate. Mother told him her son was riding in the rodeo. The cop looked into the back seat at me and then said; well he must be good, because you have to be good to ride in this rodeo.

He sure is she replied as he let us through. Mom didn't realize the cop was referring to me as being the real good rider.

This would be where my rodeo career would begin. When it was getting close to bull riding time, Ronnie asked if I wanted to get on a bull. Not wanting him to think I was scared, I said ok. I had no idea I would be getting on a bull that night, I was pretty spooked. My brother was telling me how to put my hand in the bull rope as the bull was being loaded into the chute. He also told me I needed to turn my toes out, and watch the bull's head. Ronnie had me put his bull riding spurs on my boots while he put his rope on the animal. Then I climbed up the chute gate and lowered myself onto the bull's back. I was so nervous I forgot how Ronnie told me to put my hand in the rope. I grabbed the handhold, which was braided into the rope, like

I would grab anything else. Ronnie slapped the back of my hand hard.

I told you how to put your hand in there, now turn it over! He said gruffly. Turning the hand over I slid it into the handhold with the palm facing up. Ronnie was standing on the chute gate with the tail of the rope in hand.

After pulling the rope tight, he wrapped it around the back of my hand, and across my palm. Then I closed my hand tight, and slid up close to the rope. The chute gate was opened, and when the bull leaped from the chute, I blanked out. I didn't remember anything until three or four seconds later when I hit the ground. I landed on my left side, jabbing an elbow into my ribs, which knocked all the air out of me. Ronnie had me by an arm as he was helping me up. Are you all right? He asked. I was trying to catch my breath, and said Ya, ya, yeah!

Jerry Partlow, the owner of the Diamond P Wild West Show, paid five-dollars for getting on the bull. Getting on that bull and trying to ride him was the most fun I ever had. I was so excited I didn't realize it at the time, but I was bitten by the rodeo bug, big time. I decided right then and there rodeoing was all I ever wanted to do.

On our way home my mother was telling me I was not going to be a rodeo cowboy. She was mighty mad at Ronnie for putting me on that bull. She told me how scared she was when she heard the rodeo announcer say, our next bull rider will be young Barry Brown who is only fifteen years old. Rodeo fans, this is Barry's first attempt at bull riding so give him a hand. I was not listening to a word she was saying.

It was after midnight when we arrived home, my brother Lyle was asleep upstairs. I ran up the stairs as fast as I could go, jumping on top of him yelling, I rode a bull! I rode a bull! I had the five-dollar bill in my hand waving it as I was yelling it out. Lyle and I talked about riding and rodeos the rest of the night. He had already been on a few bulls, and was ready to get on more of 'em.

The following weekend the Diamond P, would be putting on another show at the Ionia County Free Fair, in Ionia, Michigan. Ronnie told Lyle and me he could get us hired on with Diamond P. There was one exception: Ronnie said I would have to be home in time for school. Lyle quit high school the year before, so I told Ronnie there was no way I was going back to school. The heck with school, I am going to rodeo. We got into a big argument, as I stormed out of the house. You're nothing but a bum he screamed at me.

By the end of the week Ronnie was no longer angry with me. Before we left for Ionia, he told Lyle and me we had better pack our suit cases. If Jerry hires y'all, you won't be going home with me. The next day, the three of us were in Ionia riding. I chose the same bull to ride that Ronnie put me on in Saginaw; this time I successfully rode him. I was feeling mighty good now, and felt as if I had conquered the world. After talking with Jerry Partlow about Lyle and me joining up with his outfit, Mr. Partlow agreed to hire us. Ronnie then told Jerry not to let us go hungry. He assured my big brother we would have enough money to eat on. When the last performance was finished, we helped take the arena down, and loaded all the panels, fence wire, and livestock onto the trucks and trailers.

We arrived somewhere in Pennsylvania around 4:00 a.m. and immediately unloaded enough panels to set up corrals so all the livestock could be unloaded, watered, and given hay. The livestock consisted of bareback, and saddle broncs, bulls, calves, and steers. Once they were cared for, we would roll out our bed rolls and sleep a couple hours. After waking we would have to check the stocks water supply and grain them. Then if we had enough time we would walk out to the midway for breakfast.

When we returned, we would unload the buckin' chutes to set them up where they needed to be. Then we would unload all the heavy panels and build the rodeo arena, and pens that would hold all the buckin' stock for the afternoon performance. When it was over, we would tear everything down, load it back onto the trucks and trailers, then drive eighty to one hundred miles, and show again that night in another town. It got to be really nice when we had a two or three day show in the same town.

One night after the rodeo when finished with all the chores, a few of us cowboys went to a diner for something to eat. The waitress brought us all a glass of water then left. None of us could drink the water as it was sulphur water and smelled really bad. When the waitress returned to take our food order, Lyle said to her, we can't stand the smell of your water. Without hesitating the waitress replied, well, we can't stand your smell either. We all cracked up laughing when she said that. None of us realized we smelt bad, even though our clothes were dirty, and smelled of livestock manure. We were as used to that smell as they were their water.

Three weeks later my riding hand was swollen and my right knee was huge from hitting the ground so many times. Still yet, craving that next bull I never considered lying off to heal up. Once I hit the ground from being thrown off another bull, I would limp back to the chutes with my knee and hand throbbing, with tears filling my eyes from the pain. Since I was unable to use the hurt hand or the bad knee to climb the gate, two cowboys would get under me and shove me up the gate. Then I would crawl over and carefully lower myself down on the back of another bull and attempt to ride 'em. I was determined not to let the pain get in my way.

In order to rodeo you have to be able to take pain, if you can't take pain you will never make it in rodeo. This is what Ronnie told me after getting on that first bull in Saginaw. It only took a few weeks for me to understand what he meant.

The Diamond P Wild West shows were a lot of fun, but hard work. Many times we would sleep around a camp fire and one of the cowboys had a guitar. This cowboy's name was Jimmy Rogers, from California; he would pick and sing old cowboy songs. This reminded me of all the westerns I watched at the picture show and on television each weekend. Now I was living a life like they did in the movies and I loved it.

The rodeo announcer for all these shows was Snake Horse Rogers. Braymer Rogers, Snake Horse's brother was the rodeo clown and bull fighter. They were also Jimmy Rogers uncles. These two men were very funny and one of a kind. They were one hundred percent cowboys, through and through.

Movie actor Gabby Hays was traveling with the Diamond P, and was the star of the show. During intermission a stage was set up, and after being introduced to the fans he began telling stories of riding with Roy Rogers in the movies. When I was a little boy I always watched Roy and Gabby every weekend at the movies and later on TV. It was really exciting getting to meet Gabby in person, and to top that off, he was working for the same outfit as me.

A very pretty young lady, by the name of Annabelle, rode side saddle in a horse act. She would be dressed as an Indian princess with full head dress which nearly reached the ground.

When it was time for her last act, a Cadillac convertible was brought into the arena. Riding her horse at a full gallop she would jump the red and white paint over the car.

Wild West shows could be dangerous and injuries not always happened when you would expect. I had seen an act in which a cowboy would lay on the racetrack with a long board over him; another cowboy in a car would come around the track at a high rate of speed driving across the board with the cowboy under it. Then the cowboy under the board would jump up and take a bow. Once, the driver missed the board and ran over the cowboy's legs.

We showed in New York, Delaware, Rhode Island, Connecticut, and Massachusetts after the shows in Pennsylvania. Neither Lyle nor I ever got paid while riding for the Diamond P. However, Jerry Partlow seen to it that we had enough money to eat on, that was all the money we ever got. By the middle of September I was back home in Michigan, but never went back to school.

Chapter Five

During the month of January, 1960, I boarded a Greyhound bus for Gainesville, Florida to spend the winter with Ronnie, and my sister in law Dorothy. She met Ronnie at a Florida rodeo and they had married in 1959. Showing up uninvited at Ronnie's, little did I know they were having financial problems, and the last thing they needed was another mouth to feed.

This would be the first time I had ever been to Florida. During the trip south, the bus made a stop either in Kentucky or Tennessee at a gas station. Unboarding the bus I spotted a water fountain at the front of the station. Upon reaching the fountain for a drink I noticed a sign posted above it, which read, WHITES ONLY. Another sign read, NEGROS IN BACK. The restrooms were the same way. I had never seen anything like that before. Then while passing thru Alabama I noticed most all the small towns had mainly black people, and very few whites. I began thinking, if Southern folks disliked blacks so much, then why are there so many in these small towns? In Michigan it was the opposite. All blacks lived in big cities and you never saw any in a small town. In fact, I was twelve years old before ever seeing a black person when my mother took me to Detroit.

A few weeks later Ronnie had taken me with him to a Rodeo Cowboys Association (RCA) sanctioned rodeo in Jacksonville, Florida. Entered in four events he sustained a knee injury in one of them. Lying on the ground clutching his knee, Ronnie was moaning in agony. Stock contractor Foy Reynolds rushed to check on him. Foy then signaled for the announcer to call the ambulance into the arena. Short of being dead, the last thing a cowboy will allow is to be carried out of the arena on a stretcher or by ambulance. Telling Foy he didn't need the ambulance, Ronnie began to rise.

Ride out in the ambulance and I will give you $25.00 spoke Foy. Ronnie couldn't refuse the offer, and when the ambulance with its lights flashing was out of sight from the spectators, Ronnie had them stop and he got out. Foy had Ronnie do this purely for publicity reasons. The next day an article in the paper read Cowboy injured at the rodeo.

From there we went to a small amateur rodeo in southwest Georgia. The stock contractor was Cherokee Hammond. Ronnie talked to Cherokee about hiring me for his Wild West shows and Cherokee said he could use me. During this rodeo I mounted out a bareback bronc for five-dollars. This would be the first buckin' horse I ever got on. Being used to riding bulls only, I forgot they had pickup men for this event, and soon as the whistle blew I stepped off the bronc, landing on my feet. Right away I thought, oops, they have pick up men for this event.

Before Ronnie left for home, I heard him tell Cherokee to watch out for me, and not let me go hungry. Cherokee assured Ronnie he would take good care of me. Ronnie told me, back in

28

Cherokee's younger days, when he rode saddle broncs; sometimes he would hold his baby daughter in one arm while riding a bronc.

Cherokee and his wife Pearl lived in a trailer on Harry Crumbs ranch in Quitman, Georgia. Cowboys, years before I came along, named the ranch Buzzards Knob. The reason was that it was a place cowboys could come to for a free place to stay during the winter when there weren't many rodeos to go to. Ultimately they would all end up starving to death, and the buzzards would pick their bones clean.

After arriving at Crumb's ranch, Cherokee told me I could stay in the old house on top of the hill which was close to where his trailer was parked. I moved into that old house, which had one large room with three double beds, a bathroom, and a kitchen. There was no gas or heat of any kind, and no blankets or pillows, but I had my bedroll with me. There was a refrigerator in the kitchen, although it didn't work, and there was no stove to cook on, or dishes of any kind. Each day at mealtime, Ms. Pearl would call me to her trailer where she would hand me a plate of food, which I would take back to my room then return the plate after I finished. Sometimes in the middle of the night I would be awakened when several cowboys passing thru on their way to a rodeo, would come in to sleep for a few hours, then leave. I didn't know most of them but they all knew brother Ronnie.

A few weeks later a local cowboy, Larry Jones, arrived at the house asking if I would like to ride to the café with him. Once inside he ordered a coffee, I had a cup of hot chocolate. Taking the cup in my right hand I began to drink. Larry stopped me. Hold the cup in your left hand. There are far fewer left handed people in the world, therefore the cup is drunk from that side far less often and you're less apt to get any germs if it wasn't cleaned well.

I took his advice and still to this day even though I am right handed, I drink from a cup using my left hand, even my own cups.

Larry began telling about another Wild West show I could get hired on with, which would be starting up before Cherokee's outfit. I was tired of sitting around waiting for spring to come and Cherokee's shows to get going. I agreed to meet the foreman of the Circle X Ranch Wild West Show, out of Sykesville, Maryland.

The Circle X was owned by the five-times Light Weight Wrestling Champion of the World back in the 1950's, Johnny Erickson. I was taken out to Walker's horse and mule barn where the foreman for the Circle X was staying in a small travel trailer for the winter. He was buying roping calves and bull doggin' steers for the shows. I was introduced to the straw boss, (foreman) Joe Flores. Joe also knew Ronnie and sister Lorayne. We talked awhile, and then he said he would pay $45, a week to ride bareback horses, bulls, care for the livestock, and set up and tear down the arena. I agreed to hire on with this outfit, but felt bad for Cherokee, as he had been feeding me for several weeks.

Mr. Hammond was upset when I told him I hired on with the Circle X, telling me he had promised Ronnie he would look out for me. I thanked him and left. I knew I could no longer stay in that old house on Buzzards Knob, so I packed my duffel bag and moved out to the sale barn. The only place for me to sleep was in the livestock pens, which had peanut hulls for bedding. Luckily I had a couple of blankets to lie on and cover up with. I hung my green army duffel bag on the board fence. Inside were the blankets, clothes, toiletry items, and rodeo gear. Needless to say, I traveled light.

Every Tuesday was sale day, selling horses and mules. Each week I would have to re pack the duffel bag and move out of my bedroom to make way for the stock. On sale day I would earn a few dollars brushing horses. Following the sale, the pens would be cleaned out and refilled with fresh peanut hulls.

It was February, and those Georgia winter nights were sure cold. In the middle of the night I would wake up soaking wet and freezing. Those fresh peanut hulls would go to getting hot and steam would rise up soaking my blanket. The bathroom at the sale barn was built onto the restaurant with a door to enter it from the outside and was never locked. There was a large hot water heater which stayed on all the time. It was there I would spend the rest of the nights; leaning against the water heater to stay warm.

Making only a few dollars each week brushing horses, there were many days I would go hungry. Someone had told me about a river being around a quarter mile back through the woods behind the sale barn. One night I was pretty hungry and got the bright idea to go fishing for my meal. Upon reaching the river I sat down near the water's edge. With a cane pole in hand I threw the line out into the water. It was a moonlit night and I could see that the water was flowing rapidly. As I continued watching I noticed what I first thought was sticks flowing fast with the strong current. Then I realized those sticks were floating upstream. Springing to my feet I dropped the pole and ran as fast as my legs could go. What I thought were sticks at first were in fact Water Moccasins and there were hundreds of them. I never went back.

I toughed it out that winter while waiting for spring to arrive and the Wild West shows to begin I was able to hang in there purely because of my love for rodeos, and wanting to live the cowboy way of life. While starving that winter, my mother wrote to me about fresh bread and dinner rolls she just baked. I was so hungry I considered eating her letter. I refused to call home for money even though I could not afford food. I figured since I left home on my own, if I couldn't make it on my own, then I should go back home. Going home was the last thing I wanted to do.

By April, a two ton straight truck arrived to pick up a load of steers to carry back to the ranch in Maryland. Two black men drove the truck down to Quitman from the ranch. The side body of this truck was five feet high and wooden. Livestock panels were laid across the top, and fastened down with wire, to prevent the steers from jumping out. When hauling cattle, if one should get down you have to stop and get them up. If you don't, the other cattle will step all over the one that is down severely crippling or killing it. A cowboy was needed to ride back to Maryland with the two black men as they said they wouldn't get in with the steers to get 'em up if one should get down. This load of steers was straight out of the swamps of South Georgia and North Florida. They had never been around people since birth and were very wild with long sharp pointed horns. The other Wild West show hands that were in Quitman refused to ride back to Maryland with the two black men, so I volunteered to ride with them.

This would be my first time to ride in a vehicle with a black man. I rode in the middle between the two of them, but it didn't bother me at all. When a steer was down, the driver would pull off to the side of the road. I would then climb up the side of the truck to the top panels. Unwrap the wire from one corner and move it just far enough to squeeze thru. This proved to be difficult as the steers would be watching me and those directly underneath were throwing their heads up trying to hook me. Reaching down and grabbing the horns of the steers closest to me, I would hold them tight as I dropped down beside them. I had to keep doing this as I worked my way between the steers until I reached the one that was down. Then I would reach down and grab the steer by both horns, and lift its head up, until he got up. Then I would work my way back, climb out, and refasten the top panel. I had to do this several times before arriving at the ranch in Maryland. By this time I had been hit by horns, kicked, and stepped on many times, and was pretty sore but I enjoyed working with the steers.

After getting them unloaded, fed, and watered, I went to the bunk room and went to bed. It felt really good to finally get to sleep in a real bed, and it was warm too.

Two weeks later the rest of the hands arrived at the ranch. One of the shows was held at a baseball park on the ball field in Allentown, Pennsylvania. The grandstands had a high concrete wall, which was used for one side of the arena fence, leaving only one fence for us to put up to complete the arena. Most Wild West shows were held at fairgrounds on the dirt racetracks, or ball fields which were never plowed up. Since the dirt was not worked, the ground would be extremely hard.

While attempting to ride a bareback bronc I was thrown off, with my back slamming against the concrete wall. As I fell to the ground, all the air was knocked out of me. Unable to catch my breath, I laid there in extreme pain, moaning and groaning. A few cowboys ran to help me when I heard Joe Flores say to them, he's all right, he is just grandstanding. Meaning, I was faking, just so the spectators would think I was hurt. Some guys do grandstand, they are called goofs, and aren't around rodeos very long.

That night while sleeping under one of the livestock trailers, it began to rain. The floor of the trailer had not been cleaned, and was covered with manure. When the floor became saturated from the all the water, it began to drip thru the cracks of the wooden floor onto me, waking me up. Grabbing my blankets, I moved into the ball players' locker room which had a cement floor. I slept on that hard floor with only one blanket under me with my back hurting all night long. By the next day I was barely able to move. Not having any money, I was unable to see a doctor. For the next two weeks I was unable to ride or work at all. Then I began riding bulls again and helping set up the arena. It hurt my back to carry the heavy panels but I did it anyways. Two years later my back was still bothering me so I had x rays taken, and was told I had a cracked vertebrae. Don't reckon I was grandstanding after all!

We ended up in the mountains of Northeastern Pennsylvania at some fairgrounds, where we set the arena up on a racetrack. There had been a stock car race the night before and that track was hard as cement. Again we weren't allowed to cut it up at all. The bottom of my feet would sting from the rock hard track after stepping off a bull. We were told there weren't any more shows booked after the last performance...we had nowhere to go.

Come to find out the man who was hired to book all the shows for the summer, cut out. He was paid $2,000 in advance, now nobody knew where he was. We were told we would be staying there until more shows were booked.

There were only five of us cowboys left to do all the riding, roping, and all the other work it took to put on a Wild West show. None of us had any money; in fact, the most I was paid since joining up with the Circle X was five-dollars.

A burger a day is all I had to eat for several weeks. I would wash my clothes in a bucket of cold water with a bar of soap, and hang em' over a fence to dry. Before joining that first outfit, the Diamond P, Ronnie told me to wash my clothes, say yes sir, no sir, yes ma'am, no ma'am, and people would think more of me. I always did as my big brother instructed.

Each morning we would turn all the stock out so they could graze on the grass, where there was a large field with no fence around it. Three of us would have to stand around the field all day to watch the livestock making sure none of them wandered off. The older cowboys got to ride the only saddle horses. We had to stand all day long, even in the rain, so the stock could eat, and all we got was one meal a day. At least we got to sleep with a roof over our heads. It was one of the livestock barns at the fairgrounds with a nice pile of straw in it.

Charlie Jackson, aka Hump, had taken one of the trucks to Baltimore for repairs. When he returned, Hump handed Joe an envelope. It wasn't until three or four years later when I learned there were five-ten-dollar bills in the envelope. This money was to be given to the five of us, so we would be able to eat; while waiting for the next show.

Back then you could buy lunch including your drink for eighty five cents. Instead of giving us the money though, Joe sent his wife Betty to the store to buy hamburger meat and macaroni. Betty would cook a big pot of goulash each day, and when it was ready; she called us one at a time to come eat. We received one plate of goulash for the next seven days. When I learned about the money in the envelopes a few years later, I vowed I would beat the living daylights out of Joe Flores the next time our paths crossed.

One day someone from the ranch arrived seeking volunteers to work in the hay fields, back at the Circle X ranch. By this time I was ready to get out of there, and volunteered to work, we were told we would be paid extra. I worked in the fields all day long for the next week. We would load the hay wagons, and then ride them to the barn where we would unload and stack the hay bales. Within seven long days the job was finished, and I received $10 dollars for my pay. I couldn't believe that was all they paid for a week of really hard work, but I didn't say anything. During the time, I slept in the bunk house at the ranch.

It had been well over a year since leaving home and now I was ready to return. Going hungry for so long and working for next to nothing surely contributed in my decision and I was unbelievably quite homesick. The next day the bosses wife and daughter were going shopping in Baltimore. I asked if she would let me ride with them, and drop me off at the bus station. That night I packed my duffle bag, happy to know I was finally going home. During the ride into town, I began thinking about home and mom. It was then when I arrived at the Greyhound bus station; I asked the man at the ticket window how much it would cost for a ticket to Owosso, Michigan. Telling me it would take $34.00 to get me there, I asked, how far ten dollars would get me. For $9.20, you can get a ticket to Pittsburg he replied. I told the teller I would take it. After receiving the ticket, I put it into my back pocket, located a seat and never moved until the bus arrived an hour later.

After handing the driver my bag, he tossed it into the luggage area. Then I got in line to board the bus. When it was my turn I reached into the pocket for my ticket, but it was gone. Asking the driver to wait, I ran back into the station to the seat where I had been sitting. Looking all around on the floor, and in the seat, there was no ticket to be found. I returned to the window and found the same man who sold it to me. I lost my ticket to Pittsburg; how about giving me another one? I asked.

Boy! I'm not giving you any ticket; it would come out of my pocket he told me. Returning to the bus I had the driver hand me my bag.

With the duffel bag slung over my shoulder, I began walking to the nearest gas station: When I got the map, which was free in those days, I saw that I needed to get to U.S. Highway #1. I asked the attendant for directions. With several blocks to walk to get to the highway, and since I didn't have a thing to eat yet that day: I was getting awfully hungry. When I came across a small grocery store, I bought a pint of milk and a lunch cake. This left me with just twenty cents in my pocket and still six hundred miles from home.

Several hours later I was in northern Pennsylvania, standing in the rain beside the highway, when a semi stopped to give me a ride. As I climbed into the truck, I saw the driver was a black man. Hi, I said to him. I'm going to Michigan.

Well, I am going to Toledo, Ohio! I was delighted to hear this as Toledo borders the Michigan State line. I was amazed as I sat there watching this driver changing gears. His truck had eighteen forward gears. When we were climbing a hill, he would have both hands on the two gearshifts; which were next to each other mounted on the floor to the driver's right and he was steadily changing gears. At the same time he was pushing the right gear shift forward, he would pull the left one back. Back and forth his hands would go, changing one gear after the other. After topping the hill and headed back down, both his hands would be back on the shifters steadily changing gears.

Late that afternoon I began getting really hungry, but I didn't say anything to the driver. Finally, the hunger pains got so bad I had to ask him if he was going to be stopping to eat. He told me about a little drive inn restaurant close to the Pennsylvania turnpike where we would stop to eat. By the time we got to the restaurant I was so hungry I didn't think I would have the strength to climb out of the truck.

As soon as the truck came to a stop in front of the restaurant, I bailed out of the cab, and ran up to the take out window. There were two men in front of me, but I could see a menu mounted on the wall inside and saw they had a nineteen cent hamburger. I was so thrilled to know I would be able to afford something to eat.

As I was standing there waiting to place my order, I began to get very dizzy. Then I broke out into a sweat. I got out of line and walked around the side of the building where there was a bench. I ran to the bench and as I started to flop down on it, I grabbed the straw hat from my head throwing it to the ground; while tearing the snaps on my shirt open. I was on the bench all spread out with my head hanging off to one side. When the truck driver seen the shape I was in he asked, what's wrong boy?

I'm so hungry, I'm about to faint. In a flash he returned with a large coke.

I poured it down my throat so fast I don't think I even swallowed, but it cleared my head up. Then the driver returned with a double burger, which he handed to me, and in two bites it was gone. The hunger pains were gone to, but it felt like as if there was a huge hole in my stomach. I thanked the driver and tried to give him the twenty cents I had, but he refused to take it.

By midnight, we were in Eastern Ohio on the turnpike when the driver pulled onto the shoulder and brought the truck to a stop. After telling me he was going to sleep a few hours, he climbed into his sleeper. Leaning my head against the window, unable to sleep, I began thinking about home and how much I missed my mother. By mid morning we arrived at a truck stop in Toledo and the driver told me he would buy my breakfast. I had bacon, pancakes, and a glass of milk. When I finished, I asked for his name and address, and told him when I got home I would send him the money he spent on me. He gave it to me, and I told him how much I appreciated everything he done for me. I regret to say I lost his address and he never received his money. Even now, more than 45, years later I still think of the truck driver who paid for my meals, keeping me from fainting of hunger. I would love to meet this man again if he's still around.

I was standing on Highway 23, north for a few hours when a man and his son stopped to offer a ride. He said he would be getting off at the last exit in Ohio just before the Michigan State line. While sitting in the back seat, I began getting those awful hunger pains again. I was so afraid I was going to faint and thought of asking the man if he had any work I could do for a meal, but my pride wouldn't let me do it.

When I got out of the car, I could see the sign that read, Welcome to Michigan, the Winter Wonder Land. Walking under the sign, to the Michigan side, I was now feeling like I was home. Standing with my thumb out, no one would stop and the hunger pains were getting much worse. I just knew I was about to faint, so I walked over to the grassy area, where I reached down and picked a handful of grass to eat and began chewing. When I tried to swallow, it wouldn't go down; I had to spit it out. Finally a man stopped to pick me up as it began to rain again.

This driver told me he was going to Flint, which is 20, miles east of Owosso. After telling him what all I had been through, he told me he would take me to my home. This put him driving forty miles out of the way.

Barry's home! One of my brothers shouted as I walked thru the front door. Mother ran to me, greeting me with a hug and kiss. Don't get me wrong, I was happy to see my family, but eyeballing the kitchen table covered with food from supper; was more than I could bear. Later I was told how all I said was hi when I came thru the door. Then they told about how I sat down at the table and ate for 30, minutes straight. My brothers said I smelled really bad and my hair was very long. Mother said she contacted the Pennsylvania State Police, she hadn't heard from me in such a long time and was very worried about me. She was hoping the State Police would be able to locate me, and tell me to call home. I took a long hot bath and mom cut my hair.

A month later Ronnie, and Dorothy, arrived from Florida. Each summer Ronnie would be rodeoing through out the Midwest, and the Northeast. A rodeo friend of his owned a wrecking company in Toledo, Ohio. Since I was broke and in need of a job, Ronnie placed a call to Bill Paxton, asking if he could use me.

When Bill informed him he could use another hand, Ronnie hung up the phone. I got you a job Barry. Happy to hear the good news, I began re packing the duffel bag. Inside were clothes, two blankets, and rodeo gear. Ronnie was going to a rodeo in southern Ohio when he dropped me off at Bill Paxton's home in Toledo.

After working for Bill tearing down old brick buildings in town for two months, Ronnie showed up. He began telling about the Bob McKinley, Wild West show out of Farmers City, Illinois. He said if I wanted to get back to rodeoing, he would take me to where they were showing at a town in Indiana. I thanked the boss for the job and allowing me to live in their home while I was working there, but Toledo was too big a city for me and I was ready to get back riding those bulls and broncs.

McKinley was short on riders and was glad to have me riding for him. We were in Crown Point, Indiana at the fairgrounds for four performances: where I rode twenty two head of buckin' horses, and bulls. McKinley paid five-dollars for every head of stock a cowboy got on, plus five-dollars for setting up and tearing down the arena. He had his own men that fed all the livestock, which meant I got to sleep in.

I made $115.00 in those four days in Crown Point. I still slept on the ground, but never missed a meal with this outfit.

Around thirty minutes before each performance, us cowboys would have to mount McKinley's saddle horses with our chaps, and spurs, on, with a bandana tied around our necks. Then we would ride the horses out in front of the grandstand where we would sit while McKinley was on the P.A. system, telling all the fairgoers to come to the grandstands to see the cowboys.

We felt like we were in a circus freak show. In just a few minutes a pretty good crowd of folks would gather round to look at us cowboys. This was called ballyhooing. Then we would ride back to the arena where we would begin loading the buckin' horses into the chutes for the next performance. Bob McKinley would tell the people to purchase a ticket to watch the cowboys ride in the rodeo.

Mr. McKinley was a pretty good promoter; in just a few minutes the grandstand would begin filling with spectators. The last show was in September at Springfield, Ohio and there were two performances. During the first day, after stepping off the bull I just rode, I fell to the ground landing on my left arm. When I got up from the ground my elbow was hurting and then I noticed the shirt was torn and the arm was bleeding, looking closer I saw a pretty good hole in the arm just before the elbow.

The announcer for these shows was Floyd Pitzer. His wife Betty took me into her small travel trailer, where she cleaned the wound and put iodine and a bandage over it. The next day, my sister Lorayne, and brother in law Don Genest, (aka Bones) arrived for the last performance to visit with old friends and take me home.

Lorayne, and Bones, were living in a trailer park in Tecumseh, Michigan where I stayed a few months. The following weekend Ronnie, Dorothy, their son Ronnie Jr. (aka, Crow Foot,) who was only a few months old then, and Lyle, and I, went to a big one day amateur rodeo near Indianapolis, Indiana. It was called the Carey's Ranch Rodeo, with the performance beginning at 10:00 a.m. and would end at dusk, since there were no arena lights.

Unlike most rodeos where the judges draw each contestant an animal to compete on, a buckin' chute was drawn instead for each participant. There were ten chutes and there would be several sections in each event. Each contestant was drawn a chute for the section he was to compete in. All the buckin' stock was green, meaning they had never been bucked before. Whatever came into the chute the contestant had drawn, is the horse, or bull, they were to compete on. There also was an event where the cowboys were paid five-dollars to ride a buckin' horse with nothing to hold on to but the horses mane. All ten horses would be turned out at the same time, making it a pretty wild event.

Then there was the wild mule race, which was the same as the wild horse race, except these big horse mules were much ranker and meaner than any horse. Those mules would rear and try to paw your head, trying to kill you anyway they could. Kenny Williams and two other cowboys entered the wild mule race. Just before the race was to begin, they loaded the clown's trained mule into one of the chutes. Needless to say, they were the first and only team to get a mule saddled and across the finish line. They were paid the $100.00 first place prize.

Friday night on our way to the rodeo, I began feeling sick. Arriving around 4:00 a.m. Saturday, we all slept in the car. The secretary would begin taking entries for the rodeo by 8:00. When the time came Ronnie and I made our way to the entry office, where we stood in line waiting to enter. By then I was feeling really sick, so I told Ronnie I wasn't going to enter the rodeo. Then I walked back to the car where I laid down never getting up the rest of the day. My left arm was swollen so much; I had to put on a short sleeve shirt.

By dark we were headed back to Michigan, arriving at my sister's home around 1:00 a.m. I was much worse and running a fever. When Lorayne saw how huge the arm was, she awoke Bones to tell him. He got up and came out to look at it. Bones then told Lorayne to call the doctor. I tried to talk her out of it and told her if my arm wasn't any better by in the morning, then I would see a doctor.

Call the doctor right now Raynie! Bones demanded.

As she hung up the phone she said the doctor wants me to take you to the emergency room now.

After an examination of the arm, I was told gangrene was just beginning to settle in and if I

46

had waited until morning it would have been too late.

I would have had to amputate the arm said the doctor. That really scared me; it was my riding arm he was talking about. This all came about due to the injury to my arm at the Wild West show in Springfield the week before.

January 1961, I was back in Quitman, Georgia staying at that old house out on Buzzards Knob. Bruce Whatley, who was a bareback rider from Chicago, was also staying in the house. I met Bruce the summer before while riding for McKinley's Wild West show. We were both broke and would work the horse sale each week for a few dollars. One Saturday we were starving and broker than broke. I took a job at the pool hall racking balls from 9:00 a.m. until 10:00 p.m. for a measly $2.50. Bruce and I went straight to the cafe and ate it all up and were broke again.

A few days later, we got wind of a rodeo in Douglas, Georgia the next Saturday with $25 in prize money added to each event. The two of us decided to enter, hoping to win a little prize money. We caught a ride with other cowboys that were going to the rodeo. Neither Bruce nor I had money for our entry fees. We decided to go anyways, hoping to find someone to pay our fees. We weren't at the rodeo grounds long, when I heard about two guys from Idaho who wanted to pay a cowboy's entry fees for a share of their winnings. These two young men were not cowboys, they were construction workers. I talked to them about entering me in the bareback and bull riding. They agreed and handed me the money for entry fees, which were only five-dollars per event. This really had me feeling good. I was now seventeen years old, and finally entered my first contest rodeo.

In the bareback riding I drew the rankest horse in the Milton Carter herd. I really didn't want to draw this horse; I wasn't much of a bareback rider yet. In the bull riding, I drew a Brahma, pronounced as Braymer, by rodeo cowboys. I had seen this bull at other rodeos, and knew he didn't buck a lick. When it came my turn to ride in the bareback riding, I climbed up the chute gate and crawled over onto the back of ol' Sundance. Nodding my head after putting my hand in the riggin' Sundance leaped out of the chute as the gate swung open. Taking two jumps he made a small circle to the right jumping, and kicking, really hard. True to his reputation, Sundance flung me from his back, catapulting me over his head. Hitting the ground with a thud, his next jump landed a hoof on the back of my head splitting it open. I was badly dazed; the blow nearly knocked me out. Later I was told when Sundance jumped on the back of my head; he was coming back around to get me again. The pickup man's dog went after the bronc, causing it to turn off and miss me that time.

Back in those days, rodeos weren't required to have an ambulance or medical personal on hand. Luckily for me a woman watching the rodeo offered to take me to the hospital. The cowboys who carried me out of the arena laid me into the back of the woman's car; she then drove to the hospital. It took ten stitches to sew up the wound. Then my head was wrapped with several bandages making it look as if I had a turban on my head. My right arm was bleeding from being stepped on by the bronc. It was only skinned up and bruised but otherwise alright. My shirt was covered in blood, and torn to pieces. And I was still seeing a bunch of little black dots floating around in front of my eyes.

When the doctor was finished with me, I was told I owed $10. That's when I told the lady I didn't have any money, but if I could get back out to the rodeo before it was over, I still had a bull to compete on. If I won some money I would be able to pay what I owed them.

Look son, you just had a concussion, and you can't be riding anymore today, the nurse said.

Then I told her, if you will let me go, I can get a refund on my entry fee and then I can pay you. She agreed, and the woman with the station wagon who had waited for me, took me back to the rodeo.

When I arrived at the arena, the bull I was to ride was already loaded into the chutes and the bull riding was about to begin. Leaping out of the woman's car, I ran into the arena yelling, I'm back! Don't turn my bull out! Then I hurried behind the chutes where I left all my riding gear. I grabbed my glove, bull rope, and spurs, and then rushed to put the rope on the Braymer. I looked a mess with my head bandaged, my shirt covered in blood and badly torn. I knew this bull wasn't much of a bucker, but was hoping the judges would offer a reride after riding him. I rode the bull and received a very low score, but was denied a reride, and had to leave town without paying the hospital.

The following weekend, Cherokee was putting on a Wild West show somewhere in southwest Georgia. Bruce and I rode bulls, buckin' horses and threw a few steers down in the chute doggin'.

There weren't any doggin' horses, so we would load a steer into a buckin' chute. Then I would climb down into the chute grabbing the steer by its horns. When I was ready the gate was opened. The steer would run out dragging me while I was holding onto its horns. Sometimes I managed to get to my feet and throw the steer. Other times the steer would drag me all around the arena but I wouldn't turn 'em loose. Being drug by those steers like that is mighty hard on the knees.

Cherokee paid the two us $15 each. We returned to Buzzards Knob after the show. The next day Bruce took the stitches out of the back of my head with fingernail clippers.

By summer I was back up North riding for Bob McKinley. One weekend we were at the Ohio State Fair in Columbus. The arena was set up in front of the grandstands on a hard racetrack. There were two performances a day, for two days. These performances were at 7:00 and 9:00 p.m. and there was only one other bull rider besides me and I rode four bucking horses and eight bulls in the two days.

There were only three bucking chutes so I would get on the bull in the front chute. After riding him and stepping off, I would pick up the rope after it had fallen from the bull. Then I would run back to the chutes and put it on the bull in the third chute. While I was getting ready to ride, the other bull rider would be riding the bull that was loaded in the middle chute. After I rode the second time, I would climb into the bull pen behind the chutes to load three more then ride two more.

Besides being paid five-dollars for every head of buckin' stock I got on, I was also getting plenty of practice, (learning how to ride). Come fall my brother Lyle and I were living with Lorayne and Bones who had bought a ranch in Hastings, Michigan. Bones was working road construction operating a bulldozer, and got Lyle and me a job as laborers. I was making over $200 a week and bought my first car.

By February, I was back in Florida staying with Ronnie, and Dorothy. On the weekends I would compete in rodeos and break horses through the week.

One weekend I competed in a little amateur rodeo in Callahan, Florida. Cherokee Hammond was putting on this rodeo and I had drawn a very fast spinning bull. When the bull left the chute, my right knee was slammed into the corner post the chute gate hung on. When the bull ran out from under me, my body dropped to the ground. Clutching my knee with both hands I moaned loudly. The judges awarded a reride.

Cherokee said I could get on the bull at 8:00 a.m. the next morning.

That night a few of us slept on the ground in our sleeping bags. We had a nice camp fire to sleep around but late in the night the fire had gone out and it was very cold. I curled up in the night, and when I awakened around 7:00 a.m. my right knee was huge, at first I couldn't straighten out the injured leg. After crawling out of the bag, I began moving around trying to get the leg straightened out.

By 8:00 a.m. the bull was loaded into the chute. Unable to put any weight on the leg, I had to have help in order to climb the chute. Two cowboys on the gate reached down grabbing a hold of my arms and began pulling me upwards. Another cowboy was under me shoving my body up the gate. Finally, I was ready to ride. The bull took one jump out of the chute and went into a rapid spin to the right. Unable to grasp hold of the bulls hide with my right spur, he threw me to the ground in a flash.

By the middle of March I moved to North Florida, where I was staying with Kenny Williams. Kenny was a real good all around cowboy, competing in every rodeo event. His son, Speed Williams, is the Eight time Team Roping Champion of the World in the PRCA. Of course Speedy wasn't born yet. I was breaking colts for Kenny. By early May I decided to head back to my mother's place in Owosso.

Kenny had two Catahoula puppies, and asked if I would take them with me to keep for him until he came up later in the summer to rodeo. He told me Catahoulas made good working cow dogs and when he sold them he would give me half for taking care of them. I agreed to take the pups with me. One was male and the other female. Kenny had named the male Rod, and the female Reel. After being at my mother's for a week, I began training Rod, teaching him how to jump. Rod was very smart and easy to train and was with me everywhere I went. When I would get in the car to go somewhere, I'd holler load up! Rod would run and jump thru the cars open window. It wasn't long before he could jump, or climb, anything, including trees, telephone poles, up the walls of buildings and onto the roof.

My car was packed and ready to go by June. I was sure happy that Rod and I were heading for Bob McKinley's ranch in Farmers City, Illinois. Mr. McKinley would make a speech before the start of his first show at the ranch. Most Wild West shows don't pay their hired hands. When the day comes I can't pay my help, I will fold up and go home.

Sometimes we would show in two different towns on the same day, getting paid twice those days. Rod and I arrived at the ranch two days before the first show would begin. I slept in the car or a bedroll on the ground. Rod would not let anyone come near me once I lay down.

Many cowboys from all over the country had come to McKinley's to learn how to ride; they all thought they wanted to be rodeo cowboys. There were many bull riding wannabees from Texas and a kid from California. His name is Jerry

Hixson, who wanted to be a saddle bronc rider. Jerry and I were the only two cowboys that went on to compete in rodeos sanctioned by the Rodeo Cowboys Association (RCA). My goal was to become a member of the RCA one day. There were so many guys wanting to ride bulls this year at McKinley's, it would be two weeks before I got the chance to ride my first bull.

By now there wasn't but one bull rider left, other than me. Getting all the experience I could, I also rode bareback horses and saddle broncs.

All those wannabees just thought they wanted to be cowboys. Within two weeks they decided rodeoing wasn't for them. They all went back to wherever they come from, never to be seen again. After hitting those hard racetracks or getting their knees banged up from hitting the chute gate, they weren't tough enough to take the pain. If you can't take pain, you will never make it in rodeo. Even today, very few make it in rodeo compared to the thousands that try it. It takes a special breed to be a rodeo cowboy. The reason I was able to take all the pain and all those hungry days is because I loved what I was doing and I loved the rodeo cowboy way of life. I wanted to become a great bull rider so I could quit working these Wild West shows and begin competing for prize money.

One day we put on a show on the parking lot at a huge Mall in Lansing, Michigan. The parking lot was asphalt, so we had to drive the metal fence posts thru the asphalt in order to put up the arena fence. Once we were done with the fence many loads of dirt were hauled in with dump trucks.

By fall, I was back in Florida for the winter, staying with Ronnie and Dorothy. We all had to share the same bathroom. I was using a new brand of toothpaste, called Stripe toothpaste, with red and white strips. I always left the tube lying on the sink. One morning as I squeezed the paste onto my brush, the stripes were gone, it was solid white.

Hey, what happened to the red stripes, I was thinking. I figured the company short changed me and brushed any ways. Now the toothpaste had a soapy flavor to it. After brushing for several days, Ronnie asked, does your toothpaste taste any different?

Yes, ever since it run out of red stripes. Now it has a soapy taste to it. Ronnie began laughing hard. Then he explained what he done.

I squeezed all your toothpaste out, then I put my tube of shaving cream against your tube and squeezed the shaving cream into your tube. You've been brushing your teeth with shaving cream. The both of us had a good laugh then. A week later I hired on with the Circle M Ranch in Gainesville.

The Circle M, owned by Harold McCullers, was also the auctioneer at the Gainesville stockyards. There were four other cowboys working for the Circle M. Two of them rode bulls. They were Tom Buchanan and Deb Canary.

Seven days a week we broke colts, mended fence, branded and doctored cattle. There was a bunkhouse for us all to live in and we were paid

$15 per week. Somehow I made the mistake of going back to Buzzards Knob come January and found myself going hungry again.

Bruce Whatley was there, and another cowboy by the name of Wally Riddle from Texas. The three of us were staying in that same old house on Buzzards Knob, along with my dog, Rod. One day I had a few dollars and decided we should go to the grocery store where we bought a whole stick of bologna, a.k.a. cowboy steak, and a loaf of bread. The butcher let us leave the bologna in the cooler. Each day we would stop in to get three slices so we could each have a sandwich.

When there wasn't but a fourth of the stick left we took it with us back to the house. After eating we headed back into town, leaving the rest of the meat and bread on the kitchen table. We returned a few hours later only to discover Rod had eaten all our food. Wally took a pen and wrote on the kitchen wall: Wally Riddle, Barry Brown, and Bruce Whatley all starved to death because Rod ate the red and bread.

Finally, I got a job breaking colts for a man called, Cowboy Jordan, who paid five-dollars a day plus lunch. Those colts were halter broke only and none of them had ever been sacked out, or saddled. I would lead them one at a time across the road from Cowboy Jordan's barn to his arena. Then I would snub the colt up to a post, sack 'em out, saddle 'em up, then step into the saddle and turn 'em loose, riding them till they quit buckin'. I broke many horses over the years and was never thrown.

Chapter Six

I purchased my first RCA permit in 1963, while working for the Rocking R Rodeo Company owned by Foy Reynolds of Bonifay, Florida. As a permit holder in the RCA, I could only enter those RCA sanctioned rodeos which accepted permits. A full member (card holder) could enter any RCA sanctioned rodeo he wanted to. It was mainly the big rodeos that wouldn't accept permits. You had to be a full member to enter the big winter rodeos such as the Fort Worth Stock Show and Rodeo, San Antonio, Texas rodeo, the Houston Astrodome rodeo, Cow Palace rodeo in San Francisco, and of course the Daddy of 'em all, The Cheyenne Frontier Days Rodeo. My goal was to become a full member in the RCA once I thought I was riding good enough to compete against the RCA cowboys.

In March, Ronnie, Lyle, and I entered an RCA rodeo in Montgomery, Alabama. Ronnie was a tough All Around Cowboy and a RCA member. The Montgomery rodeo was accepting permits, allowing Lyle and me to enter. Barney Faircloth of Trenton Florida gave us a ride to Montgomery. Barney was a calf roper and bulldogger. This rodeo had five performances: Wednesday, Thursday, Friday, and two on Saturday.

I had drawn the rankest bull at the rodeo, which was put on by the XS Ranch out of Austin, Texas, owned by Tommy Steiner. Several

The Brown Brothers (l to r) Curt, Lyle, Barry, Dallas, Ronnie, Ronnie Jr. (aka Crowfoot)

top bull riders and past World Champions were entered at this rodeo. Dickey Cox was in the lead for the World title in bull riding at the time and would be competing at the Montgomery rodeo. We arrived on Wednesday, but I wasn't up until Saturday night. I was told all about the bull, #31, which was a big Santa Gertrudis Brahma cross, and an NFR (National Finals Rodeo) bull. I heard how he bucked off the sixteen time World Champion Jim Shoulders of Henrietta, Oklahoma.

I was really nervous seeing all those World Champions and was about to let the pressure get to me. It wasn't until about thirty minutes before time for me to get on #31, when I began thinking about how pressured up I was. Knowing I wouldn't last two jumps on this bull if I didn't get a hold of myself, I had to start thinking right and get riding on my mind. I thought about how I needed to bear down and try really hard to show everyone how good I could ride. I rode #31 six to seven seconds before he threw me off. A few of the champs came over to shake my hand. Good try kid, they each said. This made me feel good, even though I bucked off.

The following weekend we were at the Davie, Florida rodeo. To save money Ronnie and I slept on the ground at the arena. There was a bar and dance hall next to the rodeo arena. Ronnie and some cowboys went to the bar after the Friday night rodeo. I was too young to go with him so I stayed at the arena.

When I awoke the next morning, I saw blood on his face, and his nose and lips were swollen. A local threw a punch as Ronnie was on his way to the restroom. He never saw it coming, and hit the floor face first.

Saturday night during the calf roping there was a malfunction with the barrier. Foy Reynolds, the stock contractor, was at the roping box helping the judges repair the barrier. The rodeo fans were patiently waiting although it was taking a long time. The rodeo clowns weren't telling any jokes to keep the fans entertained and I noticed how quiet it was. Since the clown wasn't entertaining the fans, I decided I would.

Whistling once, I called my dog into the arena. Standing in front of the buckin' chutes, I had Rod do some tricks. I knew the fans would be watching. Taking a chute hook and holding it low, Rod jumped over it. Then I raised the chute hook higher and higher. Rod would jump it each time; the spectators began clapping. Foy began scanning the area to see what they were clapping about. When he saw my dog jumping, I had taken the choke chain from around his neck and held it out in front of me about five feet off the ground. As Rod leaped from the ground his nose would go thru the chain. When he landed it would be around his neck. Again, all the spectators were clapping. After the rodeo Mr. Reynolds said Barry, I want to hire you and your dog for the Ocala rodeo. Mr. Foy, I'm not a contract performer, and I don't really have an act put together. That's okay; I will pay you $25 for each performance. Not wanting to do it, I tried to explain to Foy I was a rodeo cowboy, not a contract performer. Since I bucked off my bull at the Davie rodeo, the $75 for three performances sounded pretty good. Okay Foy, I will do it I told him. While Ronnie and I were making the three hundred mile trip back to Gainesville, I began thinking about what I could come up with for a dog act. Rod could do several tricks already, but I needed something extra to make the act last a little longer.

Monday morning I went to a welding shop where I explained what I wanted, which would be three hoops. One was to be just big enough for my dog to fit thru, then a larger one to cover with paper, and another larger hoop built onto a stand to use as a hoop of fire. By Wednesday I received a call that the hoops were ready. When I returned home I decided to give my dog and the hoops a trial run. Once I had the medium size hoop covered with paper, I told Rod to jump thru it. Without hesitating he sailed thru it. I then cut strips from a burlap feed sack and wrapped them around the flat metal hoop. After saturating the burlap with kerosene I lit it; a nice flame burned three to four inches high all the way around. Rod jumped through the flames the first time I told him. I gave Rod a pat, figuring we had a pretty good act put together. Now we were ready to perform so I thought.

The rodeo was Friday and Saturday night, with a matinee performance on Sunday. Friday the 13th, after arriving at the arena for the first performance, I prepared the hoops for my very first Contract act. I was getting very nervous; in fact I was downright scared at the thought of walking out into the center of that arena in front of thousands of rodeo fans as a performer. I could ride buckin' horses and bulls in front of a million people, that wouldn't bother me at all. This was different though and I had caught a bad case of stage fright. I have done several radio and television interviews thru out my rodeo career but always had trouble talking once the microphone was put in front of me. Twenty minutes before time for my act, I got to thinking; maybe I didn't have enough kerosene on the hoop. Worried that it might not burn, I drenched it with gasoline. Finally it came time for my act.

Rodeo announcer Spec Lunsford from Dallas, Texas began telling the rodeo fans about me and my dog and how this was my first time as a contract performer.

I entered the arena carrying two of the hoops with Rod at my side. Lyle took the fire hoop, which was mounted on wheels, down the arena fence to wait for me to signal him when it came time for him to roll the hoop out to the center of the arena. Then light it and leave.

Folks, welcome Barry Brown and his dog Rod the announcer said.

Everyone was clapping as Rod and I entered the arena. Tipping my Resistol, with my Wrangler jeans tucked inside my Justin boots, I told Rod to sit but he just stood there staring at me. Again I told him to sit, he still refused. I picked up the small hoop and told my dog to jump thru it.

Rod just did a little hop along side of the hoop and then he took off. He ran under a gate and was gone, leaving me standing in the arena with my hoops and no dog. Everyone was laughing. This was not at all what I had planned and I was so embarrassed.

Lyle ran after Rod. Soon he brought him to me. I held up the hoop covered with paper, then told Rod to jump thru it, but Rod didn't move. I lowered the hoop to where it was only a foot off the ground. When I told Rod to jump again, he came up to the hoop, like a horse he reared up, his front paws hit the paper tearing it all apart.

Again there was a roar of laughter from the grandstands.

I dropped the hoop, motioning for Lyle to roll the fire hoop out. As Lyle lit the hoop, it went swoosh, from all the gas I poured on it. I couldn't see any of the hoop at all, and neither could my dog. The fire was burning all the way down to the ground and high into the air.

Everyone was laughing, even all the cowboys. There was this huge wall of fire. I know my face had to be redder than fire. I slapped my forehead thinking, oh no! Everyone is still laughing and my face by now is getting redder and redder. All I could do was stand there and wait for the fire to die down, but it doesn't, it just keeps roaring and seems to be burning harder and harder. All the spectators finally quit laughing and it got awfully quiet. I knew I had to do something.

Jump thru there, I scolded. Rod being smarter than I, looked at that wall of fire, then looks at me, and just stands there. Get thru there! I said a second time, but he doesn't move. Then I stomped my foot and really got after him to jump.

Rod ran towards the wall of fire and jumped. He couldn't see any of the hoop. His back legs caught the bottom of the ring where it is connected to the stand. As Rod went thru the hoop it began to fall. When he landed on the ground the top part landed on Rod's back. A puff of smoke came off it and Rod ran out of the arena.

Tipping my hat to the audience, I left the arena. Everyone was laughing, and clapping. When the rodeo was over, I told Foy Reynolds I wasn't going to work my dog the next two performances. Foy then talked me into doing another performance saying, it'll be all right.

The next morning I checked Rod, and there were a few burned spots under his belly. I treated the wounds and then covered the paper hoop. Rod jumped thru it the first time I told him. He did the same with the fire hoop which had a nice little flame all the way around it. Saturday night at the rodeo I told Foy my dog was sore from the burns and thought it would be best not to have him perform that night. Then I told him we would do the Sunday performance and he agreed. By Sunday the burns on Rod were much better. We were back in Ocala for the matinee performance.

After readying the hoops for my act, and pouring only kerosene this time, Rod and I were ready for our final performance. Entering the arena with my dog and two hoops, the gate was closed behind us. Foy had several cowboys sitting at the bottom of the gate so Rod wouldn't be able to run under it again. The grandstands were full of spectators, and I was just as nervous as I was that first day. I began the act with the small hoop and held it low. When I told Rod to jump thru the hoop, instead he did a little hop beside it again. For some reason he wouldn't jump thru. Rod ran to the closed gate. All the cowboys sitting there were waving their arms and telling him to get back.

Well, Rod took a few steps back. He then looked up at the top of that gate, which was seven to eight feet to the top. Running forward he jumped, clearing the gate by a good two feet. Everyone was laughing; there I stood in the middle of the arena with my hoops and no dog again.

Tell me something to do, I heard someone saying. Looking down, there was Pete Peterson, the rodeo clown and bullfighter, on all fours. What did you say? I asked. Pete again said, tell me something to do! Picking up the small hoop, I asked Pete if he thought he could fit thru it. I don't know, but I'll try, he replied. I held the hoop just a few inches off the ground.

Jump thru it boy! I shouted. When Pete attempted to dive thru the hoop, it got hung on his legs. After Pete pulled his legs thru the hoop, he crawled around on his hands and knees and bit me on the ankle. I began hopping around on one leg as if he had really bitten me like a dog. Everyone was laughing, thinking it was part of the act.

Picking up the paper hoop, I told Pete to jump thru it. Pete dove thru the paper making it all the way thru. Then he crawled over to me, raising one of his legs as if to be peeing on me like a dog. The crowd was laughing really hard by this time. I grabbed the cowboy hat off my head and began hitting Pete with it. He jumped up and ran out of the arena. I tipped my hat to the crowd, who was clapping loudly, and made my exit from the arena. Pete Peterson saved the day for me. Rodeo clowns are a special breed all their own.

That was the last time I ever performed with my dog as a contract act. However, I could still stand in front of the chutes with Rod doing some of his tricks, knowing people were watching, and it never bothered me. I knew it was my fault Rod wouldn't perform at the rodeo. He sensed how frightened I was and it affected him. Sometimes when a bucking chute was empty I would tell Rod to get up the gate. Rod would jump part way up the chute gate, climb to the top, jump over the chute to the other side, then jump down to the ground.

A few weeks later I was in Baltimore, Maryland for a rodeo, staying at the Lord Baltimore Hotel. George Wallace, who was the Governor of Alabama, was also in Baltimore. Mr. Wallace was campaigning for the presidential election and was staying at the same hotel. Everyday protestors were carrying signs in front of the Lord Baltimore Hotel demonstrating against Governor Wallace.

On Saturday, five of us cowboys and my dog went to tour Washington, DC. We first went to the Washington Monument. There was a long line of people waiting for the elevator to take them to the top. We decided to take the stairs, rather than standing in line. Up the stairs we climbed and climbed and we climbed some more. We didn't think we were ever going to get to the top of that monument. When ready to go back down we decided to wait on the elevator. As we exited from the monument, there was a tall white man standing out front saying, gather around folks. We are going to be having a speech for the civil rights of black folks.

Oh yeah, well I'm for the civil rights of white folks. I spoke. Then I walked across the sidewalk to a platform which had a rope around it. Rod and I jumped over the rope and onto the platform where he performed several tricks and jumps. There were thousands of tourists all around and many of them stopped to watch my dog performing. Of course I had my cowboy hat and boots on. When I finished my little act with Rod I said, okay folks be sure to vote for George Wallace, for the civil rights of white folks. Rod and I received a big round of applause. Next we visited the Nation's Capitol, and on the front lawn I had Rod performing again and made the same speech for Governor George Wallace. I don't think Mr. Wallace ever heard about it, though.

One performance during the Baltimore rodeo, New York bull rider Johnny Hastings was hit in the face by a bull's head while attempting to ride it. As Johnny lay on the arena floor unconscious, blood was shooting out his ears, mouth, and nose. I thought he was dead. He sure enough looked dead. The next day though he was back out at the rodeo, with his mouth wired shut.

Once the Baltimore rodeo had finished, I rode with Larry Lyons and Phil Heinen to Wichita, Kansas for my next rodeo. At this rodeo, I had drawn this huge freight train of a bull. It was a Holstein/Braymer cross, with huge honking muscles bulging out all over his body. I was told the last bull rider who attempted to ride this mass of muscles had his riding arm jerked out of its socket at the shoulder. Around four seconds into the ride I was slammed to the ground with a thud. Glad that this ride was over, I walked out of the arena unscathed.

By June, I was back in Michigan for the summer competing in rodeos from Iowa to New York. The Flint Hills Rodeo Company, owned by World Champions Ken and Gerald Roberts out of Strong City, Kansas would be putting on an RCA approved rodeo in Detroit, Michigan in August. There would be $1,500 in prize money added to each event, with ten performances, and permits accepted. This would be the biggest RCA rodeo I ever entered.

One week before the entries were to close, Ronnie and I were on our way back to Michigan from a Howard Harris rodeo in Pennsylvania. Ronnie asked if I was going to enter Detroit. Telling him I was planning to until hearing the entry fees were $50, I was having second thoughts about entering that rodeo. Fifteen dollars was the most I had ever paid for an entry fee. When it came time to enter the Detroit rodeo, I decided to take the chance.

There were four go rounds in the bull riding. At the time, Howard Carroll was in the lead for the World Championship in bull riding. He, as well as several other good bull riders, would be competing. Each rider would have to compete on four head of bulls. The bull rider with the highest total score on four head would be the average winner and the Champion bull rider of the rodeo.

In the first go round, scoring 165 points, I tied for third and fourth place, with Jerry Hart, Charles Wegner, and John Stokes. Each of us won a whopping $33.37. Making a qualified ride in the second round, I failed to place. Winning second place in the third round with a score of 168 points and $133.50 had me feeling a whole lot better. My fourth bull didn't buck very well, resulting in a very low score. Bud Linderman was one of the judges.

Hey Bud, can I have a reride? I asked. Nodding his head, sure he spoke. The reride rule back then was if a contestant wanted a reride, he had to ask for one. Today, contestants are not allowed to ask for a reride, if they do they can be fined fifty dollars. If a judge thinks a contestant should receive a reride, he is to award it automatically.

The reride bull I drew was a Brangus and he went in to a fast spin to the right, first jump out of the chute. I rode him for a score of 171, to win first place in the go round and $178.00. Ending up with the highest total score of 661 on four head made me the average winner and the event Champion, plus an additional $356.00. Winning a little over $700.00, I thought I would never see another poor day.

In those days the scoring system was much different than it is today. The animal was to be marked from 60 85 points and the contestants ride from 1 20. A perfect ride on the perfect animal would be 210 points. This scoring system was changed in either 1964 or 1965. Ever since then the scoring system in rodeo is 1 25 for the rider and 1 25 for the animal, for a total of 50 points from each of the two judges. A perfect ride would be 100 points, but I don't think anyone should be scored a 100. I don't believe a perfect ride can be made on the perfect animal.

The win in Detroit put me winning over a $1,000 my first year as a permit holder. I now qualified to become a full member of the RCA. Winning Detroit really impressed my girlfriend Charlotte, who was a barrel racer from Michigan. I didn't think I would ever lose her. Charlotte's parents were so proud of me; they paid for my first membership card in the RCA which cost fifty dollars.

The following weekend, Ronnie, Charlotte's Brother John Zormeier, who was a calf roper, and I were on our way to an RCA rodeo in Wisconsin. It was around 2:00 a.m. on a Saturday morning, with me doing the driving. We were on the Indiana turnpike when the generator light came on. Ronnie said the battery would go dead in just a little while since the headlights were on. So I turned them off, leaving only the parking lights on while driving 90, mph.

A Highway patrolman spotted us driving with no headlights and speeding. Pulling us over, one of the patrolmen asked, what are you doing driving without lights and doing 90, mph? So I explained our situation. He told me to follow him as I would have to see the Justice of the Peace. While following the cops, we decided to hide most of the money we had. We didn't want the officers to know we had a lot of money with us. Ronnie kept a $20 in his pocket. After we arrived at the J.P.'s, the cops told him why we were brought in. They had written two tickets on me: one for driving with no headlights and one for speeding.

I told the J.P. how we had been rodeoing and haven't won any money and the three of us were just about broke. Then I told him I was trying to save the battery since the generator light had come on. Ronnie then told them we had only $20 to our name and we were trying to make it to a service station before the battery went dead. Ronnie said he could put the brushes in himself, so we wouldn't need a mechanic, which we couldn't afford either.

The J.P. and the two cops were really feeling sorry for us by now. The Justice of the Peace said he could drop the two charges but we would have to pay court costs, but he could help us with those costs also. He charged us only five dollars. We thanked him and the cops told us they would lead us to a service station where we could purchase the brushes for the generator. After arriving at the station the cops offered to pay for the brushes.

Thanks, but we have enough money to buy them and if the gas station attendant has the wrench we need, I can put them in, Ronnie told them. Again the cops offered to pay for them, but we said no and thank you. These two cops felt so badly for us, they even apologized for stopping us.

Ronnie got the new brushes put in and we were back on the road again. We were talking about how bad the cops felt for stopping us, and how if either of them was to ever stop another cowboy; they will probably let him go.

Five days later I left Michigan for the Memphis, Tennessee State Fair and Rodeo, which would be my first R.C.A. rodeo as a member. I didn't know anyone at this rodeo, which was being put on by the Kinney Brothers. Rodeo Company.

Between the performances on Saturday, I was outside the civic center talking with the two rodeo clowns who were also the bullfighters. They were Junior Meeks and George Doaks, from Texas, who were two of the best in the business. With clown makeup still on their faces Junior asked, what's your name? Barry Brown I said. Are you any kin to Ronnie Brown? He's my brother I responded.

I thought so, you sound just like him. Junior replied.

There was a horse trailer parked next to the clowns pickup. I had my arms on top of the back gate leaning on the metal, when all of a sudden I got a heck of a shock from the trailer. Hollering as I jerked my arms from the gate, George and Junior were laughing. Then they told me how they had a wire running from a spark plug in their truck and had it wired to the horse trailer. When someone like me would touch their trailer, these two clowns would flip a switch, which would shock the heck out of anyone touching the trailer.

Once George, and Junior, were sharing a motel room with a couple other cowboys and myself. One of them was Sandy Kirby. Now Sandy was very hard to wake up and would sleep all day. These two clowns were tired of trying to wake Sandy, so they cut the electric cord off a lamp in the room. Then they cut the insulation off one end of the cord far enough back so they could wrap the bare wires around each of Sandy's big toes. After calling Sandy's name once more, they plugged the other end into the outlet, which was shocking the living daylights out of Sandy. He leaped out of the bed screaming. From that time on whenever George or Junior told Sandy to get up, he would leap out of the bed, but no one else could wake him.

Another time we were going to get something to eat, and tried to wake Sandy but were unable to. Before leaving the room we lifted one side of the mattress, rolling Sandy onto the floor with the mattress landing on top of him. Then we left the room thinking he would come along behind us. When we returned Sandy was still asleep on the floor, with the mattress still over him.

Nearing the end of the year I was competing at the Fireman's rodeo in St. Louis, Missouri. Tommy Steiner, the stock contractor, was who I referred to as a cowboy's stock contractor. He was always willing to help a young cowboy who was down on his luck and broke. Many times when I was entered at a Steiner rodeo and didn't win, Mr. Steiner allowed me to charge my entry fees. This meant he would have to pay the entry fee, which he always did. Even when I worked the labor list, he would pay me for working. Tommy Steiner always cared about the contestants and treated them with respect.

Three cowboys and I were staying at a hotel in downtown St. Louis, where we had a room on the seventh floor. My dog always stayed in the rooms with me. In the morning I would take Rod down the elevator, getting off at the lobby. We would walk thru the lobby and out the back door. There was a long enclosed glass canopy approximately twenty feet long, with another glass door at the end of it. Upon opening that door, Rod would go out to do whatever it was he needed to do. While Rod was taking care of his business, I returned to the room.

Once everyone was ready to leave for breakfast, I said to them, I need to get my dog first. We were at the elevator waiting for it to come up. When the door opened, there stood my dog. Even I was surprised. How did you do that? I asked him? He just stood there waging his tail, with a smile on his face, and never spoke a word. Talking was about the only thing Rod couldn't do.

After the rodeo that night we returned to the hotel and were in the lounge. After a few drinks, my dog and I went to the room. When I was nearly asleep, a cowboy from Houston, Texas came into the room.

Barry, can I take your dog with me to the lounge? He asked.

I guess so, don't let anything happen to him, I said. Then I told Rod to go with him. When I was just about asleep for the second time, I heard Rod barking loudly. Even though I was on the seventh floor I could still easily hear him barking. Leaping from the bed, I was dressed in a flash.

As I entered the lounge Rod was still barking. The cowboy was siccing Rod on every one in the lounge. All the patrons were on their hands and knees on tables and the bar. Not one person was sitting.

You're going to get my dog arrested I said laughingly. Rod and I returned to the room and finally drifted off to sleep.

The next morning after turning Rod out, I returned to the room for a shower and dressed for breakfast. Once everyone was ready, I opened the room door and there he was.

Rod! How did you know which floor to get off on? I bet you all didn't know Rod could operate elevators too, I said to my friends.

How did he do that they asked repeatedly. He was an amazing dog.

Rod and I were on our way to Florida from Owosso one winter when he was seven months old. It was late in the night in Kentucky when I stopped for fuel. Rod was let out to do his thing and I gave him water. Forty minutes later after leaving the service station, I realized Rod wasn't in the car. Leaving him at the station, I figured I lost my dog. Turning around, I drove 100 mph back to where I left him. Rod was near the pumps waiting for me. Wagging his tail, he was as happy to see me as I was him. From then on I could leave him anywhere or with anyone. He wouldn't leave because he knew I would be back to get him. I never liked leaving Rod but there were times it couldn't be helped.

Once I left him with a friend in Toledo, Ohio. His name is James Baum (aka Jughead) who lived in the country and had a dog pen with a very high fence. I would be picking up four other cowboys and there wouldn't be room in the car for Rod. I spent the night, and the following morning I put Rod in the pen. Jughead, was to let him out once I was out of sight. When I returned two weeks later, Jughead told me that before I got out of the driveway Rod jumped out, but never tried to run after me. He knew he was supposed to stay with Jug.

I don't see how any dog could jump out of that pen with the fence being as high as it is, exclaimed Jughead.

Ronnie, Jughead, Rod and I were on our way to a Bob Barns rodeo in Iowa. The three of us were sitting in the front seat. Ronnie was driving when all of a sudden he punches me hard in the arm.

Why did you hit me? I asked.

If you want to be a cowboy, you got to be tough and I'm going to toughen you up. Ronnie replied.

That's right said Jughead as he punches me in the other arm. Ronnie then gives me a Charlie horse and Jug hits me again. Tired of being beaten on by those two, I crawled into the back seat with Rod. My arms and legs were sore, and the two of them in the front seat were laughing their heads off.

On our way home from the rodeo we stopped at a cafe to eat. After leaving the restaurant, Ronnie had been driving for about half an hour when I realized Rod wasn't in the car.

We left Rod! I shouted.

We have come too far, and I'm not turning around. Ronnie told me.

Stop and let me out then, and I will hitch hike back to get my dog, I exclaimed. There was no way I was going to leave him.

Ronnie laughed and said he was only kidding. When we got to the cafe, Rod was waiting for us.

Chapter Seven

My mother used to attend all the rodeos in Michigan to watch her boys ride. It seemed like one of us was always getting hurt. When Lyle had the back of his head stepped on really hard by a bull at a rodeo in Southern Michigan, mom was really scared and crying. It rained a lot during the rodeo and the mud was deep. When the bull stepped onto the back of Lyle's head, it pushed his face deep into the mud. Had it not rained, the ground would have been hard, which would have shattered Lyle's face. Ever since then, I never complained if I had to compete when it began raining. There is no doubt in my mind the rain saved Lyle's life. That would be the last rodeo my mother ever attended. She couldn't take seeing her boys getting hurt anymore.

One weekend in April, Ronnie, Lyle, and I were at a rodeo in Parsippany, New Jersey, where Foy Reynolds was the stock contractor. After bucking off the bull I had drawn, I landed very hard on my left shoulder. Immediately
after hitting the ground I jumped up and began running towards the buckin' chutes. That darn bull was right on my tail wanting to hook me.

Run Barry, run! Ronnie shouted, as he held the chute gate open. As I ran into the chute the bull turned away. Ronnie noticed I had my left arm across in front of me holding it with my right hand which I didn't realize I was doing at all. Ronnie pulled my shirt open, and said, yup, your collar bone's broken.

Lyle and Ronnie still had their bulls to ride, so I waited in the car until they were through then they drove me to the hospital. After x rays, the doctor told Ronnie my collarbone was shattered and needed surgery. I spent the night in the hospital. The next morning my brothers arrived at my room. Ronnie spoke with the doctor who said I would be hospitalized for a week after the surgery. I sent for the doctor to tell him my brothers were leaving for Michigan. Explaining I wouldn't want them to drive all the way back to New Jersey in a week to get me.

I will wait to have the surgery done back home, I said to him. He then put a brace and sling on me and handed Ronnie a bottle of pain pills.

I laid in the back seat all the way home and didn't have to do any of the driving. Lorayne and Bones had bought a huge trailer park in Marshall, Michigan. They also purchased a large two story house, so all us boys could live with them. It also had a service station my brothers and I helped run through the week when there were no rodeos. When a vehicle would pull in for fuel we all would be inside the gas station playing cards. We didn't like our card game being interrupted by the customers so to get them gone fast, we all would run out to the vehicle to wait on the costumer. While one of us was pumping gas, there was no self service in those days, another would be washing the windows and one would be checking under the hood while another one would check the air pressure in their tires. Bones would stay inside behind the cash register to ring up the sale. Sometimes while we were servicing the vehicle, the customer would go inside to pay or make some other purchases, and they would say to Bones, I don't see how you can afford all this help. We all laughed when Bones told us as we were not on the payroll.

I had surgery on my collarbone in Battle Creek, spending six days in the hospital. The doctor removed a few chipped pieces of bone, then wired the collarbone back together. A week after being released from the hospital, I began judging rodeos until I could begin riding again.

Two months later I was back competing in the bareback, saddle bronc, and bull riding at the amateur rodeos. When I didn't have the money to travel to RCA rodeos, I would compete at the smaller amateur rodeos until I won enough to head back down the road on the RCA circuit. Back in those days the Association would fine a member and put them on the black list for competing in rodeos not sanctioned by the RCA. So when I entered an unapproved rodeo, I would change my name. Over the years, I was Jack Reynolds, Beep Jones, and Jack Daniel. Lyle was L. E. Gator, and Ronnie was Canton Attibury.

Once I had prize money checks made out to Jack Reynolds and had to do some kind a talking to convince the bank that Barry Brown and Jack Reynolds were one and the same person.

That summer I competed in a Tommy Steiner rodeo in Nashville, Tennessee. There were two go rounds and I won the first round on a 2,000 lb. Charbray #54. The year before I watched the great Harry Tompkins spur this big yellow bull in the neck at the St. Louis rodeo.

In the second go round I was thrown off #19, which was another Charbray. Hitting the ground hard, it cost me winning the average. During the rodeo performance Friday night, I heard there was going to be a dog show on another floor in the coliseum, Saturday morning.

Rod and I went to the show. All dogs in the building were on a leash except Rod. My dog was never put on a leash or tied. Several folks, who had dogs entered in the show, when seeing Rod, would ask, is your dog entered? Telling them he wasn't, they would say your dog would have won if he was entered.

Sometimes, after a rodeo when Rod and I were leaving the arena, a cowboy who heard about my dog would ask if I would show him how Rod could jump. Many spectators on their way out would stop to watch Rod performing his tricks, and jumps. When I was through with Rod, a man asked, who trained your dog? After telling him I had, he then said, I'm a professional dog trainer, you should be training dogs. This was told to me one other time in another city.

I never considered myself as a great dog trainer. I gave all the credit to Rod for being so smart.

By fall I was back in Owosso staying with my mother. It was Saturday morning and I was to compete at a rodeo in Pennsylvania that night. Pheasant hunting season opened and Lyle was going hunting. He asked if I would leave Rod with him, which I did. Leaving at 12 noon, I made the 400 mile drive to Pennsylvania, arriving back home Sunday morning.

Lyle began telling about what a great hunting dog Rod was. I didn't believe him and told Lyle he was crazy. Rod was a cow dog, and didn't know a thing about bird hunting. Lyle then proceeded to tell about taking Rod with him when he went hunting. As Rod was running and jumping thru the tall weeds and grass, he accidentally flushed up a pheasant and Lyle shot it. Rod watched the bird as it fell to the ground then ran to it and chewed on it a little. After getting a smell of the pheasant, Rod planted his nose on the ground and put up two more.

The next morning as I picked up my shotgun Rod got excited and began barking and jumping. You want to go hunting Rod? He really got excited then. The grass was very wet from the heavy dew. Pheasants will not run thru wet grass. Instead they will sit tight where they are and a hunter can step over them without them flying up. This happened that morning when I took Rod hunting. After walking for a while, I realized Rod wasn't around. Looking behind me I saw Rod standing and staring at the ground. Seeing the trail where I just walked thru the wet grass, Rod was standing in my tracks.

Come on Rod, I just walked thru there, there's not any pheasants. Rod continued looking down, he wouldn't budge. Then I realized he found a bird. Rod never moved until I had my shotgun ready and said, okay Rod. Then he lowered his head poking the pheasant with his nose. The bird flew up and I shot it. Rod was an amazing dog. He taught himself how to hunt. He had never been with a bird dog or ever hunted before.

November 1964, was the start of the 1965 rodeo season in the RCA following the conclusion of the Cow Palace Rodeo in San Francisco. Each dollar won at an RCA approved rodeo would count towards the 1965 World Championship standings. The rodeo season would run thru the first weekend in November of 1965. Only the top fifteen money earners in each event earn the right to compete at the National Finals Rodeo (NFR). This is the World Series of rodeo. Today it is known as the Wrangler National Finals Rodeo.

At the start of the 1965 season, I drove from Michigan by myself to a rodeo in Americus, Georgia where I won fourth place in the bull riding, which paid $42.00, then I returned home. The next weekend, John Zormeier and I went to a rodeo in Harrisburg, Pennsylvania. I tied for first place in the bull riding at this rodeo, winning over $500.00. John was hauling his roping horse Smokey in a one horse trailer.

It was a cold winter night as we were driving across the Pennsylvania Turnpike, headed back to Michigan. It was 2:00 a.m. Sunday morning, and I was driving 80 mph while John was asleep. All of a sudden the back of John's car began bouncing up and down. It woke John, he looked out the side mirror and said oh, my gosh Barry, my horse is on the road!

Looking into my side mirror I could see the outline of the horse as there were many sparks flying high into the air and all around him from all four of his shoes. Smokey was in a sitting position, with his front legs extended out in front of him, and he was sideways, sliding behind the trailer. The horse was on the highway sliding at about the same rate of speed the vehicle was traveling. There was a car coming up from behind us really fast. I pulled off onto the shoulder and brought the car to a stop.

John and I bailed out and were running towards Smokey, waving our arms at the driver in the car that was rapidly approaching. It was very dark and the driver could not see the horse which was in the center of the highway. Smokey had just gotten up on all fours when the driver of the car spotted him. He slammed on the breaks, swerving just in time to avoid hitting the horse and kept going.

John led Smokey to the front of his car so we could check him over with the headlights. Hide was torn off both knees. There were several other cuts and scrapes on all four legs.

Loading the horse back into the trailer, we got off at the next exit where we located a Veterinarian. After many stitches and bandages the veterinarian told John he thought the horse was going to be okay providing he doesn't have any serious damage to his knees. Smokey healed up just fine and a few months later John was back roping off him.

The following weekend I was competing at a Tommy Steiner rodeo in the Amphitheatre in Chicago. There were two go rounds in the bull riding and I had drawn a bull branded 1X. Three months earlier, I drew this bull at the Louisville, Kentucky State Fair Rodeo and was thrown off the second jump out. I rode him this time to win the go round. In the second round I had drawn #58, a dirty ducking, belly rolling, son of a gun and was thrown off.

After this rodeo I returned to my mother's home in Owosso where I stayed through Christmas. Then I decided to enter the big winter rodeos in Texas. I flew to Dallas, Texas for an RCA rodeo that began the day after Christmas. Still using Michigan as my home address, I would soon discover it was to my disadvantage.

I rode the bull drawn for me but failed to place. This would be the first time I ever watched the sixteen times World Champion Cowboy, the great Jim Shoulders ride in person. I watched him many times on televised rodeos. Jim bucked off his bull around six seconds and was lying on the ground, flat on his back for a good two seconds before the whistle blew. The rodeo judges still marked him though and he won the bull riding.

Raleigh, N.C. Barry Brown on "661"

Chapter Eight

When the January issue of the Rodeo Sports News was published, I was ranked seventh in the World Standings.

After Dallas, I competed at Odessa, Texas, where I bucked off my contest bull. David Glover, who was a top bull rider from Durant, Oklahoma didn't show up to ride the bull drawn for him. David knew the bull. He also knew he couldn't win any money on him, as he didn't buck much at all. This bull was a straight Brahma with a pretty good set of horns attached to the top of its head and would hook the britches off you.

I didn't know the bull but agreed to mount 'em out for two dollars and fifty cents. I rode that sorry Braymer but after stepping off him, he caught me with a horn and hooked the living daylights out of me. I took the worse hookin' I ever had at that time. The next morning I was sore all over and could hardly turn my head. I was sure glad I didn't have any serious injuries or broken bones.

I caught a ride to Fort Worth with a few bull riders and had them drop me off at the bus station where I purchased a ticket to Gainesville, Florida. Taking a day and a half before arriving at my final destination, it was a great relief to be off that bus.

Ronnie was at the station and we headed for the Homestead, Florida rodeo, four hundred miles south of Gainesville. I drew a bull to win the rodeo on, which was #31 of the Rocking R.

David Glover rode this bull at the Fort Worth rodeo a week later to win a go round. This bull was a very fast spinner to the right and I hit the turf before making a qualified ride. I also competed in the bareback riding, again failing to place. When Ronnie and I arrived back in Gainesville, he let me out at the train station as I had to get back to Fort Worth for my next rodeo.

There were no trains to Fort Worth, so I rode it to Houston from there I hitch hiked the rest of the way. This rodeo had twenty performances in ten days. There were two go rounds, with a short go round (finals) which is held during the last performance. Only the top twelve contestants with the highest total score from the two go rounds would compete in the finals. The rodeo secretary would total the three scores from the three rounds after the finals were over. The cowboy with the highest total score on three head was declared the Champion. There were usually 160 or more bull riders competing at the big rodeos.

Riding both my bulls I failed to place on either one of them and missed making the finals by one point. I scored a 57, and 58, respectively in the two go rounds. The judges didn't know how to use this new scoring system. Even in the 1970's I have won many bull ridings with scores of 70-75, points. Today those same bull rides would be scored 80-90, as the judges have learned how to use the spread.

When I was at the Dallas rodeo watching the bull riding event, #84 Wild Man, of the Harry Knight string was being bucked. After watching this bull buck, I said to the bull riders sitting with me, I would like to draw him at San Antonio.

Are you crazy, that's Wild Man! One of them spoke.

I don't care; I think I could ride 'em. Wild Man had a reputation of not only being a rank buckin' bull, he was also very mean and had injured several bull riders. He had been ridden only a few times over the years he was bucked. Most riders that drew this bull were so frightened of him, there was no way they could stay on him. Back when I decided I wanted to be a bull rider, Ronnie told me, in order to be able to ride bulls, you can't be afraid of them. You have to respect them, knowing they can hurt you.

I rode bulls for many years and was never afraid until my last year of riding 'em. Heck, I craved the challenge and loved the rodeo cowboy way of life. How could a person enjoy something if they were scared of it? Most carnival rides scare me and I refuse to ride them. Dozens of times I've been told, you're mighty brave to be riding those bulls.

Bravery has nothing to do with it, I would explain. I do it because I love the sport of rodeo. To me, those who ride Roller Coasters are the brave ones. Back in the summer of 1964, I watched World Champion bull rider Bill Kornell ride Wild Man at the Daddy of 'em all, the Cheyenne Frontiers Days Rodeo. I wasn't there but watched the rodeo on TV in a motel room, while at an amateur rodeo in Michigan. After riding Wild Man, Bill was interviewed on TV by ABC Wide World of Sports. He was asked, what is the rankest bull you have ever ridden? To which Bill replied, you just seen it. I believe it was the last time Wild Man was ridden until I rode him at the Houston Rodeo the following year.

After Fort Worth I competed at the San Antonio, Texas rodeo. I was making a real good ride on a big grey Brahma that was spinning to the left into my hand. While spurring him in the neck with my right foot the spur rowel got hung over his shoulder blade. If I would have left my foot where it was, I would have ridden him. As soon as I felt it was hung in his shoulder, I began pulling on the foot trying to get it out. When the spur came out, my foot popped out so quick that it flew way out away from the bull, which caused me to buck off just before the whistle blew. I rode my second bull but he didn't perform well enough to place on.

The following weekend, my next stop would be the Houston rodeo. 1965 was the last year this rodeo would be held at the stockyards. In 1966, and many years to follow, the Houston rodeo was held in the Astrodome. Upon arriving I was told I had drawn Wild Man in the first go round. My wish had come true, drawing the bull I wanted. I knew if I rode 'em I would win the go round. I sure needed to win. I hadn't won any money in a couple of months now. Also I had dropped out of the top fifteen in the World standings. Dallas Chartier was one of the few riders to have ridden #84 and was telling me how he rode the bull. Dallas began by telling me to set my rope way back from where I would normally put it on most bulls. He then told me a couple other things to do in order to have a chance to ride this rank bull. I noticed the great Harry Tompkins, standing off a ways from the two of us overhearing what Dallas was telling me.

When he left, Harry stepped over and said, set your rope on Wild Man like you would any other bull, and ride him like you would any other bull. Harry Tompkins was a former World Champion.

I did like Harry said. As I sat down on the bull's back I remember hearing the rodeo announcer say, well folks, the further we go the ranker they get. This next bull is the famous #84 Wild Man, of the Harry Knight string and we have a kid from Michigan who is going to attempt to ride him.

Well I did ride him! After dismounting I landed on my hands and knees. Crawling for my life, Wild Man was right behind me with his head down, about to run me down like a freight train. The chute gate was still wide open, and I was able to crawl around behind it. Wild Man turned off, going away from me then. I just knew I was going to receive a really high score. Then the announcer said one of the judges disqualified me for slapping the bull with my free hand during the ride. I couldn't believe it. I had just been cheated big time! I never touched that bull with my free hand. When I was walking out of the arena after the performance, many cowboys shook my hand for riding Wild Man. Art Reilly said, You're the only bull rider I ever seen who got on tilt while riding Wild Man and not check out (step off). As far as I know, I was the last person to ever ride the famous Wild Man.

I also competed in the Lake Charles, Louisiana rodeo during Houston. I was up at that rodeo the first of four performances. Jim Bausch, who was a tough hand riding bareback broncs said he was up the first performance; and I could ride with him.

Upon arrival at the Lake Charles Coliseum, I discovered I had drawn #25 of Tommy Steiner's. After easing down onto the bull's back, I slid my left hand into the hand hold of the rope. After wrapping the tail of the rope around my hand and clenching it tight, I called for the gate. Outside! I shouted. As we left the chute, the bull was bucking hard and began spinning to the left. Eight seconds later when the whistle blew, signaling the end of the ride, I was still in the middle of the bull's back.

I received a real good score from the judges and was sitting in first place when we left Lake Charles. I was feeling good as we headed back to Houston for the second go round. At the conclusion of the Lake Charles rodeo I ended up placing third.

The Houston rodeo had an event called the Wild Horse Race. This is a team event consisting of three contestants on each team. One contestant is called the anchor, the other the mugger, and one the rider. There wasn't but five teams entered and there were fifteen performances with fifteen go rounds. All five wild horses are released from the chutes at the same time. Each horse is haltered with a long rope attached to it. The anchorman would try and hold the horse from running off. The mugger would follow the rope up to the horse's head, grab an ear and place it into his mouth, then bite the horse's ear. This technique will cause the horse to stand still. Sometimes it works... sometimes it doesn't. Sometimes when the

HOUSTON '65   WILD HORSE RACE

Mugger reaches for the ear; the horse will rear and strike him in the face or on his head.

After the fifth go round, one team member, Paul Mayo, had been injured and had to quit the team. I was then asked by one of the other members, a former NFR bull rider, Bo Ashorn, if I wanted to be on their team. The entry fee had already been paid. I really enjoyed competing in the wild horse race and agreed to join their team. I competed in several wild horse races in the past; it was a good cowboy event. I always did the saddling and riding. Once the mugger had the horse mugged, with saddle in hand I would hurry over to the horse's side and saddle it. Once the horse was saddled, I would grab the saddle horn and swing up on the wild Mustang. The rope was then thrown to me, which I would catch and hang on as the horse took off running and buckin' down the arena. There was a judge at the other end. The first horse across the finish line with a rider on it was the winner. We won five go rounds in a row.

The Silver Spurs Rodeo used to always have a Wild Horse race. Bo Ashorn, C.T. Jones, and I would enter the contest each year usually winning it. My second bull at Houston bucked me off pretty quick, then caught me in the ribs with a horn and threw me a good fifteen feet through the air. By the next day I was mighty sore.

After Houston, I caught a ride to Montgomery, Alabama. Before entering that rodeo, I placed a call to the RCA office in Denver to have my home address changed from Owosso, Michigan to Gainesville Florida.

Billy Hand was a tough Florida bull rider and an NFR qualifier. At least Florida was on the rodeo map. Jim Shoulders was the stock contractor for the Montgomery rodeo. While there I received a call from my mother telling me I had a draft notice from the U.S. Army; and had to be in Fort Knox, Kentucky for basic training the eighth of June, 1965.

The last weekend in May I was competing at a rodeo in White Sulphur Springs, West Virginia. One day while in town, Kilos Campos, Frank Strout and I done a lot of drinking. I was arrested for disturbing the peace and spent the night in jail. The next day we were back in town for a haircut. The barber began talking about the cowboys that were in town the day before.

Those cowboys terrorized the whole town. Then he said, it looked as if the James gang hit town. The three of us were laughing, but never told him it was us.

That night at the rodeo I made a qualified ride to win first place. After picking up my prize money check the three of us drove all night to another rodeo in Otisville, Michigan. This was an amateur rodeo, and we arrived there around 11:00 a.m. the next morning. I competed in all three riding events and also the steer wrestling (bull dogging).

I was hoping to get wiped out in one of the events so I wouldn't have to go into the army. It didn't have anything to do with the Vietnam War. I just wanted to keep rodeoing. At Otisville,

I won the bareback, and bull riding, bucked off in the bronc riding, and didn't place in the doggin'. We also competed at a rodeo in Ann Arbor that night, and drove 100 mph to get there in time for the bareback riding, which is usually the first event in rodeo. I failed to place in either event at this rodeo.

By the eighth of June 1965, I was in the army. This ended all chances of qualifying for my first trip to the NFR. Just before leaving on the bus for Fort Knox, my girlfriend Charlotte said, I bet I'll be getting a Dear John letter from you!

You have it backwards; it's the soldier who always gets the Dear John I told her. Sure enough, several weeks later I received the Dear John from Charlotte.

Basic Training Ft. Knox, KY 1965

Chapter Nine

One weekend in May, while stationed at Fort Myers, Virginia in Alexandria, I rode the bus to the CowTown, New Jersey rodeo. While there, Dave Dancy, who was a two event hand, competing in calf roping, and steer wrestling, said he and three other cowboys were competing at the Otisville, Michigan rodeo the next night. Knowing I was from Michigan, and now stationed in the army, he invited me to ride along with them.

Since you're not entered, you won't have to pay for any fuel, he continued.

Knowing my brothers would be at this rodeo, I decided to go. When the Cow Town rodeo was over we headed out for Michigan.

Dave had a camper on the truck and pulling a two horse trailer. It was late Saturday night when we were about to get onto the Pennsylvania turnpike. A long haired, dirty looking hippie stood hitch hiking. Dave stopped to give him a ride. Telling the hippie to get into the camper, he didn't tell him about the three cowboys inside. Riding in the cab of the truck with Dave, as we pulled back onto the highway, he began laughing about what the cowboys were probably doing to the hippie. We both had a good laugh, as we figured they were scaring that poor hippie to death by telling him how they were going to whup him good if he ever moved.

Once we dropped the hippie off, we asked the guys in the camper what the hitch hiker did after seeing them in there. They told us the hippie sat next to the door on the floor of the camper and never moved or spoke a word.

We arrived at the Otisville rodeo before noon. Since it had been nearly a year since my being drafted, everyone was happy to see me. My brother Curt, I was told, was to be married in the rodeo arena during intermission. This was the first I heard about Curt getting married. My mother came with Ronnie, and Lyle. Sister Marlene, her husband Charlie, was there with their four children Randy, Lisa, Mara, and Ramon. After the wedding ceremony, all the cowboys lined up along the arena fence to kiss Curt's new bride, Cathy, as she exited the arena.

During the bull riding I was in the arena talking to Lyle. As the next bull left the chute, the gate was swung wide open. I was behind the gate when the bull kicked its back legs straight out very hard. Both hooves hit the gate, causing it to slam against my head, striking just above the end of my left eyebrow, nearly knocking me out. Lyle caught me as I was falling to the ground. I was told the gash would need a few stitches. Putting a band aid over the cut, I decided to wait until I got back to Fort Myers to have it sewn up by an army doctor.

It was around 1:00 p.m. Monday when Dave dropped me off at the base. When I walked into the barracks, I was told my Sargent reported me as A.W.O.L. since I wasn't in formation by 7:00 a.m. leaving the barracks I began my search for the Sargent. Once I located him, I reminded him he had asked me three days earlier if I would pull extra duty for him. He said if I did I could have Monday off. The Sergeant said that's right I did give you Monday off. I was no longer considered A.W.O.L. Then I went to sick bay and the doctor put six stitches in my head.

Two months later I was given an Honorable Discharge under medical conditions. This was due to the wire in my collarbone.

During my stay at Ft. Myers, I purchased a 1959, Chevy Impala. On my way home the engine blew up. I was somewhere in Eastern Ohio, on the Turnpike. It was 3:00 a.m. on a Tuesday morning. Catching a ride to the nearest phone, I placed a call to my good friend Jughead. In a few hours Jug arrived with a chain to tow the car back to his home in Toledo.

That Saturday the two of us went to a rodeo in Ohio where I failed to place in the bareback riding but won first in the bull riding along with a trophy buckle.

I thanked Jug for all his help and caught a ride with a few cowboys going to another rodeo in Central Michigan. Competing there the next day, I won first in both events. Winning over $500.00 for the weekend, I renewed my RCA membership and was back on the road again. It was good to be back on the rodeo trail once more with my dog Rod.

Unfortunately during my time in the Army I got to drinking nearly every day. After my discharge, I continued drinking way too much. However, on the days I was to compete, I wouldn't drink until after I had ridden. Then it was off to the bars, where I would stay until closing. Afterwards we would take beer to the room where we would play cards. It was a game called Cowboy Pitch. We would play and drink until daylight, then sleep all day.

Then back to the bars and do it all over again. Because of my drinking I have been arrested several times, mainly for public drunkenness or disorderly conduct. Once I was arrested while in the army for kicking out a window while at Fort Leonard Wood, Missouri. The cops were called, and took me to jail in Waynesville. After being locked in a cell, I began cussing the two cops that locked me up. I usually never cussed as I was taught as a little boy that it was wrong. However, when I would drink I would get as filthy mouthed as anyone. These two cops didn't like what I was calling them; entering the cell they began beating me with their fists. Trying to cover up with my arms, they continued punching.

Ok I'll quit! I shouted. They stopped then and left the cell. Another time I was locked up in Fort Worth, my friends brought a young lady to the jail whom I had never seen before. She was crying, and telling the cops she was my wife and if I missed work in the morning I would lose my job and we wouldn't be able to feed our baby. I could hear this girl from the cell. She was really good and about had me convinced we were married. It worked, and the cops released me.

Ronnie, Lyle, and I could imitate a police siren with our voices. We sounded just like a real police siren and have pulled many automobiles over using our voices as a siren. Once we were headed back to Owosso from an amateur rodeo in eastern Michigan.

I was driving, as we were rolling thru this town, Ronnie began making like a siren as we passed a car and it pulled off the road. About a mile out of town, we were pulled over by the police.

Open your hood, one of the officers commanded. When I did, both cops began looking all around and on the engine. Now open the trunk! One of them demanded, as they searched all through it. When they were unable to find what they were searching for they asked, where's it at? Where is what at? I asked. Your siren

We don't have a siren, but we heard one back in town. Then one of the cops told me someone got our tag number for pulling them over with a siren.

Do you cowboys travel thru here often? They asked. When I told them we had been to a rodeo and were on our way to Owosso, the cop said if you ever to come to this area again bypass our town. I don't ever want to see any of you in this town again.

Many times we would be running late for a rodeo and traffic would be backed up on the highway a mile or two. Knowing if we sat in line waiting to enter the rodeo grounds, we would miss the bareback riding. So the three of us would hang our heads out the window and do our siren. All the vehicles would pull off the road, leaving us a clear trail to the arena.

Here come the Browns, cowboys would say when hearing the siren. They would all be laughing as we came sliding up to the arena in the car.

Once in Belle Vernon, Pennsylvania, I pulled a Greyhound bus over. This even surprised me. I didn't think the driver could hear me. I even pulled over an ambulance in down town New York City once.

One night in Owosso, Lyle was stopped for pulling over vehicles using his voice siren. He told the cop it wasn't him.

I don't have a siren, he claimed. The next night Lyle was in town doing his siren again, when he was stopped by the same cop.

I got you this time! I was parked around the corner when you drove by with your siren going. Now give it to me!

Lyle began laughing. I can't give you the siren; I make the sound with my voice. The cop didn't believe him.

 Ok, then show me how you do it.

Taking a deep breath, Lyle let 'er rip. Unable to hold it in, the cop began laughing. Then he said, don't do it again. If you do, I will give you a ticket.

Chapter Ten

Lyle, Rod, and I, were on our way to a rodeo in Miami. Arriving around 10:00 p.m. we checked into a hotel downtown. I left my dog in the car while Lyle and I checked in. There was a sign on the desk which read, no pets allowed. When we got into our room, I removed all the clothes from my suitcase. Then I returned to the car with the empty suitcase. When I had it open, I told Rod to get in. After stepping into the suitcase, I told him to lie down. When he did, I pushed him down so he was lying flat on his side, then I closed the top down over him.

Rod weighed 45 pounds so he didn't fit easily into the case. As I carried it through the lobby and walking past the desk, Rod began moving, causing it to wiggle. I held the suitcase tightly against my leg, trying to prevent it from moving so much; hoping the desk clerk wouldn't notice the case moving. Once on the elevator, the bellhop was staring down at the suitcase when it moved but he never said anything and Rod spent the night in the room.

The following weekend during the Silver Spurs Rodeo in Kissimmee, Florida, a television crew was on hand to film a Honeycomb cereal commercial. My brother Ronnie was hired to ride buckin' horses and bulls for the commercial. This commercial was shown every Saturday morning during cartoons. Ronnie was in the process of building a house at the time and the money from the commercials paid for much his new home.

By May, while competing in the Jacksonville, Texas rodeo put on by Jim Shoulders, the bull I was attempting to ride threw me off, kicking me just above my right eye. Due to the severe blow to the head, I was semi conscious and taken to the hospital by ambulance where I received eight stitches to my brow. To this day there's still an indentation above the eye. Come morning I had a heck of a shiner and the eye had swollen completely shut. My left eye was black and blue and half closed also.

I was up at another rodeo that night in Coleman, Texas. By the time I arrived at the rodeo, I could barely see out of the left eye and had to doctor release out of the rodeo and did not ride. Four other cowboys and I left from Coleman and drove to Cresco, Iowa. They were Lewis Graves, Jim Batman, and Brothers Mike, and John Jamail.

We arrived in Cresco two days before the rodeo was to begin. There wasn't but one motel and it was filled, so we ended up staying at a boarding house in town. Our room was upstairs with a bathroom at the end of the hall. As soon as we unpacked the truck and got our clothes put in the room, we left and went to the bar for drinks, and to shoot pool. While drinking my third glass of beer, the glass broke and all the beer ran out onto the bar room floor. Of course I had picked the glass up with my teeth, which caused it to break, I think. Taking the broken glass to the bar, I handed it to the bartender. He took it and walked away.

Hey, I shouted! Aren't you going to give me another glass of beer?

No! He replied. We got into an argument, then he called the cops.

It wasn't long before a police officer walks in and starts talking to the bartender. I walked over and began to tell my side but the cop told me to wait.

After I hear his side, I will listen to your side of the story, the officer said. When the bartender finished, the cop turned and asked if I was going to go with him.

Wait a minute, you told me you would hear my side of the story, I replied.

Are you going with me or not? He asked.

No! I'm not going anywhere with you! I exclaimed. Then the cop asked where the phone was. The bartender pointed to some stairs which went down to the basement. When the cop's head went out of sight, I made my get away out the back door. As I walked along the side of the building towards the front of the bar to where our pickup was parked, there sat the patrol car. The officer's vehicle had one of those long whip antennas mounted on the back. I couldn't resist the temptation. Grabbing it by both hands, I bent it all up. Then I tied it in a knot. By the time I got to our truck, my friends were coming out of the bar. I climbed into the camper and as we left, we met two patrol cars headed towards the bar with their lights on. After we made a right turn and were out of sight, I jumped out and hid in some bushes until dark. When I thought it was safe, I made my way to the boarding house.

The next morning everyone left to get a bite to eat. Not daring to show my face in public I stayed at the room. When the guys returned they had a burger and eye makeup for me. I was hoping it would cover up the black eye and not be as noticeable. Jim Batman heard the cops were looking for a cowboy with a black eye. The makeup didn't work, so I laid low and stayed out of sight.

Later in the day when my friends returned to the room, they told me the Chief of Police was downstairs talking to the landlord. They overheard her tell him she seen me go up the stairs. I hurried down the hall to the bathroom. Jim Batman, who was a saddle bronc rider from Texas, was shaving. Looking towards the window I could see this huge oak tree, after climbing onto the window sill to jump for a limb, I chickened out. Being afraid of heights, it looked like a long ways to the ground should I miss the limb. Then I heard the chief at our room asking if I was in there, my friends told him I wasn't.

As the chief and landlord were leaving, they heard water running in the bathroom. Who's in there? She asked. I figured I was caught. Moving quickly, I stood against the wall next to the door, so when it was opened I would be behind it.

It's me, ma'am, I'm shaving and will be right out.

That's okay, she said, recognizing his voice. I waited a few minutes and then returned to our room. A while later one of the guys checked downstairs to see if the chief was gone and he was. I made my way down the stairs and out the door. While walking down the street I spotted a cowboy I knew.

Bob Scolberg and his wife from Minnesota were in their car headed for the rodeo grounds. When they seen me waving and yelling, they stopped.

Hi y'all, the cops are looking for me and I need to get out of town. Larry Lyons, and Dittman Mitchell, have a room out at the motel, can you take me there?

Sure Barry, get in, Bob replied.

Dittman was a rodeo announcer from Arkansas and Larry competed in bareback and bull riding and hailed from Lima, Ohio. Bob dropped me off at the room then headed for the rodeo. After telling Dittman, and Larry my deal with the cops, they said I was welcome to stay with them.

Larry said he was leaving in the morning for Pecatonica, Illinois. I had already entered that rodeo and now had a ride.

I was up that night at the Cresco rodeo but dared not go. This meant I had to turn my bull out but still would have to pay the entry fee plus a $25 dollar fine for not showing up. I had a good buckin' bull drawn and hated to turn 'em out. I sent a check for my fees with Larry. When they returned to the room after the rodeo, they told me it was a good thing I turned out, as there were cops all over the place looking for me.

The next morning Larry and I left for the rodeo in Pecatonica, Illinois. After Pecatonica, I headed for another one in Fordsville, Kentucky. I was to compete there Friday, then Joplin, Missouri Saturday night.

During the Fordsville rodeo I was trying to find a ride to Joplin. After asking several cowboys if they were going to Joplin, World Champion Bull Rider Freckles Brown (no kin of mine) said I could ride with him. Freckles won his first and only World Championship in bull riding at the young age of forty four, back in 1962. Freckles had a commanding lead in the World standings when he broke his neck in October 1962. The broken neck rendered him unable to compete at the National Finals Rodeo (NFR) held in December. None of the top fifteen bull riders competing at the NFR could win enough money to overtake Freckles for the World Championship title.

The NFR runs for ten straight days with ten performances and ten go rounds. The top fifteen money earners in each event earn the right to compete at the NFR for a chance to become the World Champion. The rankest buckin' horses and bulls from RCA approved stock contractors across the United States and Canada earn the right to compete against the top cowboys. This makes the NFR the greatest rodeo in the world.

During the Kentucky rodeo, Freckles competed in the three riding events as well as the bull doggin'. After the performance we packed our gear into the car and headed for Joplin. It was after daybreak when we arrived at the arena. Jim Shoulders and his hired hands were feeding the livestock. We visited with them for a little while, then we got into the car and slept a few hours.

A local clothing store was giving a gift certificate for a pair of pants to the first bull rider to buck off. I won the gift certificate but would have much rather made a qualified ride.

Freckles asked if I was going to enter the Crossett, Arkansas rodeo, which was in five days. Telling him I was, he invited me to stay at his place. Leaving Joplin, we arrived at his ranch in Soper, Oklahoma the next day. Freckles introduced his wife Eunice to me and I enjoyed tasty home cooked meals the next four days. The following day after arriving at the ranch, Freckles had me on his tractor mowing the pasture.

Come Friday we packed the car and hit the trail. It was good to be back on the road again. Freckles and I competed that night and I was again thrown off just before the whistle. We were up the next afternoon at a rodeo in Clear Lake, South Dakota.

Bill Kornell, the 1963 World Champion Bull Rider, was competing at Crossett the same performance. Bill had his own airplane and asked if we wanted to fly with him to Clear Lake. We left the motel at 4:00 a.m. on Saturday morning to fly to Clear Lake. By 8:00 a.m. we landed at the Omaha, Nebraska airport for fuel and breakfast. Before leaving we were advised there were severe thunderstorms and tornado watches out for the Dakotas and Nebraska.

I told Freckles there were plenty of rodeos to go to and I just as soon turn out at Clear Lake.

114

There was no way I wanted to get caught in a tornado while in a small airplane.

Freckles assured me if there should be an emergency with the plane he would rather be flying with Bill Kornell than anyone else. Freckles went on to say, Bill won't panic. He would fight it all the way to the ground, trying to save everyone. Freckles remarks didn't help a whole lot, but soon we were all in the plane.

Leaving the Omaha airport we climbed to ten thousand feet to get above the clouds. Two hours later, Bill informed us that we would have to land at the Watertown, South Dakota airport as they had a control tower. Clear Lake was just a grass strip with no tower.

Just before Bill began to descend thru the clouds, he radioed the tower for clearance to land. The flight controller told him, we have a passenger jet about to take off. But will keep it on the ground until you land. We will be there in ten minutes, Bill told the controller.

Once in the clouds, I couldn't see the end of the wings on the plane. By now I was getting pretty nervous. Prior to this flight with Bill, I was told he didn't pass the IFR test (Instrument Flight Rule.) It seemed as though we were in those clouds for a very long time. Then the control tower radioed Bill. Where are you? Looking at his watch he replied, we will be there in twenty seconds. You guys be looking for the airport. When we drop out from under these clouds the landing strip should be right in front of us said Bill. Then he remarked, in ten seconds we will bottom out of the clouds. With that, he began counting down, 9, 8, 7, 6, 5, 4, 3, 2, 1.

As Bill said one, we dropped out of the clouds, with the runway right in front of us, just like he said. I was amassed. I could see the jet sitting on the runway, waiting for us to land. Bill landed his plane and waited for the jet to take off, and then we left.

This time we stayed under the clouds which had only a five hundred foot ceiling but it wasn't much further to Clear Lake. When we arrived at the landing strip it looked like it hadn't been mowed in several months. After landing, Bill got someone from the airport to drive us to the rodeo arena. In spite of what I went through to get there, I was thrown off again.

After the rodeo, announcer CY Tallion, was visiting with Freckles. Who is this Barry Brown, he asked. That's my nephew replied Freckles.

It would have been to my advantage if I really was a nephew to the great Freckles Brown. It cost fifty dollars for the flight in Bill's plane and I didn't have the money to keep flying with him. I told Freckles I wasn't going to be able to keep flying with them since I was riding so badly. I was riding 'em right up to the whistle and then buck off.

Freckles said he and Cornell were talking about my problem. They both thought I was riding as good as anyone in the country but they could not figure out what my problem was. Freckles and Cornell headed west, while I caught a ride to Minnesota for another rodeo.

Chapter Eleven

Kilos Campos and I arrived at the rodeo grounds in a small town in southern Illinois for a night performance. Kilos competed in all three rough stock events and lived in Miami, Florida. While waiting for the rodeo to begin, we spotted a young lady sitting all alone in the bleachers.

Hey Kilos, let's go talk to the girl in the stands, I said. Upon reaching her we introduced ourselves,

I'm Shirley Burden, she spoke. We began laughing, telling jokes, actually we were flirting with her, trying to get the deal on. When we invited her to the rodeo dance after the performance she said, I'm Leroy Burden's wife. About that time a cowboy walks up, and low and behold it's her husband, bull rider Leroy from Shirley, Illinois.

Hi Leroy, the two of us spoke as we introduced ourselves.

We were trying to get a date with your wife. Of course that was before she let us know she was married, I said.

No problem Barry, the husband said with a friendly smile on his face.

This was a two day rodeo and since I was going to be there for both performances, I decided to work the labor list. I did this at many of the rodeos, earning enough money to cover my entry fees.

At the beginning of the first performance during the bareback riding contest, Kilos and I were behind the chutes when we noticed a good looking woman standing alone behind the chutes. As we approached her, we began shooting the bull; she was laughing and being very friendly. By now I had hold of her by the arm when one of the pickup men in the arena rode his horse up to the front of the chutes. Looking directly at me he shouted get your hands off her! We're just talking to her, what's it to you? I asked. That's my friend's wife; take your hand off her! Wife! Didn't know she was a married woman, I remarked. Turning her loose, we walked away. I heard nothing more about it until the next morning, when I entered the motel coffee shop. Seeing Kilos seated at one of the tables, I joined him.

Barry, did Ben Bates get a hold of you last night? Asked Kilos.

No, why? I asked.

He collared me up at the rodeo last night. Said he ought to slit my throat. It was his wife we had behind the chutes last night.

I could tell Kilos was petrified. Heck, he hasn't said anything to me about it. I told him.

Today would be a matinee performance and Ben hadn't said a word to me, so I forgot all about it. I was told he was a very big man who competed in the steer wrestling event. I also heard that when he gets in a fight he goes crazy. Ben Bates was one of the early Marlboro Men, who was in many commercials, as well as his picture being on large billboard signs throughout the country.

My job on the labor list was loading the calves and steers during the timed events. World

Champion Bareback rider J.C. Trujillo out of New Mexico would be releasing the cattle from the timed event chute. The calf roping was about to begin and I had the first calf ready to load when I spotted this huge cowboy approaching. While standing in the pen holding onto a calf J.C. turns, looks at me, and with a big grin on his face he shouts, Barry Brown!

Ben looks at me and says, get over here!

Thoughts began running thru my head. Should I do like he says or should I turn this calf loose and run? About that time Ben repeated himself, get over here right now! With that I climbed over the panel and stood before him.

Ben began chewing me out by asking; What were you doing with my wife last night?

I had no idea she was married, Ben, I said to him.

It doesn't matter! You sorry bull riders are always chousing on the women. It isn't right the way you all treat them! Complained Ben. I ought to cut you from ear to ear!

Deciding I better look scared, I tried putting a frown on my face.

You better wipe that smirk off yer face, or I will knock it clean down your throat! Exclaimed Ben. Then he clenched his fist.

Wow, I thought, his hand is bigger than my whole head. After a few more harsh words he turned and walked away. Climbing back into the pen, I loaded the calf into the chute. Two weeks later I heard Ben and his wife had divorced.

On my way to the Spooner, Wisconsin rodeo I made a stop for lunch in the southern part of the state. Upon entering the restaurant, low and behold, there sat Ben Bates and Judy Reed.

Come join us, spoke Ben. I was a little surprised at the invite from Ben, but did as he suggested and we got along just fine and become friends.

A few weeks later, at the Madison Square Garden Rodeo in New York City, I was making a good ride on a nice spinning bull. Around six seconds into the ride, rodeo clown Roger Mawson had a big inner tube in the arena with him. For some stupid reason he rolled it towards the bull while I was still riding it. When the tube was about to hit the animal, he hit the tube with his head causing him to quit buckin' and he run off. The judges refused to give a reride, I didn't place at the rodeo.

Howard Harris III was the stock contractor. He also served as one of the pick up men. During the bareback riding a rider was thrown off with his hand hung in the bareback rigging. The bronc began running, relentlessly dragging the cowboy. By the time the wild animal made its third lap around the arena still dragging the rider, Howard ran his horse as fast as it could go to catch up with the bronc. Once Howard was in position, he leaped from his pick up horse onto the broncs head. Wrapping his arms around the horse's neck, he threw the bronc to the ground. Several cowboys ran to the rider whose hand was still hung in the rigging. After freeing his hand, they pulled him out from under the bronc.

Then Howard loosened his grip and the buckin' horse regained its feet and left the arena. That was one wild event and cowboys talked about what Howard had done for a long time.

Howard also put on the weekly rodeo at Woodstown, New Jersey. In the rodeo world, it is known as The Cow Town, New Jersey Rodeo. Now Howard's son Grant Harris runs the weekly rodeo.

One night several of us cowboys were in a tavern in New York City. We were all sitting at a table when we heard this loud noise and glass breaking. Dickey Cox had just punched out the jukebox. It was playing a song he didn't like. With his hand cut and bleeding, Dickey wrapped a bandana around it. We were all laughing and Dickey joined us for another beer.

Later in the year, in fact it was during the month of September, I won the bull riding at the Congress rodeo in Waterloo, Iowa on Bob Barn's #54. Larry Lyons was competing at this rodeo and we were both up at Charleston, West Virginia the next night. I rode with Larry to Charleston where stock contractor Swanny Kirby was producing the rodeo.

There were two go rounds in the bull riding. We were up the second performance which would end the first go round. There were no qualified rides made the first day. Larry rode his bull, which put him winning the go round, as it was the only qualified ride made thus far. No other rides were made and I was the last bull rider out that performance. All I had to do was make a qualified ride to win no less than second in the go round.

I had drawn a long horned brindle Braymer. As he was spinning to the right away from my hand, I fell off into the well. This is the worst place for a bull rider to be, inside of the spin. I kept hanging onto the rope, hoping to hang on long enough to make a qualified ride. Being eyeball to eyeball with the bull is the last thing I remember.

When I awoke some two hours later, I could hear someone saying, wake up Barry, wake up.

As my eyes opened, there stood a nurse. Where am I? I asked.

You're in the hospital, Barry she replied. What town am I in?

You're in Charleston, Barry. The nurse responded. What state? I asked. West Virginia.

Closing my eyes, I never spoke another word, for I had lost my memory. Then I focused on a mental picture of West Virginia picturing it in my mind as it looks on the map. I also visualized where Charleston sits and got to wondering how I got to the rodeo. Then I ran it over and over in my mind, who did I come here with? All of a sudden it popped into my head, Larry Lyons. My memory was back. Opening my eyes and looking at the nurse I asked, can I go?

I guess you can, she replied. John Zormeier had come to the hospital checking on me, and gave me a ride to the motel.

Everyone was surprised when I walked into the room. They presumed I would be in the hospital for a very long time. One of my best friends, Perry Hatfield from Arizona, who was one of the best All Around Cowboys there ever was at the time, had two of his fingers bandaged.

Then I was told the bull whacked me in the mouth with one of its horns, knocking me unconscious. They went on to tell me I began having convulsions and swallowed my tongue. I was flopping around on the ground, choking to death on my tongue.

There was no ambulance or medical personnel at this rodeo which is in violation of RCA rules. Larry told me it was a good thing that Perry was there. It made him so sick he couldn't watch me flopping around and gurgling from the tongue being down my throat. Larry went on to tell me, it sounded like an axe hitting a pumpkin, when the bull's horn whacked me in the mouth. Perry ran out to help and was able to get two fingers far enough down my throat to grasp hold of my tongue and pull it back up out of my throat.

Perry held the tongue down until the ambulance arrived. While Perry was trying to grasp my tongue, I nearly chewed his fingers off.

It was thirty minutes before the ambulance arrived and my body was still flopping on the arena floor.

The next day, there were two pictures in the Charleston paper of me lying on the ground. There was a short article with the pictures which read, The Charleston Humane Association had observers at the Civic Center Saturday to guard against cruelty to animals in the Rodeo Cowboys

Association three day rodeo but the worst victims seemed to be the riders.

This is the way it is at most rodeos where there is an injury. It is usually the contestants who are injured, not the livestock. Accidents do happen though and once in a while an animal might receive an injury.

The RCA has strict humane rules for the livestock. Rodeo people love animals, this is another reason we love rodeo so much. We enjoy being around livestock, working with them, and having some of our own. It cost a lot of money to buy good buckin' horses and bulls. No stock contractor would ever allow anyone to mistreat any of their stock. Most of these animal rights activists don't have a clue about livestock.

After the Charleston injury, I returned home to Michigan for two weeks for dental work. A few of my teeth had been chipped

from the bull's horn. There were also twelve stitches in my upper lip.

By October I was rodeoing in California. I went out there soon after my teeth were taken care of. I wanted to be on the West Coast before the start of the Cow Palace rodeo in San Francisco. This is one of the biggest rodeos in the country and I didn't want to miss it. While rodeoing in California, I stayed with a bull rider I met earlier in the year at a rodeo in the Dakotas. His name is Vidal Garcia and we became the best of friends.

The day came when the entries for the Cow Palace rodeo were to close. By the time I remembered I needed to call and enter the rodeo, the books had closed three minutes

earlier and my entry was refused. However, Vidal'
had entered the day before, so I went to San
Francisco with him. This rodeo runs for ten
days. Vidal and I were broke, living mostly on
Ripple wine. It cost 89 cents for a bottle of that
stuff.

Wednesday is called Cattleman's day. The
rodeo arena is filled with tables covered with all
kinds of food for the paying patrons. Big hunks
of roast beef had been on the grill from the night
before and there were steaks of all kinds. Many
people were standing in line to buy their ticket
for the meal. Vidal and I didn't have a thing to
eat all day and no money to buy a meal ticket.
So we sat down in the spectators seats in the
coliseum, watching everyone eat.

For two hours we sat there watching all
these people filling their bellies, and ours were
 so empty. Vidal had eaten there in years past
and was telling me how good the steaks were,
knowing how hungry I was, then he would
laugh.

I got to watching the people who were leaving
after they finished eating. I noticed they were
dropping their paper plates and utensils into the
trash barrel next to the exit gate.

Come on, we are going to eat, I said to Vidal.
The two of us made our way to the trash barrel.
Reaching in we each grabbed a paper plate and
fork. Then, as we walked past the people we
were supposed to pay to get into the arena, we
held up the dirty plates and they presumed we
already paid and were going back for seconds.

126

At the conclusion of this rodeo, Vidal went to his parents' home in Santa Maria, California, and I caught a ride to Chicago for the Amphitheater rodeo. This was another Steiner rodeo where I competed in two events. I also hired on to work the labor list earning enough money to pay entry fees in one event.

Bill Earl was a bull rider from Arizona. He and I done a lot of drinking one day when we heard about a convention going on in the building for all the conventioneers. We knew that meant free drinks and perhaps food. Locating the room didn't take us long. Bill and I strolled up to the bar and ordered a beer, which was free for the convention folks. We stood out like two sore thumbs, as we were the only cowboys in the room.

Tables were set up with large bowls of chips and other snacks. Bill and I were hungry so we made a trip to the snack table. Grabbing a large bowl full of snacks each, we carried them back to the bar, where we proceeded to eat and drink. One of the men kept staring at us with a nasty look on his face. He knew we weren't supposed to be in there. After several drinks and empting the two bowls we left, with the man close behind. When he began cussing, Bill Earle beat 'em up.

Later while walking around in the building, we spotted this man sitting at his concession booth. Bill began kicking several display signs over. I finally got him to quit. We left and went back to the rodeo arena.

When I arrived at the Amphitheater the next day, I was told Tommy Steiner wanted to see me in the rodeo office. I knew I was in trouble then. Mr. Steiner chewed me out good and then kicked me off the labor list. He also had the rodeo judges disqualify me from the remainder of the rodeo. Luckily, I had already ridden both of my bulls and was sitting third in the average. However, I did have two more buckin' horses to get on but wasn't allowed to compete on them.

My third in the average held up and I left Chicago with money in my pocket. I headed for Detroit, Michigan to spend a few weeks with a few friends who were working at the racetrack in Hazel Park, near Detroit. They had a house rented to live in but no pets were allowed, so I dropped Rod off in Battle Creek, Michigan to stay with Lorayne and Bones.

A week later Lorayne called telling me Rod was dying. I left for Battle Creek immediately. Rod was very weak, but he was so happy to see me he managed to get up when Lorayne told him I was there. The next day I took Rod to the veterinarian. I told him I didn't care how much it would cost but for him to do whatever it would take to get him well; then I returned to Hazel Park.

Two days later Lorayne called to tell me Rod died. He was only six years old. The veterinarian told me his kidneys had quit working. He went on to say a dog's kidneys age twice as fast from too much hauling. He said dogs don't get let out to go to the bathroom when they need to, nor get the water they need. This causes their kidneys to age twice as fast.

We had a little funeral service for Rod, and then buried him behind my sister's house. I cried like a little baby and my mother said to Lorayne, I hope Barry will feel that way when I die. Even today, forty years later, people still talk about my dog, Rod.

When I left my sister's, I struck out for Toledo, Ohio. Jughead called and had a job for me loading horses in the starting gates at the Toledo Race Course.

One night after the races, Ronnie and Donnie Sowle, Darrel Coe, Butch Ogullsby, and I were at the bar, where I got very drunk. While sitting at the table, I was having trouble staying awake and kept trying to get my friends to leave. They had a couple of girls join them and refused to leave. Out the door I staggered. When I located our vehicle, I climbed inside to lie down. It was so cold I couldn't sleep and didn't have the keys to run the heater. Back into the bar I went, walking the best I could. Attempting to sit down, I fell over onto the table spilling all their drinks.

My friends still refused to leave, so I walked back outside and got into another car, having no idea who it belonged to. The keys weren't in it, but I was still able to turn the ignition switch and got the car running. I was staying with Jughead and his wife Lois who lived approximately 15 miles south of Toledo. Taking the car, I headed south.

Upon awakening later in the day, I began pondering my situation. Then I thought, perhaps it was just a bad dream. Getting out of bed, I peered out the window, hoping the car wouldn't be there. Sure enough, there it sat.

I felt bad for the woman who the car belonged to and assumed she had reported it stolen. Figuring it belonged to a woman, since there were two laundry baskets full of women's clothes in the back seat; I began wondering how to get the car back to the bar without getting caught. As I drove to the Interstate there sat a patrol car, parked on the on ramp I needed to take. Guilt convinced me the cop was looking for the car I had taken. Nervously I drove past him shaking in my boots, certain he would come after me. He never moved though.

There was a small grocery store close to the track where I abandoned the car. The bar where I had taken the vehicle was two blocks from where I left it.

Another night after leaving the track, Ronnie Sowle, Darrell Coe, his girlfriend and I were in another bar. Darrell was drunk. While he was gone to the bathroom, I poured beer onto the chair he was sitting on. When he returned and sat down, he quickly sprang to his feet, and began cussing and wanting to fight. Trying to laugh it off, I told him we were friends and to sit down. He continued cussing and I could tell he was about to throw a punch.

If you want to fight, let's go outside.

Soon as we were out the door, Darrell threw a round house punch. Ducking it, I hit him in the mouth. Down he went, landing face first onto the gravel parking lot. Getting up, he took another swing. Missing again, I smacked him square on the nose this time. Falling forward, his face was the first thing to hit the gravel again. The last time I knocked him down he didn't get up.

Grabbing his arms, I helped him up. Once I had him in the car, we headed for Kansas City. By the time we arrived Darrell's face was a mess from hitting the gravel so many times. When we saw John Farris, who was the arena director for the Tommy Steiner rodeo asked, what bull messed up your face?

We both laughed, then Darrell told John about the fight we had the night before. The three of us had a good laugh then.

John hired the both of us to work the labor list. We earned enough money to pay our entry fees. When I first met John Farris back in 1963, he was competing in all three rough stock events. His wife Mildred was the rodeo secretary for all of Steiner's rodeos and became one of the best rodeo secretaries in the country. Mildred also competed at the NFR as one of the top fifteen Barrel Racers of the World. She and John still continue to work for various rodeo companies throughout the country.

Not winning at this rodeo left me broke. I had planned on entering the National Western Livestock Show and Rodeo in Denver. Back in those days, the entry fee had to be paid before entry closing time. Entry fees in all events for those big rodeos were $100.00.

This would be my first time to compete at the Denver rodeo. Not having the money to enter, I began wondering how I could get the fee paid. Then I remembered when I first met a cowboy by the name of H.B. Johnson. It was during the Shreveport, Louisiana rodeo back in 1965.

After riding the bull I had drawn, this cowboy walks over and introduces himself as H.B. Johnson. I like the way you use your feet, if you ever need your fees paid, I will pay them for half yer winnings.

I placed a phone call to H. B. asking if he would pay my entry fee for Denver. He said he would, but with conditions, you will have to let me enter you at Ft. Worth, San Antonio, and Houston, too.

I was thrilled to hear him say that and was feeling really good knowing all my entry fees were going to be paid at all the big winter rodeos.

Chapter Twelve

A week before Denver, I competed at a rodeo in Orlando, Florida. It was mid January, and the weather in central Florida was sunny and warm. The Rocking R Rodeo Company produced this rodeo, where I bucked off the bull drawn for me. With Denver coming up in just a week, I sure needed a win. Now I began searching for a ride. There was no way I could afford to make the trip by myself. Jack Meli, and Dennis O'Rourke, were going and said I was welcome to ride with them.

Five days later the three of us were on the road to Denver. With close to seventeen hundred miles to travel, it took two days to make the trip. Upon arriving we checked into the May Flower Hotel. Sandy Kirby arrived in town the same day and we all shared a room together. The next morning after breakfast, while we were paying for our meal, I spotted a penny lying on the floor. Hey there's a penny, I said.

Is it heads up, asked Sandy. When I told him it was, he said, this is going to be your rodeo Barry.

We left the hotel and drove out to the coliseum where the rodeo would be held. When we got to the rodeo office, rodeo secretary June Ivory had the draw posted on the wall. We all began searching our names to see which performance we were to compete in. Everyone was listed except for me.

June, you left me off the draw sheet, I told her.

Well Barry, your entry fee arrived a day late, she replied.

Locating a phone, I called H.B. to let him know I wasn't entered. You're check arrived after the books closed, I'm not entered.

He apologized and assured me he would have the entry fees paid on time at the other rodeos. After hanging up the phone, I reached into my pocket for the penny I found. Throwing it as far as I could, swearing I'd never pick up another one. Now I was penniless, and decided to judge a rodeo to earn enough money so I could stay on the road.

The Amarillo, Texas rodeo would begin shortly after the conclusion of the National Western. Butler & Son Rodeo Company would be the stock contractor for the Texas rodeo. Jiggs Butler, along with his son, Benny, owned the company. I put in a call to Jiggs, inquiring about the judging job for Amarillo. Mr. Butler said I could have the job.

By the third weekend of February, I was at the Kissimmee, Florida rodeo. Saturday night after the performance, many of the cowboys had gone to Roscoe's bar. The place was packed with standing room only. However, I arrived soon enough to have a seat to sit on. After a few beers, I went to the restroom. When I returned, a cowboy had taken my seat.

I didn't know who he was, or if in fact he even was a contestant.

Hey cowboy! That's my seat, you need to move I insisted. As he stood up, we got into an argument. There were two other cowboys with him.

Let's step outside, he said. Then I caught a glimpse of something shiny in his hand. Figuring it was a knife I didn't budge. You coming outside with me, or not!

Nope, not until you get rid of the knife, I replied. Then I heard a click as he closed the blade. That scared me. I had no idea the blade was open.

As he handed the knife to one of his buddies, I stuck it on 'em. The blow to the head sent him sailing backwards onto a table. As he landed he slid all the way across it, landing on the floor.

Later, Larry Lyons told me he just bought a round of drinks for everyone at that table. He had just set the drinks down when I knocked the guy into it. All the drinks ended up on the floor when the table flipped over.

As the cowboy was getting up, I was there to hit him again. He went down. The fight was over as quick as it began.

The following weekend at a rodeo in Springfield, Virginia, rodeo clown and bull fighter Junior Meeks told me the cowboy I whooped was a calf roper and his neighbor back in Texas. He then told me the roper was shadow boxing every day and would be ready for me the next time we met.

Chapter Thirteen

July of 1968, Vidal and I were traveling together. Neither one of us had a vehicle, but we would always catch a ride together. We were at the Mobridge, South Dakota rodeo and while attempting to ride a bull, Vidal was jerked down onto the top of the bull's head, breaking his jaw. Vidal decided to fly home to California for the surgery.

The Mobridge rodeo is held during the week of July 4th, which rodeo cowboys refer to as Cowboy Christmas. This is due to the fact there's more rodeos that week than any other time of the year.

July 1st we competed at a rodeo in Belle Fourche, South Dakota. July 2nd at Mobridge, where Vidal broke his jaw. I went on to Killdeer, North Dakota, and competed there the next afternoon and that night in Dickinson, North Dakota. Then I caught a ride to Minneapolis, Minnesota for a flight to Florida the following day.

Brother Curt, who also rode bulls, picked me at the Tampa Airport then drove us to the Arcadia rodeo. As soon as we were off our bulls, we headed for the Silver Spurs rodeo in Kissimmee, where we competed that night. The next morning I flew out of Gainesville to O'Hare Airport in Chicago. Darrel Coe picked me up and we went to Pecatonica, Illinois for a matinee performance. I left there with Perry Hatfield, for Blue Earth, Minnesota.

We would compete on Tuesday night and then Superior, Wisconsin Wednesday. Due to severe thunderstorms and torrential rains, the rodeo was rescheduled for Wednesday afternoon. I was entered in the bareback and bull riding at Blue Earth but entered only the bull riding at the Superior rodeo.

Now that we had to stay in Blue Earth until after the rodeo on Wednesday, it was going to be nearly impossible to make it to Superior in time for Perry to compete in the bareback riding.

Finding a phone, I called the rodeo office in Superior and spoke with John Snow who was the rodeo announcer and partner in the Rodeos Incorporated, Rodeo Company. After telling him of the situation in Blue Earth, he told me they would begin their rodeo at 8:30 p.m. instead of 8:00 p.m. With an extra thirty minutes driving time, we figured we could make it.

Come rodeo time Wednesday, the arena was deep in mud. During the bareback bronc riding, I took first place on Bob Barn's Skipper. Tying for 2nd in the bull riding, I was declared All Around Champion of the Blue Earth rodeo.

After stepping off the bull and landing on my feet, Bobby Clark, who was one of the bullfighters, came up from behind as soon as I was off the bull. He then dropped two hands full of wet mud on the top of my head. We got into a mud fight and the fans loved it.

Covered in mud, I had to hose off and change clothes before Perry and I could leave. as soon as I received my prize money, we headed out for Superior.

Perry was doing 90 mph when we were pulled over by a Minnesota highway patrolman. Perry told the officer why he was speeding and he let us go. When we arrived at the rodeo arena in Superior, the Grand Entry had just begun. Perry rushed to the arena, where his bronc had already been loaded into the chute. I put his bareback rigging on the horse while Perry put his spurs and chaps on. Perry made a good spurring ride to place in the money.

I drew a bull that hadn't had a qualified ride made on him thus far in 1968. The bull was a very long horned Scottish Highlander. I saw this bull buck many times and he never tried to hook any bull rider.

After leaving the chute, the bull went into a spin to the right then immediately reversed his spin. While spinning rapidly to the left, he began drifting backwards at the same time. When the whistle blew, we were in front of the stripping chute gate. This is the gate where the buckin' stock is let out of the arena, once the rider is off. Right after the whistle blew I was thrown off away from my hand and was hung up in the rope. The bull was spinning to the left and my body was dragging on the ground off his right side with my hand still hung in the rope.

When the bull realized where I was, he came back around to the right and began hooking me. His right horn went under my body as he threw his head up, flipping me over his back. My hand came loose from the rope when I landed on the ground with the bull on top of me, savagely hooking the daylights out of me.

There were two bullfighters at this rodeo. One of them was Rick Young, from Tickfaw Louisiana. I can't recall who the other bullfighter was. They were trying to get the bull off me, but he wasn't paying a bit of attention to them. Lifting me off the ground with one of his horns, he flung me through the air like a rag doll. I ended up half way thru the piped let out gate. I went through the gate head first just past my chest. The rest of my body was standing on the ground in the arena on the other side of the gate. Frantically I tried to crawl through the gate but couldn't move. Then I tried pushing myself out, but was wedged between the pipes.

Then the bull caught me with a horn in my right side, snatching me back out of the gate. He had me on the ground again continuously hooking and hooking me some more. Then I realized he wasn't going to quit until he killed me. Luckily, he finally stopped. When he tired of hookin' me he trotted off to the far end of the arena. Two cowboys each grabbed me by an arm and drug me into the let out pen, laying me on my back.

Call an ambulance, my chest is caved in, I said to them the best I could. I was having trouble breathing and could barely speak. It felt as if my chest was touching my backbone. There was no ambulance or medical personal at this rodeo.

It was a hot dusty summer night and I was begging for something to drink. When a cowboy began to give me some of his Coke, Dwayne Martin, a bulldogger from Minnesota, (who a few

139

years later drowned after falling out of a boat) told the cowboy not to give me anything.

He may have internal injuries, Dwayne told him. Then he took some ice from the cup and rubbed my parched lips.

I continued to lie there on the ground barely able to breathe and in unbearable pain. It took the ambulance twenty minutes to arrive, which seemed an eternity. Immediately the paramedics put me on oxygen and I was transported to the Superior hospital.

Vidal was back on the trail again after having his jaw wired together and also competed at the Superior rodeo.

X rays of my chest were taken and then the technician phoned a doctor telling him the results. The doctor told the technician to transport me to Duluth, Minnesota for surgery. Desperately needing relief, I began begging for something to kill the pain, only to be informed nothing could be given until ordered by a doctor. Vidal arrived to see how I was as they rolled me out to the ambulance.

Make them give me something for pain, I said to him. Vidal began trying to tell the nurse, but with his jaw wired together even I couldn't understand what he was saying. Then he told me I had won the bull riding. I could understand him that time.

Upon arrival at the Duluth hospital, I was taken straight to x ray, still begging for pain killer. Again I was told I couldn't have anything until a doctor prescribed it. After many x rays, they finally put me on morphine, took me to a room and put me in a bed. Then a doctor came in to tell me he would operate on my chest in the morning. A tube was inserted into my nose, one in my arm and penis. I was finally able to sleep when the morphine took effect.

The next morning the doctor came into the room, telling me he had decided not to operate. He never told me why or whether or not I would need surgery. A nurse asked if there was anyone I wanted her to call.

If I am going to die, then yes, I said to her. No, you are not going to die she replied. Then I don't need you to call anyone. I didn't want any of my kinfolk driving so far to come see me. On the fourth day all the tubes were removed from my body. The morning of the fifth day I called the Duluth Airport to make reservations for a flight to Battle Creek, Michigan. Then I called a taxi to pick me up at the hospital. After getting dressed, I walked out of my room to the nurses station to tell them I was leaving. A nurse told me I couldn't leave as I had a very severe injury to my chest and besides that she said, the doctor hasn't released you.

Well, you better get him up here fast. I have a taxi on its way up here to take me to the airport. Within ten minutes the doctor arrived.

He signed the discharge papers without speaking a word to me. It seemed as though he was glad to be rid of me.

When I arrived in Battle Creek, Lorayne was waiting on me at the airport. The next day I went to see a doctor. After taking a few x rays he informed me I still had fluid in my lungs. The doctor also said my sternum was broken, and my chest was split in half. Additionally, I had five broken ribs.

Barry, there is nothing there to protect your heart. If you get hit hard enough in the chest, it could stop your heart from beating.

Then I thought, well darn, that's not good. I have wondered many times over the years why this doctor never mentioned anything about needing surgery. Plus, I was never told anything about the extent of my injuries when I was hospitalized in Duluth.

That coming weekend I judged the rodeo in Wyoming, Michigan. It was during this rodeo a friend told me he had called the Duluth hospital checking on me and was told I had a 50/50 chance of survival that first night. That was news to me, I had no idea death had come so close.

I continued judging for the next two and a half months while my chest was healing. Or so I thought. While judging rodeos I would sometimes have to climb a fence to keep from being kicked by a buckin' horse or being caught by a bull. When I would pull myself up the fence I could feel bones in my chest moving around. First there was a little pain, after a week or two my chest quit hurting, but it still didn't feel right.

Not feeling the need to see a doctor after judging for two and a half months, I began riding again, even though my chest never healed. The top half was completely disconnected from the lower half. I could push

142

the top half way in and the bottom half wouldn't move. I could do the same with the bottom half and the top half wouldn't move. I also could push the top half in and out, resulting in it moving back and forth. For the next two and a half years I continued competing in rodeos, riding bulls, and bareback broncs, even though my chest was split in half.

Chapter Fourteen

In less than a year after purchasing a 1965 Olds 98 with power windows, they all quit working at the same time. Not one of them would stay up on their own. When it would get too cold to leave the windows down, I would insert wood shims into the bottom of the glass to hold them up. Even then, there would be at least a four inch gap from the top.

As luck would have it, the heater core quit working too. This caused water to leak out onto the floor of the car. I couldn't afford to have it repaired, so I took the heater hose loose from under the hood, and then inserted the handle of a screwdriver into the hose securing it with a clamp. Now the heater no longer worked, but it stopped the water from leaking out. During the winter I nearly froze to death in that car. Once, I considered burning a bucket of charcoal in the car for heat, but never did.

One day Tom Wilson aka T.R., Gary Dymmek, and I were driving across Kansas on our way to a rodeo in Northern Iowa. We got into a severe thunderstorm late in the day. With the wind and rain blowing as hard as it was, I had to pull off the road. Since all the windows were partly opened, the rain was blowing in on us. T.R. and I were sitting next to each other in the middle of the front seat; Gary was in the middle of the back seat trying to keep dry. The three of us were soaked by the time the storm finally passed. We arrived in Iowa later in the night with the temperature in the low forties. We were all freezing! Since it was summer, we had only light jackets with us. We were miserable and stopped at every café or truck stop to thaw out.

Come November and back at the annual Amphitheater rodeo in Chicago, I drew the same bull that split my chest in half earlier in the year. I won the bull riding on him that first time, which paid $192.00. This rodeo was going to pay over $900.00 to win first. Riding the bull again, he didn't buck nearly as well as he had at the Superior rodeo and I failed to place on him.

Perry Hatfield and Dennis Rieners were there and told everyone they both had a birthday that coming Saturday. They went on to tell us their girlfriends were sending them each a birthday cake and everyone was welcome to have a piece. On Saturday the cakes arrived. One was chocolate, and the other white. Everyone was eating the chocolate cake. As I reached to get a piece of the chocolate cake, Perry whispered. Barry, get the white cake. Knowing him like I do, I did as he said. Perry later told me the icing on the chocolate cake was made of Ex lax.

A couple hours later we were sitting in the lounge at the motel. Several cowboys were sitting at tables with some girls they met. It was really funny watching all those guys as they went back and forth to the bathroom. They never did get a chance to visit with the girls. When they returned to their tables, it wasn't long before they were heading back to the restroom. The girls finally got up and left.

Chapter Fifteen

During the National Western Stock Show and Rodeo in Denver, Colorado, most of the cowboys were staying at the Mayflower Hotel in the heart of Denver. The city was inundated with hippies. When they passed by the hotel, cowboys would jump out, grab them, and then drag em into the lobby of the Mayflower. After pinning them to the floor, the cowboys would cut off the hippies hair with pocket knives and throw them back out into the street.

Prior to the opening performance of the rodeo, the Governor of Colorado was introduced. He thanked everyone for coming out to the rodeo. Then, I would like to thank all the rodeo cowboys for helping to beautify the city of Denver, by giving the hippies a haircut. All spectators and contestants were roaring with laughter at what the Governor just said.

There were two go rounds at this rodeo, with the top twelve highest scores on two head competing in the short round/finals, for the championship. In the first round I rode a bull that didn.t buck well at all and failed to place.

For the second go round the judges drew the bull I was hoping to draw. He was a red humped back muley that kicked high over its head, while spinning to the right. I just knew I would win a big chunk of prize money at this rodeo. Boy was I ever wrong. First jump out, the dad gum bull threw me off, and to add insult to injury he stepped on my right leg breaking it just above the ankle.

Medical personal laid me onto a stretcher, packed me out to the ambulance, and then carted me off to the hospital. We have to get the swelling down, before casting the leg. Therefore you will have to spend the night, I was told.

By morning the swelling was down. After X rays, a doctor said, usually, with the leg broke where yours is, we have to operate. You got lucky; the break isn't quite that bad.

O' goody, my lucks a changing, I was thinking.

Shortly after being released, I began calling stock contractors, lining up judging jobs for the next two months.

Dennis O. Rorke, Jack Meli, Sandy Kirby, and I were sharing a room at the hotel. One night while in the room on the fifth floor, Jack Meli opened the window. Then he and Dennis began climbing out. Sandy and I couldn't figure out where they thought they were going. Once they were both out the window, the two of us went to see what these guys were up to.

They somehow scaled down the brick wall of the hotel to the sidewalk below. Parked at the curb was a patrol car. Parked behind it was a vehicle with a drunk passed out in the front seat.

Opening the door, Jack, and Dennis, pulled him out and placed him in the back seat of the cop car. They returned to the room by way of the hotel elevator. Once in the room we all stood watching out the window, waiting for the cops to return to their car. Sure enough, in a short time two cops returned.

As they were getting into the front seat one of them noticed a man sleeping in the back. Both officers jumped out of their car and dragged the man out of the back seat. When they realized he was drunk, they handcuffed him and put „em back into their car and drove off. The four of us were laughing our heads off.

After seven days in Denver, I caught a ride to Amarillo, Texas where I served as one of the officials for their rodeo. When it was over I continued judging another seven weeks.

While at the Lubbock, Texas rodeo, I came across two sheets of plastic lying on the ground. Each piece looked to be a sixteenth of an inch thick, very strong and durable. They were just the right length and width to cover my chest. I got to thinking that maybe these two sheets would be enough to protect my heart, should a bull happen to step on my chest.

I took the sheets of plastic to a leather shop in Burkburnett, Texas, which was owned by the two time World Champion Bareback Rider, Jim Houston. Showing him my chest, I asked if he could build a brace out of the two sheets of plastic so it would cover my chest.

Two days later Jim called to tell me he had the brace ready. He covered the plastic with leather, sewed it together and attached buckles and straps. When I began riding again, before mounting the bull I would put the brace on under my shirt. This way it wasn't visible to anyone. Also, had I worn it on the outside of the shirt, a bull could get a horn under it, then carry me around on one of its horns.

I wore this brace every time I got on a bull for the next three years. Then Lyle's chest was stepped on by a bull at a rodeo in Detroit, Michigan. His sternum was cracked and I was worried about him getting stepped on again so I gave him the brace.

Six weeks after breaking the leg, I was judging the Lake Charles, Louisiana rodeo. By now my leg felt fine and I was tired of lugging the cast around. Figuring I could cut it off with a pocket knife, I filled the tub with water. Soaking the cast for a good thirty minutes, I began cutting. It took nearly an hour to cut the thing off. I had no idea it would be such a cumbersome task. Stepping out of the tub, I was unable to place the foot on the floor. I realized then, what big mistake I made. The only way to get around would be to hop on the good leg. Curtis Coomes injured his knee in the steer wrestling event two weeks earlier, so I lent him my crutches. Since there was a walking heel on the cast, I was able to walk just fine. Due to my brilliance, now I had no cast and no crutches.

I went to a farm and ranch supply store where I bought a stock cane as I had another rodeo performance to judge that night. I continued judging for another two weeks, and then went back to riding bulls and bareback broncs.

While competing at the San Antonio, Texas rodeo, I placed third in the second go round. I won just a little over $700, but had to send half to H.B. Johnson for paying my entry fees.

Denver · National Western

Chapter Sixteen

Now my reputation was one of being prone to injury. One day as Perry Hatfield, Sonny Ellison, (aka, Son Dog,) T R, Wilson, and I were coming into a town for a rodeo, Perry says, We better find the hospital first, so we will know where to pick up Barry. They all laughed. Boy...thanks a lot Perry. I muttered.

A few weeks later Vidal and I were at a rodeo close to the Mexico border in the South Texas town of Mercedes. During the Saturday matinee performance, two cowboys didn't show up. They were Tony Heberer and Tom Moews. Tony was the bareback riding rookie of the year, competing in bareback and bull riding. Tom and I traveled together in years past.

When the bull riding was about to begin, arena director, John Farris asked if I would mount out Tony's bull, which I did. Mr. Steiner paid $20 for getting on the bull. Had I known why they didn't show up, I would have gladly ridden the bull for no pay.

Tony and Tom competed at a rodeo in West Texas the night before, and left out the next morning for Mercedes in an airplane, owned by three cowboys. They were World Champion Gary Tucker, out of Carlsbad, New Mexico, Tony, along with another cowboy. Tony was the pilot when they got into bad weather and crashed in the hills of west Texas. It was more than a week before their bodies were found. At the conclusion of the Saturday night performance, Vidal, Sandy Kirby (aka Skurb) Bo Ashorn, and I went across the border into Old Mexico. This would be my first time to drink tequila. I drank so much of that stuff it landed me jail for the rest of the night. My trip to jail was anything but luxurious. The Police paddy wagon consisted of a 1951 Ford panel van. This must have been the economy model; the only thing to sit on was a spare tire lying on the floor inside. There were two small windows on the two back doors. A Mexican cop stood on the rear bumper watching me. Two handles were mounted on the outside of the doors for the cop to hold onto.

I was really frightened, thinking the policia were taking me out into the country to hang me or put me before a firing squad and shoot me. Of course that was if I made it that far. It felt as though this may be my final ride. I was being thrown all around inside the van, as all the roads were dirt and full of big holes. I began looking out the little window hoping to see one of my friends; I really wanted them to know what happened to me. As I was passing by the last bar on the street, Vidal came staggering out the door.

Vidal! Vidal! I shouted. When he heard me calling he looked to his right, then to the left. Once more I cried out, Vidal! He then realized I was in the police wagon.

Running into the street, Vidal began chasing after the van, shouting and shaking his fist, telling the cop on the rear bumper, let him out.

The officer told him to get back or he would put him in there with me. Vidal stopped, then waved bye bye to me. I felt a little better, knowing my friends would know where I was.

Upon arrival at the police station I was put into a large cell with a large group of Mexicans. Within minutes I realized the police wagon was merely a prelude to the less than comfortable living conditions within the Mexican jail.

There was no commode in this cell. They had compensated for that by providing a large hole in the wall to urinate in. I looked around wondering where I should sit, finding only the bare stained covered cement floor. Luckily for me, I was allowed to keep my can of snuff. Pacing and standing the rest of the night, I refused to sit on the nasty floor.

Come morning, I was taken to the Chief of Police. You speakie Espanol? the Chief wanted to know. Me no speakie Espanol. I responded. You no speak Espanol? he asked again. Me no savvy, I replied. Then I was taken to an empty cell. As soon as the cop left I went straight to the window which had no glass, only bars covering it. Then I noticed several bars broken loose from the wall. I began contemplating my escape after dark if no one came to bail me out. Only problem was, providing I busted out of there, I didn't know which way was north.

The chief sent for this old Mexican farmer who could speak English. He was to be the interpreter for the chief. When he arrived, I was taken back to the chief's office; where the interpreter explained to me why I had been arrested. I told the chief that was false, and I did pay for the item. The chief said it didn't matter, and I would have to pay a fine.

Ask the chief, how much the fine is, I said to the farmer. To which the Chief replied, $125 pesos. I about fainted, I thought it was the same as $125.00 American.

How long will I have to be locked up if I can't pay the fine? I asked frantically.

Two weeks, he replied. Then the chief asked if I could pay the fine.

No, I said, as panic set in again. Quickly pointing down while telling the chief he could have my Justin boots, he refused. Running out of options, I then offered my sterling silver belt buckle, which I won at a rodeo. By now the chief was getting mad.

This is no hock shop. You have to pay the fine just like you would in the States, he said angrily. That was that, options depleted, it was stay for two weeks, bust out, or hope like heck someone would get me outta there. I could do nothing but tell him I couldn't pay. He replied by having me placed back in the cell with the loose bars.

This time I would not be alone. Around ten minutes later, an old Mexican man who had a sack of tortillas with him, was put into the same cell. The old man was watching as I took out my Copenhagen and put a pinch of tobacco in my mouth. He spoke no English, but walked up to me with his hand out wanting a dip. When I held the can out to him, he reached in and took a big wad. Throwing it in his mouth, to my surprise, he swallowed it. I really thought he knew what it was, but he takes another big dip and swallows it too. He was much more surprised than I was. All of a sudden he runs to the window and spits and spits. He came to me rubbing his throat, Um, um, um, is all he could say, and then rubs his belly in a circling motion. Again saying um, um, um. Back to the window he ran, and spits some more, then back to me repeating it over and over. I was laughing pretty hard by then. Obviously he must have thought it was candy I had, not snuff.

Finally, Vidal showed up to pay the fine. Jerry Olson, a contract performer, who had a buffalo act in rodeo, gave Vidal $60.00 to bail me out of jail. The $125 pesos came to $9.25 in U.S. dollars. It sure felt good to be back across the border, in the good, ole USA. I won third place at the rodeo and repaid Jerry before leaving town. H. B. had paid my entry fees at this rodeo also, so I had to send him half of my winnings.

Other than being a saint, Jerry Olson competed in the steer wrestling event and finished among the top fifteen steer wrestlers of the world at least once. He was also a darn good rodeo bull fighter from South Dakota.

Jerry was the only bullfighter I had ever seen who could outrun a bull in a straight line without having to turn off. Sometimes when running from a bull, Jerry would look over his shoulder with this huge Swedish grin on his face, laughing at the bull because it couldn't catch him.

One year Jerry was the bullfighter at the Bonifay, Florida rodeo. During the bull riding, a bull jumped the arena fence after being bucked and the rider was off him. The bull began climbing the spectator filled bleachers. People were screaming and running for their lives. Many on the top row were jumping off to the ground below.

As the bull was about to reach the top of the bleachers, Jerry leaped over the fence and ran up the bleachers after the bull. Upon reaching it, Jerry grabbed it by both its horns and pulled its head around, then literally pulled the bull down from the bleachers. Jerry was a very big man and he not only could run, he was very strong. I had never seen anything like it in all my years of rodeoing, and doubt I ever will.

Chapter Seventeen

I competed in my first Canadian rodeo in Morris Manitoba, Saskatchewan in June of 1969. There were ten performances, with four go rounds in the bull riding. The last performance would be Saturday afternoon and I was scheduled to ride my fourth bull then. This bull was a big horned black Brahma. Leaping from the chute, he took one jump and then began spinning rapidly to the right. The longer I rode him the faster he would spin. Due to the centrifugal force my butt was lifted from his back. In bull rider terms it is known as jacking you up on your hand. When this happened, I immediately began pushing my riding hand hard against the bull's back, while at the same time squeezing tighter with my spurs.

I won the go round and the average to be declared the Bull Riding Champion of the Morris Stampede and Rodeo. The committee presented me with a trophy along with the prize money, and I was interviewed by a local radio station which broadcast all ten performances live. That night I competed at another rodeo in Hawley, Minnesota, where I again won first place.

Then I hooked up with bronc and bull rider Wayne Hall out of New Jersey. We were rodeoing hard and went eight straight days without sleeping in a bed. When Wayne was driving I would be sleeping in the back seat and Wayne would do the same while I was at the wheel.

Sometimes we would compete in two rodeos on the same day. Some of these rodeos were three hundred miles apart. We would have to drive wide open to get to the next one on time. We then would drive a thousand miles overnight for our next rodeo.

After that eighth day, we were able to get a room and got some much needed rest. It sure felt good to sleep in a bed for a change and bathe.

Two weeks later Wayne and I parted company. I decided to compete next at the Regina Saskatchewan rodeo with Wayne wanting to enter a different rodeo. After Regina, I was up next at the Daddy of em all, the Cheyenne Frontier Days Rodeo, in Cheyenne Wyoming.

World Champion Saddle Bronc Rider, and several times the Canadian Champion, Mel Hyland, and two other Canadian cowboys were going to Cheyenne and allowed me to ride with them. Mel had a camper on his truck, complete with a television. Late in the night, as we were travelling thru Montana, I watched Neal Armstrong take that first step for mankind on the moon.

Two weeks later competing in Harvey, North Dakota, after making a qualified ride, I stepped off the bull but was kicked in the back before hitting the ground. It hurt for just a little while and then I felt fine. A few of us spent the night in Harvey. The next morning while walking to the cafe, I had a really bad burning pain in my back. If I kept moving it would get much worse. So I would just freeze wherever I was and not move at all. In a little bit the pain would ease up and go away, then I could continue on. After the third time this happened, I decided to see a doctor before leaving Harvey.

After X rays were taken, the doctor told me nothing was broken but I was having muscle spasms. Glad to hear the good news, I decided to talk with this doctor about my chest. Opening my shirt, I began pushing in on the chest, showing him how it would wiggle.

The first thing he asked was, do you have insurance? When I told him about having insurance through the Rodeo Cowboys Association, he told me I should let him fix it.

All it will take is a little bit of wire, then you will be good as new, he explained.

I think I will wait and have the surgery done at home, I responded. The muscle spasms were increasing. Due to their frequency I decided to return to Michigan and take a couple weeks off to give my back a little time to heal.

A bull rider rode with me from Harvey to his home in Minnesota. It was around 4:00 a.m. traveling on I 94 in Northwestern Minnesota, when I run into the worst fog I had ever been in. There was zero visibility. When we entered into the fog I was doing 80 mph in the left lane while passing an eighteen wheeler pulling a flatbed loaded with hundreds of crates of live chickens.

It was pitch black, total darkness. The only thing visible was the glare from the headlights bouncing off the fog back into my eyeballs. As soon as I removed my foot from the accelerator the car began back firing loudly. Quickly hitting the brakes I brought the vehicle to a halt. As we rolled to a stop, we were sitting in the left lane.

The fog consumed the semi leaving me with no idea where it was.

Soon, a young man and a young lady appeared at my window. They told me it was a good thing I stopped. Their vehicles were right in front of me. When the young lady entered into the fog she brought her car to a stop in the left lane. Then the young man being unable to see her vehicle ran into the back end of her car.

Calmly, I told the cowboy who was with me we had better get my car off the road. I don't believe either one of us truly realized the danger we were in. He was walking in front of the car pointing which way for me to steer the vehicle when all of a sudden he disappeared into the fog. Stopping the car, I blew the horn. When he appeared at the driver's door, I told him he had gone out of sight and to sit on the hood to point the way. We got the car onto the grassy area well off the interstate. We were very fortunate no traffic had come along at the time.

Once out of the car we headed in the direction of voices we could hear in the dense fog. After locating the other drivers, the trucker handed us all a few flares he had in his truck. We stuck the flares into the road in a few places hoping to warn other drivers that might come along. Although once we were only a few steps from the flares, we couldn't see them.

Then we all heard an air horn blowing as another semi truck entered the fog. All of a sudden there was a loud crash as this driver run into the back of the flat bed trailer. We all hurried to check on the driver.

When we got to his truck he was slumped over the steering wheel, not moving or saying anything. There were chickens everywhere, clucking and cackling and many of them were dead. Of course the dead ones weren't making a sound! The chicken hauler returned to his truck to retrieve a pry bar. When we got the driver's door pried opened, the driver who was slumped over the steering wheel gave out a loud sigh of relief as he fell over onto the seat. His left leg was pinned between the seat and the door.

I told my friend we needed to get out of there and get some help. We hadn't gone far and were out of the fog and it was daylight. We had no idea it was daylight, it was still pitch black in the fog. The two of us were amazed.

After just a few miles, I came upon an exit that had just one old farmhouse sitting a short distance off the highway. I banged on the door of the house several times. Finally, a big goofy looking man wearing bib overalls with no shirt opened the door. I told him what happened and then he asked, what do you want me to do about it? I thought, Boy, what a dummy.

Call an ambulance or the state police! Again he asked, what do you want me to do about it?

I was flabbergasted. Returning to the car, I said to the bull rider, I can't believe anyone could be so ignorant. It was another twenty miles or more before we came to another exit. The both of us figured the cops were out there by now, so we continued on our way.

Chapter Eighteen

Within two weeks the back healed. Cabin fever had done set in and I was ready to get back on the road again. Catching a ride with identical twins Ronnie and Donnie Sowle, we headed out for North Washington, Pennsylvania. Midway through the performance a heavy fog rolled in, covering three fourths of the arena. During the saddle bronc riding within three seconds into the ride, the broncs with their riders still aboard would disappear into the fog. This made for a short ride for the contestants as the judges had to score them after they went out of sight. Even if a cowboy was thrown off before the mandatory eight seconds, the judges couldn't see it happen. That is unless the horse came back out of the fog before the buzzer sounded.

During the timed events, the timers had to leave the timers booth and walk to the far end of the arena in order to see when to start their stop watches.

Competing there Saturday night, I was scheduled to ride the next day in South Bend, Indiana. It was early Sunday morning when the Sowle brothers dropped me off at the Pittsburg Airport. There were no late night flights, so I spent the rest of the night in the airport. Ronnie and Donnie returned to Michigan.

Upon arriving at the rodeo in South Bend, I learned I had drawn bull #11, Bar Fly. Rodeos Incorporated was the stock contractor, and their bull Bar Fly had been ridden only once in the three years. I rode em and won first place.

Trophy Buckles were awarded to each event champion.

Bar Fly was a very strong jump and kicker. He never went in to a spin but was so rank that when he did get rode, the rider always won first place, beating out the spinners.

By the next day, little bumps covered the entire length of my riding arm. After each bull ride they continued to grow and my arm was hurting more. I decided to return home and rest the arm after my next good win, so I kept riding.

Finally, I won second place at Louisville, Kentucky, which paid over $700.00. Instead of laying off to give my arm a rest, I entered many more rodeos. I was riding well and drawing good buckin' bulls, so home was the last place I wanted to be. I left Louisville and went to the Indiana State Fair and Rodeo in Indianapolis.

The Bob Hope show was starring at the fair and would be performing in front of the grandstand on the racetrack. There were three rodeo performances in front of this grandstand also. Rodeo performances were during the day with the Bob Hope show at night. Many of us cowboys decided to see the show. After all, contestants had free admission.

Back at the room everyone was showering, changing clothes, and began drinking. We had three hours before the show would begin. By the time we got out to the fairgrounds, I was mighty drunk. It was dark by now and the next thing I remember, two Indiana State Police officers had a hold of me. It wasn't until the next morning when I found out what happened. I was in bed at the motel and woke up with someone asking me where Perry's car was.

Don't ask me, I didn't have it, I said to him. Then I was told, I got tired of waiting for Perry at the motel and drove off in his car and drove to the fairgrounds. Perry was in the room now and told me when he came in at 4:00 a.m. and seen the bandage on my chin, he figured I wrecked it. Not remembering taking his car was one thing, but I didn't even know there was a bandage on my jaw.

My friends then told me how I tripped over a rope which lay across the racetrack. There was an old man sitting on a chair at one end of the rope. When a vehicle came along he would lower it to the ground. While attempting to step over it, my feet got tangled in the rope. Tripping, I fell face first onto the hard track. I never tried to break the fall with my hands so my jaw was the first thing to hit the track, splitting it open. Regaining my feet, I looked at the old man accusing him of jerking the rope up as I was stepping over it, tripping me. As I ran towards him waving a clenched fist, he jumped up and began running while calling for help.

This is when the State Police grabbed me. My friends were trying to get the police not to arrest me, telling them they would take me to the first aid station to get my chin sewn up.

My shirt was covered in blood and I was still bleeding badly, so the cops agreed to let me go.

While lying on a cot in the first aid room, I passed out. I awoke as the doctor was shoving a needle thru the skin. Reaching with both hands,

I took hold of his arm to stop him. Then I passed out again and the doctor finished the job by inserting 14 stitches in the bottom of my jaw

Later that night while still at the fairgrounds, I met up with Judy Reed who was a barrel racer from Illinois. Judy offered to take me a back to the room as I forgot I had Perry's car. He found it safe and sound the next day. Later in the day when I seen Judy she was wearing a turtleneck shirt.

You're a hell of a lover when you're drunk she said. I didn't remember being with her either.

Chapter Nineteen

My arm continued to worsen and had lumps from the wrist all the way up through my bicep. After making another ride, the arm would be in so much pain, I would run back to my riggin' bag which was behind the chutes. In it was a can of ether and pain pills, along with my riding gear. Scrambling as fast as I could for the ether, I would spray the entire length of my arm. This would freeze it giving much needed relief. Then I would take two pain pills and head for the next rodeo.

During the Amboy rodeo in southern Minnesota, I had drawn bull #100 again, of the Bob Barns string. He was a big, stout, horned brindle, which I had ridden three or four times over the years, winning first place each time. I was glad to have drawn him again. In a way, I was kind of dreading riding him this time. I knew how my arm was going to feel after the ride. Even though I made a qualified ride to win first again, the arm was in such excruciating pain I couldn't enjoy the win. It was hurting so much that I was unable to pull the riding glove off my hand. I was out of ether and the pain pills didn't help at all.

Leaving the rodeo grounds alone, I headed for another rodeo in the town of Virginia, Minnesota. It was in the 30's that night and my arm was throbbing so bad, I hung it out the car window trying to freeze it. I was willing to try anything that might bring some relief from the pain. The cold air didn't help, so I stopped and bought a six pack of Budweiser and drank them all as fast as I could. Once I finished the last beer my arm was feeling much better.

With more than 300 miles to drive, I didn't arrive in Virginia until after daylight the next morning. When I reached the Civic Center, I laid down to sleep a few hours. That night after riding, my arm wasn't hurting as much as it had been. The rodeo committee had a complimentary room with food and a keg of beer for the contestants. After a few beers I went to the car where I slept for the night.

The next rodeo would be at the Minnesota State Fair in St. Paul, which was five days away. To my surprise when I stepped off that next bull, my arm wasn't hurting at all. It completely healed, with a few days rest.

From St. Paul, I made my way down to Fort Madison, Iowa where I finished in fourth place. Vidal was competing there also, but was thrown off.

This rodeo had four performances, in as many days. Each day one of the committee men would have a free feeding at their home for all contestants. It was their way of saying thank you cowboys, and cowgirls, for coming to our rodeo. Contestants such as me, who choose to rodeo for a living, eat in restaurants ten eleven months out of the year. It is really nice to get a home cooked meal like the ones we had at Ft. Madison, Iowa. Additionally the committee was well aware of how costly it is for the contestants who chose to rodeo for a living. In those days we had no sponsors and had to rely on what we won to pay all expenses, which were gas, motels, food, laundry, and most important, entry fees. As the saying goes in rodeo, Chicken today, feathers tomorrow

Vidal and I decided to enter a little one performance rodeo in Sibley, Iowa. This rodeo had only $80.00 in prize money added, per event. The two of us figured it would be an easy rodeo to win money at, as we didn't think any top hands would bother entering such a small rodeo, especially since the big rodeo in Omaha, Nebraska was being held the same weekend. This rodeo is called the Aksarben Rodeo, which is Nebraska, spelt backwards. Neither Vidal nor I had a vehicle but were able to catch a ride to Sibley with a couple of bronc riders who were going to the Aksarben rodeo.

When we arrived in Sibley, they dropped us off at an old hotel as there were no motels in this town. It was late in the night, so after checking in, we went to bed. The next morning we walked to a café where we had T Bone steaks, eggs, and a Budweiser for breakfast. The rodeo wouldn't begin until 8:00 p.m. and we had all day without anything to do, so we headed for the nearest bar.

We drank and shot pool until around 5:00 p.m. Two women came into the bar and joined us for some drinks. After leaving the bar, we grabbed a six pack of beer to take to the room with us. The four of us walked to the hotel and after a few beers, the girls left. Vidal and I grabbed our riggin' bags and walked to the rodeo grounds, which wasn't but only two blocks from the hotel.

After arriving at the arena we discovered there were several top cowboys who were competing in this little rodeo. I began feeling miserable and weak from drinking all day. This was the first and only time I ever done any drinking on the same day I was up, before competing.

I tied for second and third place in the bareback riding. Myrtis Dightman, who was a black bull rider from Houston, Texas and one of the top bull riders in the country at the time, had drawn the same bull as I. There was more bull riders entered then there were bulls at this rodeo, so some of the bulls had to be bucked twice. Myrtis drew the bull first and competed on him during the rodeo and I got on him after the performance. Myrtis bucked off, but I rode the bull, to win first place. I was crowned the All Around Champion, as I won more money than any other cowboy that competed in two events or more. After receiving my prize money, we carried our riggin' bags back to the hotel. Then we went back to the bar where we had spent most of the day.

Cotton Young, who was a steer wrestler from Alabama and who a few years later would become my brother in law and Joe Crane a saddle bronc rider from Illinois, were in the bar and invited us to join them. We sat at their table where there were two young ladies sitting.

When I was about to pay for the two beers I ordered, Cotton told me he had a tab and to charge them to him. While Cotton and Joe were shooting pool, Vidal and I began shootin' the bull with the two girls. After a few beers, we invited them to our room. One of the girls had a car and drove us to the hotel. We laughed at Cotton and Joe the next time we seen them, as they had to pay for our beers and we made off with their girls.

Chapter Twenty

I spent the month of December at my mother's place in Michigan, to be home for Christmas. The Madison, Wisconsin rodeo was held in January, one week before the Fort Worth, Texas rodeo. Ronnie, his brother Donnie, and I entered Madison.

One night after the rodeo, we were all back in our motel room and I was in the bed. Ronnie and Donnie were still drinking and were out in the hall. Jim Houston was sharing the room with us and the two of us were watching a movie.

Ronnie came running into the room telling me they needed help. He said there were several guys out in the hall trying to pick a fight. I jumped up and ran out of the room to help my friends. When I got out into the hall those other guys were at the far end going into their room. I just had to open my big mouth, and began telling those trouble makers they had better get in their room and not come out. When one of them stepped out into the hall, I continued mouthing him and he began running towards me. When he was getting close I could see this feller was pretty darn big. Grabbing the fire extinguisher from the wall, I began hosing him down.

When he was about to reach me, I threw the extinguisher at him. With a huge muscular arm, he batted it out of his way. Then he jumped on me. He had his arms wrapped around me, holding me tight. As we fell to the floor I had a good hold of him. We lay on the floor with neither one of us able to move. To my surprise he said, I quit! Then he turned me loose, so I turned him loose.

When we both were back to our feet, he asked, Why did you spray me with that stuff? Before I could answer, he threw a punch hitting me just below my bottom lip, splitting my jaw wide open. Then he returned to his room. As I walked into mine, blood was flowing down my shirt. Jim told me I better go to the emergency room and have my jaw sewn up. Telling him I couldn't afford it, he told me I was going to look like a freak if I didn't get it taken care of. Then Jim handed me his health insurance card and Donnie drove me to the hospital. It took fourteen stitches to close the wound.

The next day, Ronnie, and Donnie returned to Michigan and my bottom lip was five times its original size. I rode to Fort Worth, with Dennis Rieners, aka Ringtail, from Arizona. A few years later Dennis won a World Championship as a saddle bronc rider. He also starred in the rodeo movie Bronco Billy.

Some cowboys stayed in Madison for the next performance and when it was finished they came to Fort Worth. When they arrived, they told me the guy that busted my jaw came out to the rodeo the next night looking for me. They went on to tell me this guy said he felt bad for hitting me. He told them he was a weight lifter, and he wanted to apologize for hitting me. I thought that was mighty nice of him, but it didn't make my lip look or feel any better.

There were several of us sharing a room during our stay in Ft. Worth. One of the cowboys in the room became a country music singer a few years later. His name was Chris Ledoux. Chris had his guitar with him and would pick and sing while the rest of us would be playing a card game called cowboy pitch. Sometimes Chris would play cards, but his passion was riding buckin' horses and singing. Many times after a rodeo performance we would sit around the pool at the motel and drink, while Chris, Ivan Daines, Mel Hyland, and Monty (Hawkeye) Henson would pick and sing.

Chris was singing Copenhagen Angel long before it was recorded. In 1976 Chris Ledoux won the World Championship title in the bareback bronc riding. Then he went on to become a top recording artist.

During the Houston rodeo, most of the cowboys were staying at the White House motel. One night I was sitting in the lounge drinking my first beer. It wasn't long before I heard some ruckus going on in the lobby. Rising from where I had been sitting, I went to see what was going on. As I stepped out of the bar into the lobby, two cops had a hold of bull rider Tommy Tidwell. Tommy broke loose from the cops and began running, but the cops caught him quick and handcuffed him. Then I saw World Champion calf roper Ernie Taylor talking to the cops, asking why they were arresting Tommy. After telling Ernie the reason why, he told Tommy to go with them and he would come bail him out. Turning towards the cops he boldly told them there better not be one more mark put on Tommy or I will sue you!

As the cops were taking the bull rider out, Texas bulldogger Dewayne Newton told them if they were taking Tommy they would have to take him too. The cops spun him around, handcuffed him, and hauled the two of them off.

Suddenly it looked to be like twenty cops came busting through the door and into the lobby. Turning around, I found my way back into the lounge. While sitting at a table by myself, a few of those cops came into the lounge and said for me to get up. After telling them I didn't have anything to with it and didn't have a clue what they were talking about. He didn't believe me, more like he didn't care. I was handcuffed and taken to jail where I spent the night. Ernie Taylor told the cops he would sue them, yet they did nothing to him. All I did was stand and watch what was going on; I never uttered a word. The next morning someone bailed me out. Several other men and I were sharing the same cell. When this cop unlocked the cell gate and called my name, I walked out. I was wearing a new black $100.00 Resistol felt hat. The cop asked a few questions, then stopped and sternly said, take your hat off when I am talking to you! I did as ordered and removed the hat.

When the cop finished with his questions he turned and began walking, telling me to follow him. As I began to walk I put the hat back on, following behind him.

When the cop looked over his shoulder, seeing the hat on my head, he quickly turned around knocking it off my head with the back of his hand, saying, I told you to take that hat off! Picking my hat up from the floor, I carried it to the desk where I was to receive my belongings.

While standing behind the cop who knocked my hat off, I was looking at the pistol strapped to his hip. I wanted to grab that cop's gun and fill him full of holes. You don't mess with a cowboy's hat.

Being on the rodeo trail eleven and a half months out of the year, living expenses really add up. To cut cost a cowboy would check only himself into a motel and ask for two double beds. He was still only charged for one occupant. He then would get seven more cowboys to stay with him. When everyone was ready for bed, the mattresses would be pulled off and put onto the floor. There would be two on each mattress and two each on the box springs.

In Shreveport, Louisiana one night after the rodeo, I was in my car headed back to the room at the Horseshoe Motel. There was a stop sign just a half block from the Coliseum, which I didn't see. When I run thru the stop sign I ran into another car, hitting it in the back door. When the car stopped, it was two or three hundred feet through the intersection. I immediately stopped when I hit the car and was sitting in the middle of the intersection. The other driver was out of his car looking at the damage done to his vehicle, then he looked at me.

I got to thinking how I didn't have any insurance, run a stop sign, and been drinking. Mashing down on the accelerator, I skedaddled out of there. To get to the motel I had to make two left turns, which put me crossing back over the same street the wreck occurred on. My car still sounded like an army tank. As I crossed over the street where the other car was sitting, I eased off the accelerator figuring the driver would be listening for the car and would know where I was.

Upon arriving at the motel, I parked in front of the room where shrubbery grew between the curb and sidewalk. With a headlight knocked out and damage to the fender, I pushed the front of the car tight against the shrubbery. I was hoping if the cops should happen to drive thru looking for a car with a headlight out, they wouldn't see it.

The next day when leaving Shreveport, I was really nervous and thought the cops would be out and about looking for me. Being easy on the accelerator, trying to keep the car as quiet as possible, I sneaked out of town and drove to the next rodeo.

While at the Baton Rouge rodeo, I came down with the flu and couldn't afford to see a doctor. Perry Hatfield was there and after telling him how bad I felt, he suggested taking me out to Clark Holden's ranch. Clark rode broncs and had a horse ranch near Baton Rouge. Perry told me we could get a needle and syringe from Clark and he would give me a shot of livestock Penicillin.

After telling Clark what we needed, he told us all he had was Terramycin. This is a type of antibiotics used in livestock.

All the needles have been used on the horses, Clark told us.

That's alright, we will boil it in hot water first, spoke Perry.

When he had the needle and syringe ready, he asked, where do you want it? Give it to me in the arm, I said.

No! I would rather give it in the hip, Perry told me.

Again I said, put it in the arm. He insisted I let him give the shot in my butt. Finally, I agreed and pulled my Wranglers down and bent over. I could feel the needle as Perry gave me the shot but he pulled his hand away fast. Are you finished already? I asked.

No, it didn't go in he replied. The needle was dull, since it was previously used on five head of horses. Perry then drew his hand with the needle in it way back and then drove it home. The needle went in this time and the medication was injected.

We visited with Clark for a while and then we drove back to town. The next day, due to the shot, I could only sit on one cheek. I began to worry that I might not be able to sit on the bull's back the following day. When it came time though, it was feeling better. I made a qualified ride to place in the money. That one shot of Terramycin worked and I was feeling much better.

World Champion bull rider Ronnie Rossen was competing at the rodeo. He had drawn a bull branded YD, which stood for Yellow Dog. YD was a pretty good jump and kicker and he seldom would go into a spin. Having very long horns, I never seen him come close to hookin' anyone. In fact if the rider or clown got in his way, YD would always run around them and out the gate.

While Ronnie was riding YD, he began spurring the bull very hard. During the ride Ronnie had both feet far out from the bull's sides and was jerked down onto the top of its head, smacking Ronnie in the face. When he landed on the arena floor, he was out colder than a cucumber.

YD continued on to the far end of the arena where he immediately turned around and just stood there. By now medical personal were attending to Ronnie and a stretcher was brought in to carry him out. All the while Ronnie was being attended to; YD stood watching from the far end of the arena and never moved. I had watched YD buck many times over the years at other rodeos. He would always make a big circle and run out the gate as soon as the rider was off his back. It was like the bull knew Ronnie was hurt. Everyone was watching YD. It looked as if he had tears in his eyes and felt bad for the bull rider. As soon as Ronnie was carried from the arena, the bull began trotting back towards the other end of the arena where everyone was standing, then he went out the gate. We all were amazed by the bull's actions.

A day later I was back in Florida, competing in two other rodeos. During the Silver Spurs rodeo friends were telling me they were going to enter Bob Barnes' rodeo in Buffalo, Minnesota and asked if I wanted to travel with them. To split expenses I left my car at Ronnie's. A few weeks later none of us had won any money and my traveling partners decided to return home.

There were no PRCA sanctioned rodeos in Florida at the time, so I caught another ride to the Fort Smith, Arkansas rodeo. This rodeo had four performances, Wednesday thru Saturday night. I was to compete on Wednesday. Being penniless, I paid the entry fee with a hot check.

The Fort Smith Rodeo Committee has a free barbeque for the contestants each day, so I got to eat at least one meal a day. I bucked off the bull drawn for me and caught a ride to Hugo, Oklahoma where I was to compete Thursday night.

The bull at this rodeo didn't buck much at all and I got on him during the slack after the rodeo in pouring down rain. I could have turned the bull out without having to pay a fine since it was the slack and not a paid performance. Being broke, I never considered that option. Instead, I was hoping the judges would offer a reride. No such luck though as the judges said no to a reride. I had to write another hot check at this rodeo.

Next, I was up in the slack Friday night in Madisonville, Texas. Again, I had drawn a bull that wasn't much of a bucker.

I sent another hot check with a bull rider that was going to Madisonville and rode to Fort Worth, where I stayed with a friend. Saturday night, I competed at Mesquite, Texas.

My last rodeo for this week would be in Strong City, Kansas on Sunday. During the Mesquite rodeo, I was trying to find someone who was going to Strong City. Unable to find anyone going I began thinking I would have to turn out at the Kansas rodeo. No one I asked was going and didn't know of anyone who had entered that rodeo.

Midway thru the performance though, I got lucky. A calf roper heard I needed a ride and said I was welcome to ride with him and his wife. After thanking him, I informed him I was broke and wouldn't be able to pay for any of the gas. Then I promised to pay him when I won some money. He said if I could help with the driving, I wouldn't have to pay for any of the fuel. I tied for fourth place at Mesquite but had to leave before picking up my winnings. With the rigging bag slung over my shoulder, I hurried from the arena. Bo Ashorn was standing at the gate as I made my exit.

Hey Bo, pick up my check, I'll see you in Ft. Worth Monday.

The calf roper and his wife had their horses loaded and were sitting in the truck with the engine running, waiting on me. I jumped in and we struck a lope for Kansas, arriving there before noon the next day.

At Strong City I drew a big Brahma bull that come from the Cow Town Rodeo Company in

Woodstown, New Jersey, owned by Howard Harris III. I believe this bull's name was Playboy. The big Brahma seldom was ridden, as he would one jump most of its riders. This was my last chance at winning any money to cover all the hot checks I had written for entry fees, which I had to do at this rodeo also.

Sandy Kirby was entered and said to me I will tell you how to ride the bull if you would like me to.

You bet Sandy, tell me, I quickly responded. This Brahma would squat way down low with his front legs extended out in front of him as soon as the rider began to sit on his back. Usually when a bull isn't standing correctly in the chutes, the rider will not nod his head until the animal is standing properly.

Sandy told me not to jack with the bull, and to take him squatting. Then he went on to tell me when a bull rider has someone poking on the bull to get him to stand, this makes him mad and he blows out of the chute hard and fast and kicks over his head, and the rider hits the ground. If you take the bull with him squatting, he can't blow out of the chute nearly as hard or strong.

I did as Sandy said and won third place on the braymer. The prize money check from this win was enough to cover all the hot checks and left me with enough money to rodeo on another two weeks.

By now my chest was really loose and I could feel it wiggle while walking. Mother kept after me to get it fixed, she was really worrying about me. Every time I would turn over while sleeping, I would wake up as my breast bones were rubbing against each other and would snap and pop. I began to worry about getting my chest stepped on by a bull and it killing me. This was causing me to buck off bulls I should have ridden.

December of 1970, I decided to have my chest repaired, and went to a Veterans Hospital in Ann Arbor, Michigan. While showing my chest to a doctor he began shaking his head.

I have never seen a chest like yours, he responded.

That's not good for me I thought. He then assigned me to a room. During the first two days, nurses and doctors would come to my room after hearing about my chest. Every one of them asked if they could see it. After showing them, they left the room shaking their heads.

X rays were taken every day and even at night. Finally, the VA doctor decided to take me to the University hospital before a board of doctors to examine my chest. As he told me, he couldn't figure out how to repair it. There were approximately twenty five to thirty doctors in the room. After hearing my story as to how the injury happened, they each came up to feel my chest, pushing it in and out, then they would shake their heads.

Then I was taken back to the VA Hospital. Finally, one day my doctor called me into his office to tell me they would be doing surgery at 7:00 A.M. the next morning. He, along with the university doctors had come up with a plan to repair the chest.

We decided to put two pins vertically into your chest. After a period of time we'll remove them.

Okay, I'm ready, I said.

At 7:00 a.m. the following morning, my doctor came into the room to tell me he cancelled the surgery.

I just don't think it's the best way to fix your chest. Something just isn't coming out right in the x rays.

Doc, I think I know what the problem is. If I could shove the top of my chest in and hold it for the x ray, I believe you would get what you're looking for. Then he told me to go on down to x ray and he would call the technician to advise him to do whatever I told him.

When I was standing in front of the x ray machine, I had the technician wait until I tell him when to take it. As I placed my fingers against the top half of my chest, I pushed it in and then said, ok, take it. After developing the x ray, he brought it to me and said it wouldn't work as all the bones in my fingers were in the way. Do you have a board I could use?

I don't know, but I will go look for one, said the technician. A short while later he returned with a 2 x 4 approximately two feet in length. I moved back into position for the x ray. Then after placing one end of the board against the top half of my chest, I grabbed the other end of the board with both hands and shoved my chest way in. After taking a deep breath, I said, ok take it.

Around five minutes later, the doctor called me to his office. As I entered, he said, that's it! He wanted me to see the x ray, which showed the top half of my chest had dropped down and was two inches behind and below the bottom half of the chest. Returning to my room I waited while my doctor took that x ray to the university doctors.

The next day, I was told they come up with a plan to fix my chest. He went on to tell me they had no idea whether or not it will work as this would be the first time for this type of surgery and I would be making medical history. He explained it all in detail.

We are going to take a few chips of bone from your left hip. Then we will mash those pieces into powder. Next, we will spread the powder along both halves of your breastbone; as this will help it to mend together faster. Then, we will take a larger piece of bone from the hip and shape it into a pin, and then wire it vertically into the center of the chest. Then we will wire both sides of the chest together. The doctor continued on. It will take at least a year for it to heal, but you may never be able to ride again if the surgery doesn't work.

But, I knew right then if it didn't work, it wouldn't keep me from competing in rodeos. I was riding with my chest split in half for over two years and there was no way I was about to quit. So I asked the doctor, Will I still have use of my arms if the surgery doesn't work? After telling me it wouldn't affect the usage of my arms at all. I said, let's go for it then. He informed me they would be taking pictures of my chest before, during, and after the surgery, and would film the whole process.

At seven the next morning the surgery began and seven hours later it was over. There were four doctors that worked on my chest.

When I awoke in the recovery room, I saw a nurse and my sister Lorayne. There were two surgical tubes inserted into each side of my chest and held in place with stitches and skin around the tubes. At the other end of the tubes were two one gallon jugs. These jugs were filling up with fluid being drained from my chest.

The next night after surgery, two nurses came into the room telling me I wasn't coughing enough and I still had quite a bit of fluid in my lungs. Then one nurse held my arms as the other one began feeding a surgical tube into my nose. I could feel the tube as it went down my throat and then curled around in my chest. With the other end of the tube hanging out my nose, the nurse began yanking up and down on it. This made me cough and cough, very hard. It felt as if it was going to tear everything apart in my chest. The tube was then removed from my nose, and the nurses left the room.

I sat on the edge of the bed and tried to cough all night long. I vowed that night; no one would ever tube me again. Two weeks later I was back home.

Chapter Twenty One

January came and I began calling stock contractors, lining up judging assignments. I knew there was no way I could sit around for a year waiting for the chest to heal and be away from rodeos for such a long time. My first judging job was the San Antonio, Texas rodeo in February.

I was staying with Claude and Sammy Groves at their parents' home in New Deal, Texas between rodeos. This was saving a lot of money as I didn't have to stay in motels. I never gave any thought as to how bad it may have looked to the other contestants that Claude and Sam were traveling with one of the rodeo judges. Cheating for them or anyone else was the furthest thing from my mind. I hated it when a crooked judge cheated me. My goal when judging rodeos was to be the best judge there ever was.

However, a few cowboys did start a campaign to stop me from judging and I was told World Champion saddle bronc rider John McBeth had accused me of splitting with Sammy Groves. Sam was riding broncs as well as anyone and was among the top fifteen in the World standings.

At most of the rodeos I judged, and Sam won money, the other judge usually scored him higher than I had. The six times All Around Champion of the World Larry Mahan asked if he could catch a ride to the next rodeo he was entered in and I was judging. Larry began telling how the RCA office had contacted him and asked what he thought about my judging. He told them he thought I was doing a good job and thought I was honest.

Phil Lyne, another All Around World Champion had done the same as Larry and caught a ride with me, and told me the same thing as Larry Mahan had. I judged the Helldorado Days Rodeo in Las Vegas, Nevada that spring.

There was a Rodeo Cowboys Association Board of Directors meeting during the rodeo. I was told the board was going to be checking me out. After the final performance of the rodeo, I was told the board had decided I was off on one horse. Personally, I thought that was some mighty good judging on my part; to be off on only one horse out of three to four hundred head. The board wanted to make those that were complaining about my judging happy, so I was told I would no longer be allowed to judge rodeos adding $1,000 or more per event.

I left Las Vegas and was to judge the Miami, Oklahoma rodeo the following weekend. There were five other cowboys that rode with me from Las Vegas to Oklahoma. It was late at night and we were in Northern Arizona. The heater still wasn't working, nor was the windows and they weren't all the way up. We were all freezing as cold air was blowing in on us from everywhere.

Bo Ashorn was one of the cowboys riding with me. He suggested we stop and get all our dirty socks and underwear out of the trunk and stuff them into all the cracks where air was coming in. We had socks and underwear stuffed at the top of all four windows. I am sure people thought we were really a bunch of weirdoes. It helped a little but we were still mighty cold all night long, but no one had to worry about the driver falling asleep.

After the Oklahoma rodeo, I was to judge another, which had $900.00 added per event in Montgomery, Alabama. John McBeth was entered and there were three go rounds in the saddle bronc riding.

After the final performance of the rodeo, I was on my way to the motel and stopped in at the Palomino bar. When asked what I would like, I replied, I drink Bud cause I'm wiser. Then I noticed John was in the bar. I never spoke to him, but instead walked over and sat down at the bar. John came over and placed a hand on my shoulder.

"Brown, you handled it like a man."

What are you talking about John? I asked. Well Barry, after arriving here at the rodeo, I learned you were one of the judges. I thought there was no way you were going to let me win anything; so I started to get back into the car and return home. I'm I glad I stayed though, I won exactly what I was supposed to.

I told him he should go to the RCA office and check all the judges. score sheets, from all those rodeos where Sam won money. Then he would see the other judges were always higher on him than I, except for maybe four or five rodeos.

I was sure you were cheating for Sam, I'm sorry, said John.

I judged almost every RCA rodeo in Texas through spring. I also judged rodeos all over the country, from California to New York, until August. It now had been nine months since the surgery and my chest was feeling like it had healed. I never went back to my doctor for an evaluation before entering my first rodeo. This was in Deadwood, South Dakota where I rode the bull I had drawn but he

didn't buck well enough to win on. The picture on the book cover is this bull.

The next weekend I was competing in the Sikeston, Missouri rodeo. The Sikeston rodeo committee has a party after the first performance for all the rodeo contestants. They would rent a room at the motel, set a commode up in the room, then fill it with a mixed drink they called Chicken Blood . After being given a cup, we would dip it into the commode stool to fill 'er up.

During the rodeo on Saturday night, I had drawn a good bull from the Rodeo's Incorporated string by the name of Frito Bandito. The great Freckles Brown was one of the judges. I scored eighty points to win first place. Sandy Kirby was at this rodeo and told me my eighty point ride was the fourth or fifth highest score ever made. I also received a silver buckle for being the Champion Bull Rider.

The Rodeo Sports News, is a publication for RCA members, and rodeo fans. Today it is known as the Pro Rodeo Sports News. It has a listing of coming rodeos and where and when they will be held. It also prints the results of past rodeos, complete with pictures, and the amount of money the contestants win at each RCA sanctioned rodeo. When the results for the Sikeston rodeo were printed in the Rodeo Sports News, the headline read, "Barry Brown, Comeback Cowboy of the year." This was due to the surgery I had on my chest and the fact that I made medical history, and was still able to ride and win. The Sports News article continued on and said, Barry made one of the greatest comebacks in all of sports. The Rodeo Cowboys Association selected me for the Comeback Cowboy of the Year award. I was the first recipient of this award, given by the RCA.

Comeback Winner Of '71-Barry Brown

By October I was at the Bonifay, Florida rodeo competing in the bareback and bull riding but wouldn't compete until Sunday. It was Saturday night and the Grand Entry had just begun. After the arena gate was closed, I walked up and leaned on the gate watching the Grand Entry. Someone came up from behind putting a hand on my right shoulder and jerked me back away from the gate. As I was turning around to see who had grabbed me so hard, I threw my right arm up, which caused the person who had a hold of me to lose their grip, causing their hand to come off my shoulder. After turning around, I realized it was a sheriff deputy that grabbed me. Speaking harshly, I said, don't grab me like that again! The deputy told me I was supposed to be able to recognize an officer of the law. Telling him I didn't have eyes in the back of my head, he asked if I was a contestant. "Yes I am!" "Let me see your membership card!" He demanded. You had no right grabbing and snatching me back the way you did. I'm not showing you anything! He then informed me as to how he was taking me down town, and asked if I was going with him.

I quickly responded I'm not going anywhere with you! Well then, I'm going to my car to call for back up; you're going to jail, the idiot said. When he left for the patrol car to radio for help, I went into the arena and headed over to where my future brother in law Cotton Young was standing. After telling him what just happened, we swapped hats. Mine was a black felt and he was wearing a silver belly. Cotton told me where he parked his truck which had a camper shell on it. I went to the far side of the arena, climbed over the fence and walked to the parking lot which was filled with thousands of vehicles. When I located the truck, I climbed into the camper where I laid for the next two hours.

After the rodeo, Cotton drove me to my motel room. When a few of my friends returned to the room, they told me several deputies were asking where I was. The deputy I had the confrontation with told them he was going to get me, even if he had to shoot me. He also said he would be at the contestants' gate on Sunday checking all the contestants' identification as they arrived for the rodeo. That night at the room, my friend Ernest Davis began telling about all the long haired hippie types who were milling around behind the buckin' chutes. He went on to tell about the cops clearing them all out of the area, which was for contestants only. Ernest saw me leaning on the gate and told how he got the deputy's attention and then pointed to me. He was telling the cop I wasn't supposed to be in there either. What began as a joke, nearly turned into a deadly situation. Ernest and I had a good laugh about it though.

Arriving two hours earlier than usual on Sunday, I knew no one would be at the gate checking contestants so early. When rodeo announcer, Hub Hubble arrived at the arena and seen me behind the buckin' chutes, he told me he heard about my run in with the law. Hub said he talked with stock contractor Matt Dryden of the Circle D Ranch in Marianna, Florida and rodeo secretary, Mildred Klingeman, about my situation. They agreed for Hub not to use my real name when I was to compete. The rodeo fans would be told I was Tex Hawkins, from Texas. Before the rodeo began, someone was telling me the deputy at the gate was checking contestants' identification and had a sawed off shotgun with him.

As I started up the chute gate to mount the buckin' horse, there were many deputies standing above on the catwalk. They were all watching as I sat down on the horse I was about to compete on. Not one of them had a clue I was the one they were looking for.

After the bull riding, I got out of town and headed for another rodeo.

Barry Brown   ?? Caution   Deadwood S.D. 9?

Come November I was back at the Chicago rodeo. Vidal and I had been at the bar and there was a restaurant next door. After leaving the bar we were sitting in a booth at the restaurant. Bill Earle was in the booth in front of us, when two plain clothes detectives began trying to pull him out of the booth. Bill was kicking and pulled a knife on them. They finally got him handcuffed and while standing in the middle of the floor, another cowboy from Arizona jumped up from where he was sitting, ran over and punched one of the detectives.

They grabbed him and put handcuffs on him too. Vidal was passed out the whole time but woke up and raised his head just as I stood up to tell the cops they had no right punching Bill the way they had. Just then one of the cops pulled out a can of mace and sprayed me. It got Vidal too and he immediately put his head back down. Our eyes were burning really bad and we couldn't see a thing. A little while later a paddy wagon arrived. I watched from the booth as the two cowboys were put into it.

Shaking Vidal awake I said to him c'mon, we're getting out of this sorry place. As we walked outside, I saw the cop who punched Bill. I began telling him again he had no right to hit Bill the way he had. A man standing next to the cop in a short sleeve shirt slapped me upside the head with a slapjack. I went down, as it nearly knocked me out. I jumped right back up and told the man I was going to my car to get a gun. I didn't even own a gun at the time.

He told the cops what I said and they threw me in the paddy wagon with the other two. The three of us spent the night in jail and were released the next morning after paying a twenty five dollar fine.

When the rodeo was over I decided to return to Michigan for Christmas. It was late at night and before I got out of Chicago a cop pulled me over and claimed I was speeding. I could tell this cop was drunk, so I offered him twenty dollars to let me go. He took my twenty and I drove to Michigan.

33 Barry Burns on Rafter "Fuzzy Bruin" (August 78) Jackson Ms. '81

Chapter Twenty Two

January, I was back in Fort Worth for their rodeo and when I went into the rodeo office to check the mail, there was a Western Union Telegram from Columbia Pictures with my name on it. It had an 800 number to call Columbia Pictures in New York City. I couldn't figure out why Columbia Pictures would want me to call them. Then I decided they sent it to me by mistake.

I called the number anyways and gave my name. I believe you sent this telegram to the wrong person and it was probably meant for the six times All Around Champion of the World, Larry Mahan, I said to the woman on the other end of the phone.

The lady said, no, you're the one. She then asked if I would be at the San Antonio, Texas rodeo.

Yes, that is my next rodeo to compete in, I replied. Then she told me which hotel to check into and said for me to charge all my meals and have my laundry done there and Columbia Pictures would pick up the tab. She went on to tell me that movie actor Cliff Robertson would be at the Saturday night performance of the rodeo and would be introducing me to the rodeo fans.

When I arrived in San Antonio I checked into the hotel and for the next ten days I lived like a king. I met Cliff Robertson at the rodeo Saturday night and after he introduced me to the fans, I walked out into the arena. Cliff presented me with a trophy which was given by him and the Rodeo Cowboys Association. These words were engraved onto it: "To Barry Brown, for perseverance over great adversity."

Cliff went on to tell the spectators about my surgery and what all I had been through. Columbia Pictures would be releasing a rodeo movie titled J. W. Coop. It was based on an All Around Champion Cowboy who had been in prison for ten years. After being released, he went back to rodeoing and was still able to ride and win.

Cliff Robertson came up with an idea to promote the movie. Columbia Pictures had been in touch with the RCA in 1971, to select a cowboy as Comeback Cowboy of the Year. Columbia Pictures then used me for publicity on the movie when it was being released in various cities around the country and there was a Pro Rodeo in town. I left San Antonio and competed next in El Paso, Texas, Baton Rouge, Louisiana, and Kissimmee, Florida.

While at the Silver Spurs Rodeo in Kissimmee, I was interviewed by the Orlando Sentinel News Paper. When the article came out in the Sunday paper, the headline on my article was "BIONIC BULL RIDER." This is where I got the title for my book. After the Silver Spurs Rodeo, I was to meet with Cliff Robertson at a steakhouse in Miami the following Friday.

I left Kissimmee with my friend Billy Yarborough, who was also a bull rider, living in Davie, Florida, which is close to Miami. While in Davie, I was interviewed by the Miami Herald paper. Then I met with Mr. Robertson at the steakhouse where he had several handicapped children present. Mr. Robertson was very involved with handicapped children. I was to speak to them about perseverance and overcoming adversities in their lives.

My meals and hotel expenses were paid for by Columbia Pictures. The next day I had to catch a flight to Houston, Texas for the Astrodome Rodeo. Columbia Pictures paid for my flight to Houston also. That ended my venture with Columbia Pictures and Cliff Robertson.

One night during the Houston rodeo, Wayne Hall, Tom Hazeltine, and myself were in a bar drinking. I had gone to the restroom and as I was coming out the door, a man was going in. As we met we bumped shoulders and when this happened, his hand grabbed me in the crotch. I turned and grabbed him by an arm and slung him across the bar room floor. He slammed into a table and slid across it, as he fell to the floor on the other side the table flipped over on top of him. After crawling out from under the table, he came running straight towards me. When he got close enough, I stuck it on him and down he went. As soon as I hit him, one of his buddies punched me in the nose and it began to bleed. This guy then went to saying, what are you doing hitting a blind man? He repeated this a few times.

Blind man? I asked. I thought he was a queer. By now Wayne was at my side, when a security guard approached saying, it was an automatic $250.00 fine for fighting in bars in Houston. I told him how this guy grabbed me in the crotch and I thought he was a queer.

Wayne told the guard they would leave and take me straight to the motel where we were staying. He agreed to let me go then and I was really feeling bad for hitting a blind man. I was thinking that maybe when our shoulders bumped, it caused his arm to swing forward hitting me in the crotch with the back of his hand.

That night while lying in bed, I run it over and over in my mind about the blind man I punched. There was no doubt in my mind he had actually grabbed me, as his hand was cupped when he did. Besides, there is no way a blind man could have jumped up after landing on the floor with the table on top of him and run straight to me like he did.

Later that spring while at the Mineral Wells, Texas rodeo, Walt Garrison, who was the great running back for the Dallas Cowboys, was also a steer wrestler. Walt was working for the U.S. Tobacco company and had been in many commercials for Copenhagen snuff. The U.S. Tobacco Company was to film a commercial showing Walt bulldogging a steer. The commercial was filmed one night after the rodeo.

A movie camera was strapped to Walt's head so as to give a view of what it looks like to bulldog a steer from horseback. Many spectators stayed to see the commercial being made. After the camera was mounted onto Walt's head, he mounted the bulldogging horse and backed it into the doggin' box. When the steer was released, the horse ran to catch it, and just as Walt began to lean to his right and slide off the horse's back onto the running steer, he suddenly fell to the ground missing the steer.

The camera, which was strapped to Walt's head, was so heavy, that when he reached for the steer the camera pulled him straight to the ground. Everyone was laughing. Then a much smaller camera was mounted to Walt's head and he was able to catch the steer this time and throw it down. The commercial was a success.

The last week of June, T.R. Wilson and I were in Mobridge, South Dakota. We arrived four days before the rodeo was to begin. Every day we drove out to the Missouri river to swim and kill time. When we left the river, we returned to our room to change clothes, and then head for the Silver Dollar Saloon. After drinking several beers one afternoon, I took out my buck knife and proceeded to pluck a silver dollar out of the floor.

We were the only ones in the bar at the time, so the bartender had no problem seeing what I was attempting to do. Coming out from behind the bar, he grabbed me by the arm that was holding the knife. What do you think you're doing? He asked. I'm getting me one of these silver dollars. I replied. After chewing me out, I returned to the booth. When we finished our beer, I called to the Barkeep, bring us another round. I will no longer serve you! He said. Exiting the booth I moseyed up to the bar. Hey! Come here. I snapped. When he was standing in front of me on the other side, I reached across grabbing him by the front of his shirt with both hands. Then I pulled him up across the bar, and told him he better give us a beer or I was going to whup him when he got off work.

T.R. and I left then and went to another bar next door. Later that night we returned to the Silver Dollar. The bartender met us at the door and handed each of us a beer. We never had to pay for another drink the rest of the night.

One day in August, on a flight to Douglas, Wyoming where I was up that night at the rodeo, a man sitting in the seat next to me asked if I was riding in the rodeo. After telling him I was, he told me country music singer Marty Robbins was playing at the rodeo and he was a guitar picker in Marty's Band. He told me his name was Son Duffy, and I introduced myself. As we were about to land in Douglas, he told me to look him up after the rodeo and he would treat me a steak dinner.

After the rodeo we went to a steak house where Mr. Duffy was asking all about my rodeoing. When I finished telling him, he told me I should go to Hollywood and be a stunt man.

I told him I didn't know anything about the business. Son Duffy then said to me,

Barry, the movie business is just like the music business, it isn't what you can do, but who you know. He then said he knew all the right contacts and could get me in the movie business.

I thought about it, but not for long, as I told Mr. Duffy I loved rodeo and was going to keep rodeoing like I was. I thanked him for the offer and never saw him again.

Sandy Kirby, Bo Ashorn, two other cowboys and I arrived in Fort Worth one night from a rodeo in Iowa. We headed straight for the bar, where we stayed until closing. I'm not sure where Sandy parked his truck for the night, but he slept on the front seat and the rest of us slept in the camper. I awoke in the morning when I heard Sandy cranking his truck.

Then he drove to a restaurant across the highway from where we slept. Everyone was awake by now and when Sandy parked his truck in front of the café, we all bailed out, with our cowboy hats on and our Wranglers tucked inside our Justin boots. The front of this café was all glass and I noticed many of the people inside eating were looking at all us cowboys as we fell out of the camper.

It rained during the night and there was a big mud puddle not far from the camper. When I saw the brown muddy water, I decided to brush my teeth. Returning to the camper, I grabbed my toothbrush and toothpaste. When I was at the muddy hole, I dipped the brush into the dingy water, then put toothpaste on it and began brushing my teeth. When my friends saw me brushing, they all got their brushes and did the same. Everyone in the restaurant was watching, as we brushed our teeth in that muddy brown water.

By September, I was competing in the bareback and bull riding at the Minnesota State Fair in St. Paul. I had a very good bucking bull drawn in the bull riding. The bareback horse I had drawn bucked me off and kicked me upside the head, just above my left ear before I hit the ground, knocking me out momentarily.

When I came to, calf roper C. T. Jones had his fingers in my mouth. He told me I was having convulsions and he was holding my tongue down. I was taken by ambulance to the St. Paul hospital. After lying on a bed in the emergency room for some time, I began calling for a nurse.

Finally, one came into the room and I was sitting up. I explained to her how I had a bull to ride at the rodeo and I needed her to get a doctor in there to sew up my head. Finally, a doctor came in to sew me up. It took thirteen stitches to close the wound. He then wrapped my head to where it looked like I was wearing a turban.

After being released, I called a taxi and went back to the Fairgrounds. I was hoping to make it back in time to compete in the bull riding. There was a lot of traffic and thousands of fairgoers.

The cab was stopped in traffic and I could see the coliseum where the rodeo was being held. It looked to be about two blocks away. Checking the cab meter to see how much I owed for the ride, I tossed the driver his fee. Leaping from the cab, I ran fast as I could. People were looking at me like I was a mad man with the turban on my head and the left half of my shirt covered with blood.

When I reached the arena I was mighty disappointed. The rodeo was over, and the arena was being taken down. I had been at the hospital much longer than I figured. I left town and headed down the road for the next rodeo.

The following weekend I was in Eau Claire, Wisconsin. Rodeo announcer John Snow who also announced the St. Paul rodeo asked what all happened to me after being hauled to the hospital. After telling him the whole story and about how hard I tried to make it back for the bull riding, he began repeating the story to the rodeo fans as I lowered myself onto the back of another bull. He finished by saying, so goes the Saga of Barry Brown.

A week later during the Ft. Madison, Iowa rodeo, Perry was attempting to pull the stitches out of my head with fingernail clippers. There were scabs over the stitches from the cut in my head. Once Perry began to pull them out, my head was really hurting and began to bleed. Then I soaked my head in the shower to soften the scabs and the stitches came out easily then.

By fall I was back in Florida staying with my good friend Phil Heinen and his family. Phil was a good bareback and bull rider and a former Champion in the bareback riding at the Daddy of „em all, The Cheyenne Frontier Days Rodeo. He also qualified for the NFR. Phil had bought some land near Summerfield, Florida, and I was fencing it off for him through the week and competing in PRCA rodeos on the weekends.

Barry Brown   24 (Minick)   Omaha 1974

Chapter Twenty Three

When January arrived, I decided to enter the Fort Worth, Texas rodeo. L e a v i n g Florida, I drove to Montgomery, Alabama where I caught a ride with Ernest Davis. Ernest competed in the steer wrestling event and had his own bull dogging team of horses. As we pulled onto the highway with the horse trailer behind the truck, we had gone only a couple of miles when we came upon a roadblock.

Alabama had three inches of snow the night before. A highway patrolman came over to the vehicle to tell us the road was closed due to all the snow. I told him we were competing in the Fort Worth rodeo and we could not wait for the snow to melt. The officer then informed us we would be traveling at our own risk if we continued on.

I said to the cop, I thought I always traveled at my own risk whenever I got behind the wheel. He moved the roadblock and we drove to Ft. Worth, arriving there a day before the first performance.

One night we went to a bar that had free draft beer night, with a one dollar cover charge. I got pretty drunk and ended up in the Ft. Worth Jail. Upon arrival and being checked in, a lady asked my name and other information. When she asked for my social security number I couldn't remember it, so I gave her my sister Lorayne's phone number who was living in Florida at the time. The two arresting officers ran to where I was standing, and one of them said, wise guy huh! Then he punches me upside the head, knocking me to the floor. Both of them went to beating me and kicked and stomped on my ribs and chest. Then they picked me up off the floor and propped me up against the desk in front of the lady and said, Now, do you remember that number?

I was very sore from the beating, but still could not remember my social security number. Finally, I told the woman I couldn't remember it. The two officers then took me to a cell and locked me up.

I come to the conclusion, if you make the cops mad, they will beat you, regardless of the color of your skin.

The next morning Ernest paid a $25.00 fine and I was released. Back at the motel I began thinking about what I had gone through the night before. I was tired of all the trouble I had been in over the years and did not want to be locked up ever again. I knew the drinking was my problem and decided to quit. For the next twenty two years I never went into another bar nor did I drink any alcoholic beverages and it paid off. I began riding better than I ever had. I was more consistent and winning more, although I failed to place at Ft. Worth.

It was tough not drinking the first month or two when I quit. TV stations would sign off at midnight in Louisiana and Texas and I was used to staying up most of the night. While everyone was out partying, I would be alone and bored to death.

During Baton Rouge, our room was next to the lounge. The band was playing loudly, which I could hear from inside the room. When the TV went off, there was nothing to keep me entertained. It was pure boredom but I knew if I joined my friends I would end up drinking. I toughed it out though and it paid off.

Ernest and I returned to Alabama where I stayed for two weeks to spend time with my girlfriend, Margaret. Then I returned to Florida where I was staying with Phil Heinen. I lived with them until May and competed in every RCA rodeo in the state that winter and spring and won most of the bull ridings I entered. By November, I was named the Bull Riding Champion of Florida and received a nice plaque from the Florida Cattleman's Association. It had my name on it and read, "Bull Rider of Florida 1973."

During the Houston rodeo I competed on my first go round bull during the Saturday matinee performance and was to compete at the Silver Spurs Rodeo in Kissimmee during the Sunday morning slack. John Gloor, and Larry Turner were to compete there during the performance. John had a van and I asked if I could ride with them to Kissimmee.

After John said I could I asked if he would mind driving straight through since I was up in the slack in the morning. Then I told him we would have to drive 90, mph all the way to make it in time to compete. I also told him we would have to gas and go each time we needed to fuel up and we wouldn't have time to stop and eat along the way. John said that was fine with him and we would drive however we needed to. Then I called the rodeo secretary at the Silver Spurs rodeo to tell her where I was and how I was going to try and make it in time for the slack.

The secretary said they would hold my bull to last. The PRCA rule book states, "If a contestant is not ready to compete when it's his turn, stock will be turned out, and once stock is turned out it cannot be brought back." A few cowboys at the Houston rodeo told me, we couldn't make it to Kissimmee in time for slack. I told them we could, but it would be close and we would make it with fifteen minutes to spare.

As soon as the three of us had ridden our first go round bulls, we grabbed our riggin' bags, ran to John's van and headed for Florida. Around 2:00 a.m. I was driving when we crossed into Alabama and was pulled over by a Highway patrolman for speeding. Since I had an Alabama driver's license I was given a citation and let go.

Around 4:00 a.m. we were in North Florida and John was at the wheel. Larry and I were in the back asleep. We awoke when hearing a cop talking to John after pulling him over for speeding. The police officer asked John if he was sleepy.

Yes sir, I am, he replied. The cop said he thought so because the van was weaving on the highway. Then he told John to get one of us up to drive and he wouldn't give him a ticket for speeding. After telling the cop I would drive, he let us go. Little did the officer know it was the wind causing the van to weave.

I drove the rest of the way to Kissimmee, which was more than four hundred miles. As we reached the parking area at the arena, I brought the van to a sliding stop. As I bailed out the driver's door, Larry tossed the rigging bag to me. Slinging it over my shoulder, I ran into the arena. That's when I heard someone say, Barry, you missed the slack. It ended 45 minutes ago.

I couldn't figure out how I could have miscalculated the driving time by so much. After thinking about it for awhile, I remembered that daylight savings time went into effect early Sunday morning, due to the so called oil shortage. Daylight savings time began much earlier that year. I allowed for the time zone change where we would lose an hour for it, but not another hour for daylight savings. We lost two hours that night instead of just one for the Eastern Time Zone, or I would have made it in time to compete.

After John and Larry competed on their bulls during the rodeo that afternoon, we got into the van and drove back to Houston for the second go round.

Chapter Twenty Four

Later in the year during the Hugo, Oklahoma rodeo, I was trying to find a ride to Cherokee, Iowa where I was to compete the next day. Bobby Berger was a very good hand in all three rough stock events and said he was going and I was welcome to fly with him in his plane. A few years later Bobby won a World Championship in saddle bronc riding.

Bobby had a motel room and two other cowboys were staying with him. Sunday morning one of them drove us to the airport, which was a grass strip with no control tower. The sky was dark and cloudy and severe thunderstorm warnings had been posted. Once we were airborne, Bobby flew his plane to the Indian Nation Turnpike which went north nearly to Tulsa.

The clouds were very low and Bobby was going to follow the Turnpike to Tulsa. The further we went though, the lower the clouds were getting and they were darker and stormy looking. I was getting pretty nervous and told Bobby there would always be another rodeo to enter. Then I suggested we turn back. Suddenly we came to a solid wall of black clouds that went nearly to the ground as we were over the hills by now.

Then Bobby began circling the plane in a tight circle with the nose of the plane pointed upward. Around and around he flew the plane while he was looking up at the clouds. I couldn't figure out what he was doing, so I asked him.

Then Bobby said, I'm looking for a hole thru the clouds. He went on to say, sometimes there will be a small opening thru the clouds and the sky will be visible and he was going to fly the plane up thru the hole. After a few minutes of circling his plane, Bobby gave up and flew back to Hugo.

After landing, we grabbed our suitcases and rigging bags and hitchhiked to the motel. The two cowboys were still asleep. Shaking them awake Bobby said, Y'all got to drive Barry and me to the Tulsa Airport. We don't have much time, so hurry and get dressed! He then called Tulsa checking on a commercial flight to Omaha, Nebraska. It was going to be a photo finish to make it in time to catch the flight. Driving 100, plus mph all the way, we made it with only minutes to spare.

Bobby was a model for Lee Rider Jeans and had a friend who lived in Omaha that worked for Lee Riders. Bobby's friend was going to pick us up at the Omaha airport, and drive us to Cherokee.

Shortly after departing from Tulsa, the wind was blowing hard and there was a lot of lightning. As the jetliner was climbing it began bouncing around really hard and I could feel it drop some but it continued to climb. Once we were over 40,000 feet into the sky, we were above the clouds and the sun was shining brightly. Later that day, we heard Tulsa had been hit by a tornado.

Bobby and I arrived in time to compete at the rodeo, where I won fourth place.

212

Another time, I competed at the St. Paul, Minnesota rodeo on a Friday night and was to compete in Douglas, Wyoming the next afternoon. Three other cowboys were riding with me. Bobby Berger was bragging about how we would be driving all night, while he's sleeping in a bed all night. He began to laugh as he said, and I will still be in Douglas before y'all.

Bobby had his plane and was flying to Douglas in the morning. Around noon the following day we were fifty miles east of Douglas, when we spotted an airplane sitting alongside the highway. As we passed by the plane I recognized it and told the guys with me, That's Bobby's plane.

We all began wondering what happened. When I seen Bobby at the rodeo I asked him, why's the plane sitting alongside the highway?

I ran out of fuel, and had to set 'er down on the road. Naturally, he became a little nervous when the plane's engine conked out and forgot to put the landing gear down. He realized his mistake as the plane skidded down the highway on its belly. A motorist came along and helped Bobby push the plane off the highway, then took him to Douglas.

Chapter Twenty Five

During the Wyoming, Michigan rodeo, I was scheduled to compete Wednesday. This rodeo had four performances which were Wednesday thru Saturday night. It was a two go round bull riding. I asked to be up the first performance. In rodeo the rules for two go rounds states that if you start the first go round, you end the second go round. This meant I would compete Saturday night on my second bull. This is what I wanted, as there were two other rodeos I planned to enter for the weekend.

I was thrown off in the first go round but stayed in Wyoming, Michigan until after the second performance Thursday night. I was catching a ride with Sandy Kirby, who was up Thursday night in all three riding events and soon as he was thru competing we left for a rodeo in Edina, Minnesota a suburb of Minneapolis.

This rodeo was a two go round bull riding also. I was up on my first bull Friday night and had my second bull during the Saturday matinee performance. Then back to Wyoming, Michigan for Saturday night and Richmond, Virginia on Sunday.

At Edina, I tied for first place in the first go round with Jerome Robinson but should have won it easily by myself. The bull I rode was named Judge. This bull took one jump out of the chute and went into a spin to the right, jumping and kicking really well while spinning. Judge was a twenty one point bull. Jerome's bull was a seventeen to eighteen pointer as it scattered across the arena, then turned back and perhaps made two rounds before the whistle.

Saturday morning I made reservations for a flight out of Minneapolis to Grand Rapids, Michigan. It was going to be a photo finish making it to the airport in time to catch my flight and a photo finish to the rodeo arena in Wyoming to make it in time to compete there.

Andrea Moon agreed to drive me to the airport and had her car parked close to the rodeo arena in Edina. Andrea was a time keeper and rodeo secretary.

As soon as I was off the bull, I ran behind the chutes, grabbed my riggin' bag, leaped over the fence and jumped into Andréa's car. While I was putting my glove and bull rope into the bag, Andrea was driving as fast as she could to get me to the airport before my flight departed. I was still wearing my spurs, as I knew I wouldn't have time to put them on once I got to the rodeo in Wyoming. I picked up the flight ticket that morning. When Andrea dropped me off, I ran as fast as I could into the airport, with a cowboy hat on my head and spurs strapped to my boots. As I went thru the metal detector, my spurs set it off. Security stopped me and had me remove them. I had to run a long ways to my plane, and they were just closing the door when I hollered, wait for me! I made it just in time.

When I arrived in Grand Rapids, Darrell Coe was waiting for me. While he was driving, I put the spurs back on. When we arrived at the rodeo the bulls were already loaded in the chutes and the bull riding was about to begin.

I hurried and put my rope on the bull drawn for me. By now I was feeling pretty good, since I made it in time to compete but was thrown off for the second time at this rodeo, before making a qualified ride.

Then I caught a ride with Perry Hatfield to Richmond, Virginia for a Sunday afternoon performance. I rode a good spinning bull to win first place. I also won the second go round at the Edina rodeo and first place in the average. I now had four days off until my next rodeo which was in Salt lake City, Utah on Thursday; then Ogden, Utah Friday; Cheyenne, Wyoming Saturday afternoon; and another rodeo in Wisconsin for Sunday. Then back to Cheyenne for the second go round.

At this time I didn't even own a vehicle. My fiancé told me that before we could get married, I would have to have a pickup truck and a camper, as she wasn't staying in motels.

Chapter Twenty Six

Perry and I stayed with Marty Stein and his wife Ann, from Washington, Pennsylvania. The two of them were competing at Richmond and invited us to spend a few days at their home while waiting for the time to head for the next rodeos.

I told Perry about needing to buy a pickup truck. The next day, we went to a Ford dealer in Pittsburgh. I decided on a new F 250 three quarter ton camper special that was on sale. It listed for $3,800, but I got it for $3,250. Since I wasn't from the area, the salesman told me Ford Motor Credit would finance the vehicle. I was to return on Tuesday to pick up my new truck.

Tuesday morning I returned to the dealer, where the salesman informed me Ford would not finance the truck. He then told me not to worry; a local bank would finance it for me.

Really? I asked. Even though I don't live here, a local bank will finance it for me?

Yes they will, the salesman replied. After calling several banks with no luck, I told the salesman about having a checking account with the Owosso Savings Bank, in Owosso, Michigan.

The salesman called the bank for a loan approval, but this bank refused to finance the vehicle. Then I remembered something my brother Curt told me months earlier.

Curt had a small carpet installation business and was hired to install carpet for the loan officer in his home. When he finished the job, the man asked my brother if he would allow him to make payments instead of paying for it all at one time.

Curt agreed, allowing him to make payments. Then Curt told me, he bet I could get a loan anytime if I mentioned his name to the loan officer. I called the loan officer at the bank in Owosso and after telling him my brother had an account there, he asked who it was. Curt Brown, I replied. Oh, I know Curt! You do? I asked trying to sound surprised he knew my brother. He told me how Curt installed carpet in his home. I asked if there was any way he could put the loan for the truck temporarily in Curt's name. I went on to tell him, because of the business I'm in, it will be two weeks before I can get back there to sign the papers.

I have never heard of such a thing. Besides, Curt probably wouldn't do it, he spoke.

Call Curt, and tell him the deal, and he will sign the papers, I said.

By Wednesday afternoon, I was back at the Ford dealer. The salesman I was dealing with said, I know you were planning to be somewhere else on Thursday, but we have decided to let you take the truck even though the papers for the loan hadn't been signed. He told me how they were taking a big risk, and I would have to go straight to the bank in Owosso to sign the papers first. If that is what I need to do, then I will do it and not go to Salt Lake City, I told him. How long will it take to get to Owosso? He asked.

It isn't but 350 miles, I will be there before daylight.

Ok then, here's what I want you to do. At ten tomorrow morning I want you to call me from inside the bank.

Yes sir, I said. Then he handed me the keys to my new truck.

I returned to Marty's home and loaded my clothes and riggin' bag. A Pennsylvania cowboy was entered in the bull dogging at Cheyenne and was going to ride with me from Pittsburgh to Cheyenne. I planned on dropping him off on my way to Salt Lake City. We left Pittsburgh at 5:00 p.m. Wednesday. I knew there was no way I could drive to Salt Lake in time to compete at the rodeo by Thursday night.

The next morning we were in central Iowa, where I stopped to call the banker in Owosso. I'm in Des Moines, Iowa. The dealership back in Pittsburg allowed me to take the truck. Due to the business I am in, it will be two weeks before I can get back there to sign the loan. I promised the salesman it would be done this morning. Get a hold of my brother and have him sign the papers! With that, I hung up the phone before he could respond.

By noon Thursday we were in Omaha, Nebraska. Driving straight to the airport, I boarded a plane for Salt Lake City. The cowboy with me drove the truck on to Cheyenne. After arriving in Salt Lake City around 6:00 p.m. I caught a taxi to the Salt Palace.

This is the civic center where the rodeo was being held. Country singer Chris Ledoux was competing in the bareback bronc riding. Asking when he was up at the Ogden rodeo, He replied,

Friday. He then said he was up during the Saturday matinee performance at Cheyenne, which was the same as me.

Good deal, can I catch a ride? I asked. You bet T.R. will be going with us, spoke Chris.

The bull I had drawn was #66 Brayford of the Swanny Kirby string. When it came my turn to ride and after I had lowered myself onto the bull's back, the flank man spouted, get off him kid! Once I was off the bull's back and out of the chute, the flanker put the hot shot to #66, making sure the bull was awake and ready to buck.

Once I was ready to ride, the gate swung open. The bull leaped from the chute jumping and kicking very hard. After the second jump he went into a spin to the right away from my hand. (Most riders hope the bull will spin into their hand. It didn't matter to me which way they turned back, just as long as they did.) He was jumping and kicking really hard and was a very strong bull (lots of power).

A little before the whistle he jumped out of the spin, which jerked me into my hand. I was just a little off center and began wondering if the whistle had blown. I noticed during the bareback, and saddle bronc riding, it was impossible to hear the timer's hand held whistle, with the fans cheering so loudly. Instead of making a move to get back into the center of the bulls back, as I should have, I was wondering if the whistle had blown and just sat there. The bull took another jump straight ahead which put me further into my hand. I figured the whistle must have blown, so I opened my hand and landed head first onto the arena floor. My body folded up, causing my ribs to separate.

I was in severe pain as I curled up lying on the ground holding my ribs. A few cowboys ran to help. As they were rolling me onto my back, bull fighter and cowboy life saver George Doaks shouted, be careful, it's his chest! George knew all about the injury to my chest.

I told George it was my ribs and not the chest. Then I was carried behind the buckin' chutes, and laid down. First aid personal came to see how I was, and perhaps pack me off to the hospital.

I'll be fine, it's just my ribs, I said to them.

When the bull riding event was completed, several bull riders came to check on me. Swanny Kirby asked if I was ok. Looking up, I said to him, Swanny, you don't know me, but do you remember when you put on the rodeo in Charleston, West Virginia back in 68, and a bull rider was whacked in the mouth and swallowed his tongue?

Yes I do.

I was that bull rider, and this is only the second rodeo of yours I ever competed in, and you have crippled me at both of them.

That was the greatest bull ride I have ever seen he said. While ol' #66 was spinning, I was spurring 'em with both feet, one foot at a time. This caused me to get on tilt when he jumped out of the spin as my right foot was out of him, from the spurring.

One of the judges came over to check on me. Did I make it? I asked. Just as you hit the ground the whistle blew he told me.

If judges back then timed the event as they do today, more than likely I would have received a score. You would have been at least 94, points the official said. I was really disappointed in myself for not doing the things I needed to do to ride #66, two more jumps. Once I was able to get up, Chris, T. R. and I went to the motel. We were in the room for just a little while, when I took a pinch of Copenhagen and put it in my lip. I used to take huge dips but when Chris looked at me he began laughing and said, dad gum Barry, you look like a Buddha. Looking in the mirror, my lower lip was pushed way out and appeared deformed from all the Copenhagen packed in it. Chris was right; from then on I began taking smaller dips.

Friday evening we arrived at the Ogden rodeo. As I attempted to lift my rigging bag from Chris's vehicle he called Rodeo Rose, my ribs hurt so bad, I asked T.R. if he would carry it to the buckin' chutes.

Before the first performance began, a severe thunderstorm moved in. It was raining very hard with lots of lightning and strong winds. I thought there was going to be a tornado. The rodeo performance was canceled and moved to Sunday.

The three of us left Ogden and drove onto Cheyenne for the Frontier Days Rodeo.

I had drawn a bull that wasn't a very good bucker. Around the six second mark, my ribs were hurting more than I could bear so I stepped off him before the designated eight seconds. By now it pained me just to take a breath. I began to run towards the chutes, knowing once I removed the bandage from around the ribs the pain would subside.

Cowboy life saver Wick Peth was close by when making my dismount. When I began running due to the pain, Wick thought I was scared of the bull and he began shouting run! Run! He's going to get you! At first I thought he was serious, so I tried to run harder, which caused more pain. I didn't appreciate what he did but never said anything to him about it.

Knowing I wouldn't be able to compete in the next go round, I went to the rodeo office to inform the secretary I would be turning out my second bull and would send a doctor release to the RCA office in Denver. I would also have to send a release for Ogden, and the Wisconsin rodeo.

While in the office I noticed there was a letter for me. It was from a doctor at Children's Hospital in Wilmington, Delaware with a phone number for me to call. Unable to figure out why a doctor in Delaware wanted me to call him, I placed the call. Once I had him on the phone, he informed me as to how he was one of the doctors who helped with the surgery on my chest. He wanted to know if I thought the surgery worked or not, in case there should be another chest injury like mine. He wanted to know whether to fix it like they did or to try something different.

I think y'all done a great job, and my chest feels stronger than ever I commented.   That's good to hear Mr. Brown.

Would you mind having another x ray taken

and mail it to me? I will reimburse you for the x ray.

I don't mind at all doc. I'm leaving Cheyenne today going to Michigan and will get an x ray in two-three days. As soon as I was off the phone I left the rodeo office, located my truck, and drove straight thru to Owosso.

Salt Lake, City Utah.. Bullfighter, George Doaks.1973

James Fain, Photo,

Chapter Twenty Seven

Arriving at my mother's the next day, we visited for a while and then I got some much needed sleep. Monday morning I was at the bank signing papers for the loan. When I saw Curt later in the day he began telling how worried the loan officer was.

Curt! Every time your brother called he was in a different town and different state. He will have the truck worn out before he gets here to sign the papers.

Four days later I was judging a three day rodeo in Hamilton, Ohio. After this rodeo, I drove down to Opelika, Alabama. My fiancé and I were going to get our blood tests so we could be married.

I arrived in Opelika on Monday and check into a motel. Since I had driven straight thru from Ohio, I went to bed early. The following morning, Margaret came to the room saying her father said I was welcome to stay in their home. He didn't like the idea of her visiting me at the motel.

By Thursday my ribs were still hurting pretty bad, so I decided to take another week off from rodeos. The next afternoon however, Margaret informed me her father was mad because we were getting married. Since she was 17, and me 29, Margaret said we would need to wait until her next birthday in three weeks. You probably ought to leave now though, she said.

My first thought was, where do I go?

Then I retrieved the Rodeo Sports News from my truck to see if there were any rodeos to enter for that weekend.

Crossett, Arkansas and Kankakee, Illinois rodeos were adding a $1,000 to each event but the entries had already closed. The only rodeo in the whole USA that hadn't closed their books yet was in Evergreen, Colorado adding only $300.00 per event. Since I needed somewhere to go, I entered it for the second performance, which was Sunday.

I left Opelika Friday afternoon. Twenty one hours later, while crossing the Panhandle of Texas, I fell asleep at the wheel. I woke right back up and was in the oncoming traffic lane, about to hit a station wagon head on. I quickly pulled over into my lane just in time.

It wasn't long when I woke up again, just before running into the back end of a car going the same direction. Hitting the brakes, I managed to stay awake until the next town which was Vernon, Texas.

After checking into a motel, I left a wakeup call for 10:00 p.m. It was now 3:00 p.m. Saturday, the first performance of the Evergreen rodeo was about to begin.

Entering the room, I headed straight for bed and was out like a light. It seemed like no time at all when the phone rang. It was my wakeup call. Crawling out of bed, I took a shower, got dressed, and was back on the road again, headed for Colorado.

By 8:00 a.m. Sunday, I was in Western Kansas not far from the Colorado State line. I stopped and placed a phone call to enter another rodeo for Tuesday night in Coffeyville, Kansas.

It was around 12:00 p.m. when I arrived at the rodeo grounds in Evergreen. As I prepared for the bull riding, I rubbed the ribs with liniment and then had a cowboy wrap them with an ace bandage.

While riding the bull the judges had drawn for me, my ribs were hurting so much I had to jump off before making a qualified ride. I ran back behind the buckin' chutes and as fast as I could to remove the shirt. The ribs were hurting and the ace bandage was making it worse. I could hardly breathe and having the ribs wrapped was hindering them more than helping.

After the rodeo, I got back into the truck and headed for Coffeeville, Kansas in the Southeastern corner of the state.

By 9:00 p.m. in western Kansas, I stopped and checked into a room for the night, arriving in Coffeeville Monday evening. The county fair was going on and all the motels were full, so I slept in the truck.

I had drawn a real good buckin' bull #1, Gibb of the Sonny Linger Rodeo Company out of Montana. My ribs were feeling much better as I sat down onto Gibb's back. Nodding my head, the chute gate swung open. Gibb took two jumps out of the chute and went into a spin to the right. Around six to seven seconds the bull's head hit the end of the chute gate, causing him to hesitate. He then took one step backwards and began spinning to the right again. I lost my momentum when he hesitated and was thrown off just before the eight second whistle. This cost me winning first place at Coffeeville.

These days, the contestant would receive a reride for the foul. Back then it wasn't considered a foul unless it had been my leg that hit the gate.

Back in the truck and on the road again, I headed for the Jaycee BootHeel rodeo in Sikeston, Missouri. There would be four performances each night, Thursday thru Saturday, with a matinee performance on Sunday. Perry Hatfield had a room so I stayed with him.

Chapter Twenty Eight

The bull riding was a two header (two go rounds). I was to compete Thursday night on my first bull and Sunday afternoon in the second go round. I drew two really good bulls and knew I could win the bull riding if I got 'em both rode.

When I found out I was up Thursday and Sunday, I got out the Rodeo Sports News to see what other rodeos I could compete in Friday and Saturday. Finding four other rodeos, I got on the phone to enter Sioux Falls, South Dakota for Friday afternoon; Shakopee, Minnesota Friday night, and Burwell, Nebraska for Saturday afternoon, then on to Wahoo, Nebraska Saturday night and back to Sikeston for Sunday.

At the conclusion of the first performance at Sikeston, I was sitting in first place. The bull I rode was #20 Jigs'. He was a real good black horned Brahma that spins to the right with a lot of buck and hard kicks.

It rained very hard during the rodeo and my clothes were covered in mud. Before heading out I had to change. I entered those rodeos thinking there would be plenty contestants needing a ride. No such luck though not one other soul was going.

It must have been close to 11:00 p.m. as I pulled away from the arena, making my way to South Dakota. By noon Friday I arrived at the rodeo grounds in Sioux Falls. Having two hours to kill until performance time, I made my way out to the fairgrounds for lunch. Returning to the arena, I visited with friends until time to prepare for another bull ride.

This one was just mediocre, but it left me sitting in third place with one performance left. Since I had a 250 mile drive to my next rodeo that night, as soon as I was off the bull I grabbed my rope and equipment bag, then hurried to the truck. It felt good to be behind the wheel again headed for another rodeo. Even though I've been up for two days now, I wasn't the least bit tired. Somewhere along the way I stopped for supper.

By the time I arrived in Shakopee, the event was in progress. The bull drawn for me to compete on was #100 of the Bob Barns Rodeo Company out of Peterson, Iowa. He was a big, strong, motley faced, muley brindle that spun to the right. When the whistle blew I was still in the middle of his back and took over first place. There were still two performances left, which meant someone else could move me down.

Climbing into the truck, I headed west for Burwell, Nebraska. By 4:00 a.m. Saturday, while passing thru Sioux Falls, I began getting very sleepy so I drove out to the rodeo grounds where I slept in the truck until 8:00 a.m. Then I continued on to Burwell. During this rodeo Paul Mayo, and Randy Magers asked if I was going to Wahoo, as they were needing a ride.

Sure thing, I'm by myself so there's plenty of room I said to them, thinking at the time how I could get a little sleep by having one of them drive. I still had an all night drive to make, back to Sikeston.

After riding at Burwell, I was sitting sixth with one performance left. It wasn't but 160, miles to Wahoo, so I decided to do the driving. This would be the third and final performance for this rodeo. Making a decent ride, I wound up in third place. After receiving my winnings, of $342.00, I began the long drive back to Sikeston.

By 7:00 Sunday morning, I was on I 70, in Western Missouri. The radio in my new truck quit working, there was no air conditioner and the hot August sun was shining directly into my eyes. I was dippin' Copenhagen, smoking cigars, and trying to sing to stay awake.

The first rest area I came upon, I pulled in to throw cold water on my face, hoping to remove the sleepiness I was feeling. I could have stayed and slept for two hours, but was afraid of over sleeping, causing me to miss the rodeo. As I was leaving the rest area, there was a guy, and a girl, hitchhiking. O'boy! I got a driver now. Or so I thought. Picking them up, they began telling of how they had been out there all night trying to catch a ride. They went on to tell me how tired they were and they were coming from Colorado. I didn't dare let one of them drive then, so I fought it on into St. Louis. After dropping the two of them off, I had gone perhaps ten miles when I spotted another hitchhiker. I just knew I had me a driver this time. As this hiker was climbing into the truck, he says, Thanks for the ride man. I'm going to New Orleans. With that, he leaned his head against the window and was out like a light.

Oh no, not him too, I was thinking. Driving fast would usually help keep me awake, but by now it wasn't working. Without realizing it until checking the speedometer, I would be doing 30 mph. I stopped several times for coffee and to throw cold water on my face, and doing whatever I could to stay awake. When I arrived at the Sikeston exit, I dropped the hitchhiker off and went to Perry's room. It was 11:00 a.m. by now. I took a long cold shower, shaved, and changed clothes. This would be my first bath since Thursday. Then I went to the motel restaurant where I ate a big steak, thinking I needed to get some protein in my body.

By 1:00 p.m. I was out at the rodeo, which would begin in one hour and I was very sleepy. A good friend, and sometimes traveling partner, J.W. Farington, aka Roe Hoe, who was a calf roper and bulldogger from Cullen, Louisiana had a camper on his truck.

When I seen him he was on one of his horses. J.W. I'm going to take a nap in your camper. Wake me in an hour will you?

Ok, he replied.

While lying on the bed about to fall asleep, I got to thinking how tired I was, and if I slept for just an hour, I would feel much worse than I already did. With that thought, I got up and went to the arena, waiting for the bull riding to begin. I rode this bull to win the go round. I also won the first go round which made me the average winner and Champion Bull Rider. I was presented with a solid silver buckle. This was the second buckle I won at the Sikeston rodeo in three years. The prize money I won totaled $590.00.

After receiving the buckle, two bull riders, whose names I don't recall, asked if I was going to Grundy Center, Iowa. This was a one performance rodeo on Tuesday. I told them they were welcome to ride with me but I wasn't leaving until the next day.

I was going to get some sleep and was on my way to get a room and go to bed. By 7:00 p.m. I was asleep and didn't awake until noon Monday. The two cowboys caught a ride with someone else.

After eating, I called each of the rodeo secretaries in the other towns where I competed over the weekend. I failed to place at Sioux Falls or Burwell. However, I won first place at the Shakopee rodeo which paid over $400.00 along with winning third place at Wahoo. I had been on six bulls over the four days and rode them all. I drove a total of 2,100 miles, and went without sleep for four days and three nights, except for the four hours I slept in the truck early Saturday morning.

On my way to Grundy Center, for the Tuesday rodeo there, I made a stop to call and enter the Springfield, Illinois State Fair Rodeo for Wednesday. I also entered a rodeo in North Washington, Pennsylvania for Friday night and Boston Massachusetts Saturday, which was a two go round bull riding. I had my first bull there on Saturday afternoon and my second bull Saturday night, and then the Kentucky State Fair Rodeo in Louisville the next day.

My winning continued as I placed third at the Iowa rodeo. Late that night I made my way to Springfield, arriving by dawn. After locating the arena, I parked under a tree for shade and went to sleep. Waking a few hours later, I drove to one of the livestock barns where there were showers. By the time I finished, the matinee performance was fixing to start. The cool shower and clean clothes left me feeling refreshed and ready to ride.

There were thousands of fair goers, young and old, milling about. Animals of all sorts were being readied for judging.

Making my way to the arena, I located the entry office to pay my fees. Then checking the draw sheet to see which animal I would be competing on, a smile came over my face. My draw would be the same bull I won the second go round on at Sikeston, just three days earlier. He was a big brindle with a lot of buck while spinning. I made another successful ride on him at Springfield and was placing first with two performances yet to go.

John Sandeen, who rode bareback broncs out of Minnesota, was working for Rodeo's Incorporated, who were also putting on the rodeo in Louisville the coming weekend.

Earlier in the day, Arkansas barrel racer Joann McKim asked if I were going to North Washington. She wanted someone to help with the driving.

I asked John if he could drive my pickup to Louisville. Then I said I will see you there on Sunday.

Sure thing Barry, I'll take good care of your truck, John replied.

Joann pulled her two horse trailer with a Winnebago. By the time I reached her rig, the horses were loaded. The two of us pulled out and headed east for Pennsylvania, arriving there on Thursday.

This rodeo runs five days, Tuesday thru Saturday. Kim allowed me to stay in her motor home Thursday night, so I wouldn't have to pay for a motel.

Friday night after riding my bull, which didn't buck much, I caught a ride with cowboys from the Northeast that were going to the Boston rodeo. Along the way we fueled up at a truck stop, somewhere in New York. A trucker asked if we were rodeo cowboys. After telling him we were, he asked where all I had been and where we were headed. Once I told him where all I had been the past ten days, the truck driver said I thought us truckers done a lot of traveling, but nothing like you rodeo cowboys!

We arrived in Boston Saturday morning. Competing on both bulls that day, I was thrown off in each of the two go rounds. I spent the night in Boston then caught an early morning flight to Louisville. As I entered the rodeo office the secretary handed me a check. It was my winnings from Springfield for first place. I made another nice ride at this rodeo to win second.

Photo by Bern Gregory

Chapter Twenty Nine

Country music singer George Jones was performing at the Kentucky State Fair. He had come to watch the rodeo and visit with the cowboys. During one of the events, he was in the arena wearing a short sleeve shirt, which is against RCA rules. Arena director John Farris told the Possum he could not be in the arena wearing a short sleeve shirt, so George left.

After the rodeo, he invited several of us to come to his show that night. After telling us which door to come to, he would let us in. When we arrived at the stadium where George Jones was performing, we knocked on the door. When it opened it was the Possum, George Jones, who let us in.

C'mon in boys, he said. Suddenly throwing his hand up in front of me he shouted, all except you, no short sleeves allowed. At first I thought he was serious, but then he and all the band members began laughing.

While on the road, I spoke to Margaret by phone many times. She insisted I set a wedding date.

Margaret, right now there are so many rodeos to go to, I don't know when I will have enough time off for us to be married. When I have three to four days in a row where there aren't any rodeos for me to compete in, I will call with a date.

Monday after the Louisville rodeo I drove up to Indianapolis for the Indiana State Fair and Rodeo. I wasn't to compete until Wednesday night. I had drawn a very good spinning bull that was easy to ride. I messed up though and fell off, which cost me winning the contest. I then drove to northern Minnesota for a rodeo there on Friday night in the town of Virginia.

Failing to place again, I drove all night to southern Illinois for another rodeo in Du Quoin. I won first on #11 Bar Fly of Rodeos Incorporated. This would be the third time I had drawn this bull. The first time was at the Pulaski, Wisconsin rodeo, where he had thrown me off the first jump out of the chute, stepping on my right leg. In just a little while the leg had swollen and I could barely walk on it. That night, Wayne Hall, Tom Hazeltine, and I slept in the car next to the highway somewhere in Wisconsin. By morning my leg was huge and turned all kinda' pretty colors in the night.

We were headed for the Gerry, New York rodeo next and decided to take the ferry across Lake Michigan, rather than driving around the lake. There weren't any boats leaving until the next day, so we slept in the car that night. I left Du Quoin and drove all night to Vinita, Oklahoma to compete there the next day.

I called Margaret to tell her we could get married the following Tuesday after the Vinita rodeo. Then I told her we would have to leave the same day for Saint Paul, Minnesota.

Vannis Heddin, who was a bull rider from Arkansas, rode from Du Quoin to Vinita with me. I made a pretty good bull ride at the Vinita rodeo and should have placed, but didn't. Then I headed for Alabama to get married. It was around 5:00 p.m. when I got out of Vinita. By Monday morning I was 140 miles from Opelika, when I ran out of gas. I was out of cash and had no credit cards, only checks.

I called Margaret to tell her where I was and had run out of gas. She and her father drove to where I was to give me money for gas. By the time we got to Opelika I was ready for bed.

We were married Tuesday morning in Margaret's home church of Providence Baptist in the small community of Beauregard, Alabama. After we said our I do's, we went back to Margaret's parents' home to pack our clothes.

My father in law G.E. (Sonny) Young had a small camper he bought for us. The camper was in Texas and a cowboy friend of her family was coming to visit them and brought the camper to us, but it had some damage as it fell off the truck in route from Texas.

Every hundred miles or so, the back of the camper would spread out and would be almost off the truck. Then I would pull off the road, where Margaret and I would push on each side of the camper at the same time shoving it back together.

After we had it mounted onto the truck, we packed and left for Minnesota. Four and a half hours later we were in Nashville, Tennessee where we stayed for the night. Wednesday we drove all day, arriving in Paw Paw, Illinois that night to visit my sister Gloria and brother in law Bernard Cowles, who was pasturing a church there.

Margaret and I spent all day Thursday with Gloria and Bernie at their home. That night we left and drove to St. Paul, arriving at the Fairgrounds around 4:00 a.m. I always enjoyed returning each year for the St. Paul rodeo, as the Minnesota State Fair was one of my favorites of all.

Friday night at the rodeo, I made a qualified ride to win second place. The next night I competed at the Huron, South Dakota State Fair Rodeo. I had drawn a bull called Fools Gold, which was a Scottish Highlander that had gone all year without a qualified ride being made on him. He also was a National Finals Rodeo buckin' bull. This bull would spin as fast as any bull could and faster than most. He had a reputation for pulling riders down onto its head. He did this to the great little bull rider Randy Magers, two weeks earlier at the Virginia, Minnesota rodeo.

Every time I watched this bull buck, he would go one or two jumps out of the chute, and then go into a very fast spin to the right. When I got on him at Huron, he took one jump and made a round to the left and then reversed directions, rapidly spinning to the right. The longer I rode him the faster he got. Around the seven second mark the bull was spinning so fast it began standing me up on my riding hand. This causes the rider to lean forward and his feet to pull out and go behind his body.

The rider then will come down onto the back of the bull's head. It is one of the last places the contestant wants to be.

Being jacked up on my hand, I began pushing against its back with my riding hand. At the same time I would squeeze tighter with my legs. This continued for some three to four seconds longer. Finally my feet came behind me and down onto the bull's neck I went, in a prone position on top of Fools Gold's back. He continued spinning faster and faster. My body was then slung off him feet first. I went sailing off his back. As my head past his back legs, the bull kicked out, striking me just below my left eye. The blow flipped me completely over and I landed flat on my back.

As I was getting up, I heard the whistle blow, which was closer to fifteen seconds then the mandatory eight. Jim Beaman, a bull rider from Colorado was one of the judges.

Jim, the whistle was mighty long.

I know it was Barry, but you weren't there when it blew, so I can't mark you.

Many of the bull riders thought it was wrong. Some told me I would have been at least 94 points. Marvin Paul Shoulders won the bull riding with a 78, point score. It paid over $600.00 to win the Huron rodeo.

I finished the year ranked 17th in the world standings, missing the top fifteen by only $482.00. If a qualified timer had been hired, I would have qualified for my first National Finals Rodeo.

It was obvious to all the bull riders I had ridden the bull much longer than the required eight seconds. With it being so obvious, the

241

judge should have checked with the timer but he didn't.

The next time I seen the bull riding director Jerome Robinson, I began telling him about what happened at the Huron rodeo. Jerome said he heard all about it and the board of directors were checking into it. He also said one of the fair boards committee men timed the bull riding and probably didn't have a timers card. This is against RCA rules and this person should have never been allowed to be the timer. I never was told the outcome of the board's findings.

My next stop would be in Prairie Du Chien, Wisconsin the next day, then Palestine, Illinois that night. My head and face were really hurting, so Margaret had to make the all night drive to Wisconsin. I rode my bull there and as soon as I was off him, we hurried to the truck and had to drive really fast to make it in time to compete at the Palestine rodeo.

Afterwards, Margaret and I drove to my mother's place in Owosso. She wanted to meet her new daughter in law and had a wedding reception for us.

We stayed four days with my mother and then left for Fort Madison, Iowa. One day Margaret was driving and pulled off the highway to let me take over. In a little while, I asked her to hand me the cup sitting on the dash in front of her. It was my spit cup, which was about half full. As she snatched it from the dash, it spilt all over her. When she realized what it was, she began yelling over and over, Copenhagen spit! Copenhagen spit! She was madder than a wet hen and demanded I stop the truck. As I pulled off the road she jumped out and began taking her clothes off, right there beside the truck in broad daylight. I had to climb into the camper to fetch her clean clothes. I thought it was funny, but Margaret didn't.

We had driven a total of 17,000 miles the first two months we were married. Margaret drove only 1,500 of those miles.

Chapter Thirty

I competed in rodeos from North Carolina to Florida, to Albuquerque, New Mexico then to Stone Mountain, Georgia, Milwaukee, Wisconsin, Omaha, Nebraska, Oklahoma City, Memphis, Tennessee, back to Florida and then to the Cow Palace rodeo in San Francisco, California.

T.R. Wilson rode to San Francisco with us from a rodeo in Florida. From there, Margaret and I went on to Portland, Oregon, James Town, North Dakota, and Chicago.

It was a cold November day when we left Portland, going to James Town. While driving across Idaho we had to cross over a pass to get into Montana. This pass went over a mountain at a high altitude. The Interstate wasn't completed yet and when we reached its end, we had to take a two lane road up and over the mountain. It was raining as we began our drive up the mountain.

We hadn't gone far when Margaret said, Barry that sign said the road is closed.

I told her it was okay, it's only raining. In just a little while though, the rain turned to sleet, then to snow. By the time we reached the top it was a blizzard and we could barely see a thing. Once across the pass, it was all downhill and in no time we were out of the snow and it was raining again.

I believe if we had been just five minutes later, we wouldn't have made it over the pass and would have been buried in the snow. After

Chicago we returned to her parents home in Opelika.

In order to make it in time to compete at most of those rodeos, we had to drive straight through from one rodeo to the next and made many all night runs.

It was now the end of November and my truck wasn't but four months old and had over 38,000 miles on it. I had many more miles on my body in those four months, as I left my truck to catch rides and flew to some of the rodeos.

We stayed at Margaret's parents place through Christmas and lived in the camper as we didn't have a home of our own. After Christmas, we packed up and headed down the road again.

Chapter Thirty One

By the end of December 1973, Margaret and I were on our way to the Sand Hills Rodeo in the West Texas town of Odessa. By now we had a nice over the cab camper, which was fully self contained.

Margaret decided to compete in the barrel racing event, so we were hauling two horses with us this time.

I won third place at the Odessa rodeo, but was thrown off just after the whistle had blown. My right arm had been stepped on and I was in a lot of pain. Medical personal tried to get me into the ambulance for a ride to the hospital.

I told them my wife was with me and how I couldn't leave her alone. I knew she would be frightened, so I had them drop me off at the camper where Margaret doctored the arm. The next day I could barely lift it, so Margaret had to hook up the trailer and load the horses. She drove most of the way to Denver until it began to snow, then I took over.

Neither one of us placed at the Denver rodeo. Twelve days later we were on our way to Homestead, Florida, which is forty-five miles South of Miami. Margaret won the barrel racing event and I took first in the bull riding.

My father in law was at this rodeo and after I had ridden the bull he asked if I thought I was Jim Shoulders, due to the way I spurred 'em.

The rodeo committee presented buckles to each of the event champions in the men's events but not in the barrel racing. Margaret was mad and didn't think it was right.

We left Homestead and headed for the Fort Worth, Texas Livestock Show and Rodeo. In those days the barrel racing event was by invitation only, so Margaret didn't get to compete.

Next we went to Lafayette, Louisiana. I had drawn Black 6, which was a Brangus bull that just a few weeks earlier had been voted on and tied with another bull as the rankest buckin' bull in the world for 1973. This bull would take one jump out of the chute and then go into a very fast spin to the right with a lot of kick.

After the first round, Black 6, slid me back off my rope just a little. This loosened me up and I began spurring with both feet. Somewhere between seven and eight seconds, my riding hand came out of the rope. As it came out of the handhold, which is braided into the rope, my riding hand slid straight up the tail of the rope. I was still spurring with both feet, and holding onto the tail of the rope.

The rule reads that as long as the rider has any part of the rope in his hand when the whistle blows, he is to receive a score. The only exception to this rule would be if the rider's feet touch the ground before the eight second whistle. If this happened, he would be disqualified.

The rodeo fans were cheering loudly as the rodeo announcer told them all about what a great bucking bull Black 6, was and how he was seldom ridden.

My riding hand slid all the way up to the end of the tail of the rope. My hand continued going up and came completely off the rope. By then my hand and arm were straight and well above my head. This caused my body to tip to the left as the bull was still spinning rapidly to the right. I was thrown off and landed flat on my back under #6. Both hind legs were high in the air when I landed beneath him. Then both legs came down with its hooves landing hard on my chest. Springing to my feet I ran for safety.

Then I looked to see if the judges were scoring me; I never heard the whistle blow. One gave a score but the other judge refused, saying I didn't make it. This judge was Billy Tom Steiner, who was the son of stock contractor Tommy Steiner.

Bonnie Boston was the time keeper. She told Billy Tom I made a qualified ride but Billy Tom refused to give me a score. I was told by other cowboys the reason he wouldn't mark me was that they wanted their bull, Black 6, to go unridden in 1974, so he could win the title of bucking bull of the year out right, by himself.

Sleeping in the camper that night, my chest had swollen a little and I felt a little sick to my stomach. Other than that I was fine. Many a bull rider has been killed from having their chest stepped on. However, because of the surgery I had on my chest three years prior, not one bone was broken. All the wire and pieces of bone that was wired into my chest made it much stronger.

I once talked to a doctor about having the wire removed from my collarbone. That doctor told me I should leave the wire in as my collar bone would be much stronger.

Ever since the Lafayette incident, I have always thought there should be a rule saying a Stock contractor's son will not be allowed to judge his daddy's rodeo.

By May, Margaret and I were competing at the Fort Smith, Arkansas rodeo. Deciding to enter the Helldorado Days Rodeo in Las Vegas, Nevada, I also entered Roswell, New Mexico. I was up at Fort Smith on Friday and then flew out of Tulsa Saturday morning for Las Vegas.

While in the rodeo office paying my entry fees, I noticed an update of the top fifteen from the PRCA office with me in fourteenth position. I then realized I had a chance to finish the year among the top fifteen, which would qualify me to compete at the World Series of Rodeo, the National Finals Rodeo.

I bucked off the bull at this rodeo just before the whistle, which cost me winning first.

World Champion bull rider John Quintana, told me about the big horned brindle I had drawn. He warned me that towards the end of the ride the bull will get you in the well.

I had ridden him for about seven and a half seconds when he dropped me inside the spin. The bull was spinning to the left into my hand. As I was sliding down his left side I was looking him right in the eye. Since swallowing my tongue back in 1968, I knew I had to protect my face. I turned my back to him as he threw his head at me, hitting me in the middle of the back with one of his horns. It hurt for just a little while but nothing like if it had been my face.

The next morning I flew to Roswell, where I rode my bull but failed to place. Roswell was a matinee rodeo, so I flew out that afternoon for Tulsa where Margaret picked me up. She had been staying with friends while I was gone. They were Lee and Dixie Wheaton from Mounds, Oklahoma. Lee rode bulls and Dixie ran barrels.

The next weekend we were competing in Amboy, Illinois. For the next three to four weeks, we would be competing in rodeos on the weekends in North and South Dakota, Minnesota, Wisconsin, Illinois, and Iowa. Then during the week days we were back in Oklahoma and Texas.

While at the Wichita Falls, Texas rodeo where I won third place, a good friend from Charleston, Arkansas Denny Flynn, who was a very good bull rider, was telling me he was thinking about quitting rodeo and was going home. Denny rode bulls as good as anyone in the country. I told him about all the rodeos Margaret and I had been going to and he could travel with us. Then I told him we were going to the Sioux Falls, South Dakota State Prison Rodeo next, as soon as the Texas rodeo was over.

Denny agreed to keep riding, and said he would travel with us. When we arrived at the South Dakota State Prison the next morning, the Prison guards told us to keep our camper locked, as we had silverware which consisted of some knives.

We were allowed onto the prison grounds inside the walls of the prison. There were prisoners walking all around and Margaret was frightened. She told me there was no way she was staying in the camper with it parked inside the prison walls. We had driven all night, and needed to get some sleep. Leaving the horses, and trailer inside the walls, we stayed at a motel close by. Returning that evening for the rodeo we had to pull through the prison gate and park inside the prison.

Civilian spectators were seated on one side of the arena with the prisoners on the other side. Hardened criminals were placed into a wire cage to see the rodeo.

Denny had drawn a real good spinning bull which he rode and was winning the bull riding.

I drew a new bull Bob Barnes recently purchased from an amateur stock contractor in South Dakota. I was told this bull had been bucked 205 times without a qualified ride ever being made on him. I rode the bull, to beat Denny for the title of South Dakota State Prison Champion Bull Rider.

Our next rodeo the following day in Illinois was rained out. By Monday we were back in Texas. A couple weeks later, Denny began traveling with other cowboys and went on to qualify for the NFR.

During the 1975 rodeo season Denny was severely injured at the Salt Lake City rodeo. After stepping off the bull he had just ridden, it caught Denny with its horns tossing him high into the air. The bull stood still watching Denny

251

as he was coming down on the top of its head. Just as Denny was about to land on the bull's horns, it threw its head up causing one of its horns to pierce him. As the horn entered his body, it pierced his liver. Denny was hospitalized in serious condition.

Once Denny was well, he was back riding bulls and qualified for the NFR again, where he won the ten head average and was crowned the National Finals Bull Riding Champion.

Chapter Thirty Two

Back in those days a bull's horns were never tipped. Most of them came out of the swamps of Florida, Louisiana, and Texas. Their horns were long and very small at the tips making them sharp. Many of these bulls would hook anything that moved and the stock contractors loved 'em as it was exciting for the fans watching.

I never gave a thought about bulls horns, but once off the bull and he was coming after me, then I would become concerned about those sharp horns, and run for my life. All I thought about before getting on the bull was making a qualified ride.

Joe Pasenni was a stock contractor from Illinois and loved for his bulls to hook the cowboys. Each time one of his bulls left the chute Joe would yell out, buck em'off! Buck em' off! When the bull rider bucked off, Joe would yell, now eat em'! Eat em'!

It didn't bother us bull riders none, we would laugh at Joe, we thought he was funny. The following year after Denny's injury, a rule was passed. All horns must be tipped, and can be no smaller than a quarter. Today they cannot be smaller than a fifty cent piece.

Margaret and I were at the Elkhorn, Wisconsin rodeo, arriving two days before the rodeo was to begin. It was July and there were plenty of shade trees to park our truck and camper under. A day before the first performance, two committeemen came to our camper with a newspaper reporter, asking if we would mind being interviewed as they wanted the publicity for their rodeo. So we did the interview.

We were up during the first performance Friday night. We then left out the next morning for a rodeo in East Dubuque, Illinois for Saturday night and then Sunday we competed at the Hawley, Minnesota rodeo. I ended up winning Elkhorn, and Hawley, but failed to place at East Dubuque.

By the fourth of July we were in Kissimmee, Florida. When it was over we returned home to Opelika. Margaret stayed with her parents while I left in the truck to continue rodeoing.

At Sidney, Nebraska I rode a real good horned brindle of Mike Cervi's. I don't remember this bull's number, but he turned back to the left and was jumping and kicking really hard while spinning. Just as the whistle blew, I was thrown off. My riding hand hit the ground hard but I won the bull riding.

After receiving my check, I drove to Dodge City, Kansas to compete the next afternoon. By the time I arrived the hand was badly swollen. I considered turning out, as I could barely close my hand but it's hard to turn a good bull out at a great rodeo like Dodge City. The bull's branded number was #777 and appropriately named Three Sevens of Harry Vold's.

I rode the bull only a few jumps before losing my rope. I was unable to grip the rope tight enough to hold onto it. Then I returned home to get Margaret and the two of us were back on the road again. Every time we would stop to eat,

Margaret would have me order first and then she would say I'll have the same thing.

I told her she didn't have to eat the same thing I did and to order whatever she wanted. Margaret wasn't used to eating in restaurants. When she was rodeoing with her parents, they lived in a camper, where her mother fixed all the meals.

Early one morning as we were driving through Junction City, Kansas we stopped for breakfast. When looking at the menu, I saw they had a Jalapeno Omelet and ordered one.

I'll have the same thing, replied Margaret. She had no idea what she was ordering. When the waitress brought our omelets, they were green from all the hot peppers in them.

I noticed two waitresses standing behind the counter watching and waiting for Margaret to take a bite. One bite was all it took. Shoving the plate in my direction she said you can have mine, too!

The two waitresses and I were laughing our heads off. From then on Margaret never ordered the same thing as me.

By September we were in Spencer, Iowa for the county fair and rodeo. This was a one performance rodeo on Thursday night, then Barrington, Illinois Friday, which would be the last rodeo for the weekend.

During the summer, I dropped out of the top fifteen. While in the office paying my entry fees, secretary Donita Barns had an update of the top fifteen in each event. Checking it I found my name in fifteenth place. Leaving the office, I hurried back to the infield.

After telling Margaret the good news, I checked the Rodeo Sports News for any other rodeos I could enter for Saturday and Sunday. There was only one rodeo in the whole country whose entries hadn't closed yet but would be in a few hours. It was the Washington State Fair Rodeo in Puyallup. There would be ten performances with $3,000 per event added money, no permits accepted. Locating a phone, I entered the Puyallup rodeo for Sunday. Then I made reservations for a flight out of O'Hare Airport in Chicago Saturday morning to Seattle.

When entries closed, there were only nine other contestants who had entered. Hanging up the phone, I told Margaret, with only ten bull riders entered; I know I can win enough money to at least pay all the expenses. The secretary had informed me there would be four go rounds.

At the Spencer rodeo, I drew good ole #100 of Bob Barns again. Making another successful ride on him for the third time, I took first place each time. Friday night, I won third at the Barrington rodeo. This was an outdoor rodeo and it was very cold and snowing.

Saturday morning Margaret dropped me off at the airport and drove back to our home in Alabama. This would be the longest trip she ever made by herself.

After arriving in Seattle, I rode a shuttle bus to Puyallup, then rented a car and checked into a motel.

Sunday at the rodeo, I got on and rode my first go round bull. I received a low score as the bull did not buck much at all. In fact most of the bulls at this rodeo didn't buck, including the bull I had ridden in the second go round. The stock contractor was Christianson Brothers.

The following Wednesday night I competed at a rodeo in Idaho and was thrown off. I returned to the motel in Puyallup and went to bed. Competing in the third round Thursday, I finished in fourth place. I wouldn't compete in the fourth round until Sunday.

After the performance I caught a ride to Bakersfield, California for a Friday night rodeo produced by the Flying U and owned by cowboy Cotton Rosser from Marysville, California. Bucking off there, I caught another ride to Albuquerque, New Mexico with Bob Marshall who was a World Champion Steer Wrestler from California. With a 700 mile drive ahead of us, we arrived in Albuquerque Saturday evening.

In a few hours I was sitting on the back of another bull. Eight seconds later the ride was over and again I failed to win.

Now I had a decision to make. The last performance at Puyallup would begin roughly in 14 hours. The only way to make it would be to fly out Sunday morning, but then I would have to fly to Omaha, Nebraska for Monday. I decided to turn my fourth go round bull out at Puyallup, even though I was sitting second in the average after three go rounds and only one point behind the leader. There was too much cheating going on at that rodeo. I figured there was no need to let them cheat me again.

Sandy Kirby once told me, after he competed at a few rodeos in the North West, how bad they cheated out there and I should never go. I should have taken his advice.

A barrel racer at the Albuquerque rodeo was going to Omaha and needed someone to ride with her and help drive. She said if I could help with the driving, I wouldn't have to pay for any gas. Since I was running low on funds I turned out at Puyallup and rode with the barrel racer to Omaha.

Chapter Thirty Three

Six days later I was competing in Brooksville, Florida on Sunday and then the Dallas, Texas State Fair Rodeo that night. After the Brooksville rodeo, I caught a ride with a few Florida cowboys who dropped me off at the Tampa Airport where I caught a flight to Dallas.

Before boarding I called my friend John Zormeier, who was now living in Keller, Texas and would be at the Dallas rodeo on Sunday. I told him what time my flight would be arriving.

The weather was really bad when the plane arrived over DFW and we circled the airport for thirty minutes before getting clearance to land. John was waiting for me and the two of us ran as fast as we could to his car.

John drove like he was driving a NASCAR on the track. I knew it was going to be a photo finish making it to the rodeo in time for me to compete.

When I got to the arena, the bull I had drawn which was YD (Yellow Dog) of Tommy Steiner's had already been loaded into the chute. Handing my rope to another bull rider, I asked him to put it on YD while I put my spurs and chaps on. I made it with only minutes to spare.

I rode YD, tying with two other contestants for a third, fourth, and fifth place split. This rodeo had what is called a long go round, and a short round, or finals. In the long round every contestant rides one bull. The twelve highest scores would compete in the finals on Monday night, which would be televised by CBS Sports Spectacular.

The PRCA bull riding director Jerome Robinson was one of the bull riders that tied with me in the long go round. This put us going into the finals tied for third, fourth, and fifth, with another bull rider.

It wasn't until the following spring I heard Jerome had ridden a bull in the long go round at Dallas that he never should have been allowed on. The judges were wrong in their decision to let Jerome have the bull he wanted. What I was told happened from other bull riders, was that Jerome received a reride. Jerome was also up the same performance as I in the long round.

After I had ridden my bull, I was behind the chutes putting my equipment away, when Jerome received the reride. There were two bulls in the reride pen, which the judges were to draw from for Jerome's reride. One of the bulls was #24, Roanie. This bull was in the draw and had just been bucked before Jerome received a reride. Roanie wasn't a very good buckin' bull and Jerome knew this. He also knew he didn't stand a chance of placing in the long round if he drew #24 for a reride.

I don't remember what the other reride bull was, but I do know that he didn't buck well enough to place on either.

There was a good buckin' bull standing in the chutes that a bull rider didn't show up to ride. Jerome knew this bull and he also knew he could place on him if he could convince the judges to let him have that bull for his reride.

After the judges told Jerome what the two reride bulls were, Jerome told them #24, had just been bucked and if he drew him the stock contractor wouldn't want to buck him again so soon. The other reride bull was in the livestock barn and if Jerome were to draw him, he would have to wait for the bull to be brought to the arena. Jerome then told the judges to let him have the bull that was turned out, which the judges did.

Since Jerome was the bull riding director, the judges cheated for him. If it had been me or most any other bull rider, the judges would have drawn a reride from the reride pen. If I had drawn #24, and Tommy Steiner did not want to buck him again so soon, I would have had to ride him at 8:00 a.m. the next morning. Also, if I had drawn the other reride bull, I would have had to wait until he was brought in and loaded. No way would I have been allowed to get on the bull that was turned out, nor should I.

The way the judges did what they did for Jerome was completely against the rules. Nothing was ever done to Jerome or the two judges for what they did at Dallas. By helping Jerome the way they did, some bull riders were cheated at this rodeo, including myself.

These judges knew what they did was against the rules as they were well experienced in rodeo. Both these judges were bull riders. One was a past World Champion and the other had been an NFR qualifier.

Several months later, I was talking to World Champion Bull Rider Butch Kirby about what I heard Jerome did at the Dallas rodeo. Butch told me Jerome had done the same thing at the Houston rodeo the following year, 1975.

Back at the Dallas rodeo for the finals, I drew a pretty good bull but he didn't buck well enough for me to win on. I never placed in the finals or the average. Eight times bull riding Champ of the World, Don Gay, won the short round and the average. Jerome won second in the average and I believe he won second in the short round. Jerome won a pretty good bit of money at the Dallas rodeo but he shouldn't have won a dime.

Back in 1973, after winning the bull riding Thursday night in Spencer, Iowa, my wife and I headed for Abilene, Texas. I was to compete there on Saturday and Ponca City, Oklahoma Sunday. By Friday afternoon we were on I 35 in Oklahoma, when I saw an exit sign for Ponca City.

Margaret, we might as well head on over to the Ponca rodeo. We have plenty of time to make it to Abilene.

The Ponca City rodeo had three performances, which were Friday and Saturday night, with a matinee performance Sunday. There was well over one hundred bull riders entered. Twelve bull riders were out in each performance. All the other contestants had to ride after the performance on Friday night, which is called slack. Jerome Robinson rode his bull during the Friday performance and received a reride.

I didn't stay for the slack or for Jerome's reride. We left and drove to Abilene where I competed on Saturday. After the rodeo we drove back to Ponca City.

I didn't know the bull I had to get on but he ended up being a pretty good jump and kicker that spun to the right. I didn't win any money but thought I could have placed.

Grabbing my rigging bag from behind the chutes, I began making my way towards the truck when I heard someone ask another cowboy who had won the bull riding. He replied, Jerome Robinson.

I stopped dead in my tracks and thought to myself, how could Jerome have won the bull riding, when he wasn't here today to get on his reride draw?

The rules for rerides then were, reride animals are to be drawn first, then draw the stock for the contestants. If a reride is awarded and the animal drawn for the reride had already been drawn for a contestant in the same go round, the contestant that had drawn the animal first gets to compete on said animal before the contestant who had drawn the animal for a reride.

The bull Jerome was allowed to have for his reride was drawn for contestants all three performances. According to the rules, he could not get on the bull until after the rodeo Sunday afternoon. When Jerome checked with the judges to see what bulls were in the rerides, he was told they forgot to draw a reride pen. This was a Walt Alsbaugh rodeo.

263

This stock contractor had very few bulls that bucked very well at all. His best bull at that time was one branded with the letter P. and named Arnold.   This bull was the one all good bull riders wanted to draw as they knew the bull couldn't throw them off. They also knew they were going to win first place every time they rode him.

Gary Kirby, aka Butch, had drawn P Arnold and was to compete on him the first performance. Butch did not show up to get on the bull; he was up at a larger rodeo in the Northwest on the same day.

Since there had been no rerides drawn, Jerome told the judges to let him have P Arnold. Then he told the judges he could not be there Sunday to get on the bull as he had to be at a board meeting in Albuquerque on Sunday. He also told the judges he would take full responsibility.

So the judges allowed Jerome to get on the bull Friday night after the rodeo performance. Both those judges should have been fined for not enforcing the rules. Jerome should have been fined big time for cheating. He also should have been kicked off the board.

I was told when Jerome got to the board meeting; he told the other board members what he had done during the Ponca City rodeo. He was given a slap on the hand and told not to do it anymore.

What a joke!

Again bull riders were cheated out of money from the way things were done. When I heard

Jerome won the bull riding, I dropped my riggin' bag and walked back to the arena to ask the judge how Jerome could have won the bull riding, when he wasn't here to compete on his reride bull today.

Ed Costell, one of the judges, was near the buckin' chutes saying good bye to Walt Alsbaugh. They shook hands and then Walt told Ed, Remember, don't worry about a thing. Jerome said he would take full responsibility for it.

After hearing this, I knew there was no need in saying anything. I turned around and walked back to the truck and headed down the road to another rodeo.

Three months after my chest surgery, I was one of the judges for the Lubbock, Texas rodeo. Ed Costel judged it with me. During the saddle bronc riding event, Hawaiian bronc rider Darrell Kong, won the first round on a really good bronc. Sammy Groves. horse barely bucked. I remember marking the bronc a measly 13 points. The other judge marked Sam's horse an 18. I couldn't believe it.

In the second and final round, Sam had drawn the same bronc Darrell won the first round on and Sammy won the second round on the horse. When Ed and I totaled the two scores together from all qualified rides, Sam was winning third in the average.

That boy is winning way too much average, spoke Ed. Then he tried to get me to lower Sam's score in the second go.

That was a buckin' son of a gun Sam just rode. I'm not changing my score, I told him. The reason he's placing so deep in the average is because you loaded that dud he rode in the first go round. If you had scored the horse like you should have, Sam wouldn't have placed in the average.

Barry, North Washington, PA 1064

Chapter Thirty Four

After the Dallas rodeo, I competed in Liberty, Texas. Bobby Mayo, who competed in the bareback riding, failed to place. The two of us got to talkin' and he told me how he hadn't had a thing to eat that day. Then he asked if I could loan him some money. I didn't have but ten dollars on me but gave him half of it.

A few years earlier when Bobby was winning consistently and I wasn't, he asked Sandy Kirby why he was always hauling those dead weights. He was referring to me and a couple other cowboys. Now here in Liberty, Texas Bobby was broke and needing some help, just as I, and most rodeo cowboys do at some time or another.

I left Liberty and caught a ride to Poway, California for their rodeo. I was still in 15th. place in the World standings. After making a qualified ride at the Poway rodeo, I stepped off the bull, landing on my hands and knees. The bull was about to hit me when the bull fighter ran between me and the bull. Placing a hand on my back and the other on the bulls head, he pushed off my back and the bulls head. This boosted him out of the way of the bull.

When he pushed on my back, it shoved me flat to the ground. The bull saw me and hit me in the middle of the back. He didn't know he was supposed to follow the bull fighter. Then he began pushing against my back with the top of his head. It felt as if he was pushing me into the ground. He kept pushing harder and harder and wouldn't stop.

I was beginning to get really scared, as he continued pushing down on my back. Finally, he quit and left. I jumped up and ran to the fence. I thought I was okay, but while walking to the vehicle I was travelling in, a terrible pain hit me in the back and I fell to the ground.

If I moved at all the pain would get much worse. It felt as if someone stuck a knife with a hot blade into my back. I would lie completely still and in just a little while the pain would ease up and go away. Then I was able to get up and continue on with whatever I was doing.

The next day I was still having those pains. I went to the hospital where x rays were taken. A doctor told me I had a pinched nerve in my back.

The Cow Palace rodeo was to begin in just a few days, with ten performances in ten days. It starts the last weekend in October and runs thru the first weekend of November. Rodeo is unlike most all other sports, there are no seasons for rodeos as there are pro rodeos year round.

When I arrived in San Francisco five days later, I was still having problems with the back. I was worried it wouldn't be well in time to compete on my first bull.

A. J. Swaim was a bull rider from Washington State and was ranked sixteenth in the World standings. I finished the year in seventeenth place when the regular season ended in 1973. A. J. finished sixteenth that year and missed making the top fifteen by just a couple hundred dollars. A. J. was interviewed by the Rodeo Sports News after finishing sixteenth in 1973. In the article, he vowed to make the top fifteen in 1974.

I saw A. J. at the Cow Palace rodeo where he asked how much money I had won thus far. After telling him how much I thought I had won, he told me how much he thought he had. I told him it sounded like he either had me by $50 or I had him by $50.

When the performance came for me to ride my first bull, I wasn't able to due to the back injury. I talked to the judges and they agreed to hold my bull back for two more performances.

Two days later I was still having those awful pains and had to turn the bull out. By now I was broke and decided to fly home. I knew my chances for finishing the year in the top fifteen wasn't likely.

A. J. had two good bulls drawn at the Cow Palace. He also entered a rodeo in Harrisburg, Pennsylvania and Sioux Falls, South Dakota. Points from those two rodeos would count towards the 1974 World Standings as they were held before the completion of the Cow Palace rodeo. A. J. told me he had good bulls drawn at every rodeo.

The bull he had at the Harrisburg rodeo was the bull I had ridden at the Landover, Maryland rodeo back in May. At that time before I got on the bull, I was told it hadn't had a qualified ride made on him in five years. I was scored 85, points and was winning the rodeo for a few performances. I left the Maryland rodeo before it was over to compete in Birmingham, Alabama and Tulsa, Oklahoma the next two days.

The bull was Top Cat, of the Cow Town Rodeo Company, out of Woodstown (Cow Town), New Jersey and owned by Howard Harris III. This bull was at the 1974, NFR and threw off Sandy Kirby and Bobby Berger. I was the only bull rider who made a qualified ride on Top Cat in 1974.

Back in the summer of 74, I saw Sandy at a rodeo in Spooner, Wisconsin. He told me I should have won the Landover rodeo. I knew John Davis had won the bull riding, but I didn't know what bull he had ridden to beat me. Sandy told me he rode #1 Lizard.

I had seen this bull buck many times and he has never bucked until just a half second before the whistle. He would be at the far end of the arena, which means he had to cover a lot of ground. He would make maybe one round to the right before the whistle blew. When Sandy told me what bull John had beaten me on, I knew there was no way he should have beaten me.

One of the judges for the Landover rodeo was Chip Golding. He was at this Wisconsin rodeo, too. In fact he rode there with Sandy. When I saw him, I grabbed hold of him by the front of his shirt. I told him I heard how he cheated for John at Landover. He denied it. After I told him Sandy told me all about it, he tried to apologize. I shoved him back and walked away.

After arriving home from San Francisco, I waited until the Cow Palace rodeo had been over for two weeks. Then I called the RCA office to see who ended up fifteenth in the standings.

It's you, Barry, I was told. I beat out A. J. by only $27.00. He bucked off at all those rodeos, trying to beat me out for fifteenth place. I hung up the phone. It was now the middle of November and the NFR would start in three weeks.

Chapter Thirty Five

In those days each contestant had to pay their own entry fee to enter the NFR. I was broke and my wife was nearly six months pregnant with our first child. I called Brother Curt, he agreed to loan the money to pay the entry fee, which was $100.00.

The day came when it was time to head for Oklahoma City. I had to be there two days prior to the first performance. Margaret stayed home and was coming out the middle of the next week.

The NFR has ten performances and there are ten go rounds. I stayed with a friend that was competing at the NFR in the bull riding also. He was a Canadian cowboy by the name of Brian Claypool. Brian allowed me to stay with him at his motel. He knew I was broke and wouldn't be able to pay any room rent.

I told him my wife would be coming out with our truck and camper and then I would be staying with her. Brian even paid for a few of my meals. Around two years later, he and two other cowboys were killed in a private plane crash in Oregon. It was months later before their bodies were found.

At the National Finals, I rode five of the ten bulls I had drawn. I split a fourth three ways on one of them to win a grand total of $62.00. I never won another dime at the NFR.

In the 7th go round, I rode a bull called Tarzan of the Mon Can Rodeo Company, and should have won first in the round. This bull had only one qualified ride made on him during the year, coming into the NFR. Don Gay drew this bull in the third go round and bucked off him within three to four seconds of the ride.

This was the year Don won his first World Championship. John Quintana placed in this go round on a fat, hoggy, brindle that went into a slow spin dragging its butt (no kick) which slid John way back off his rope. The last two seconds of the ride, John was sitting on the flank.

Barry Brown on Tarzan, NFR 1974

I didn't see it, but I was told the ride I made on Tarzan was shown in 1975 on television when advertising the National Finals Rodeo. It's also on the VCR tape titled Most Spectacular Rides of the 1974 NFR.

In the eighth round I rode a bull by the name of Muley, which belonged to the Bob Aber Rodeo Company out of North Dakota. John Quintana rode Muley in the fifth go round and scored 76 points, which won him second in the round. When John rode the bull, it was halfway down the arena before it went into a spin and only made two rounds before the eight second buzzer. When I rode the same bull it went into a spin to the right, first jump out of the chute. While Muley was spinning, he was drifting backwards, which makes it more difficult to ride. When the buzzer blew the bull was still spinning and backing up.

I scored only 74 points on him and didn't place. Sandy Kirby won fourth in this go round and could have received a reride as the bull didn't buck at all.

I also should have placed in another round. The 1974 National Finals Rodeo was the worst judged rodeo I had ever competed in.

After the finals, we returned home. I decided to call the RCA office to log a complaint against the Judges. Hugh Chambliss was Secretary Treasure of the RCA. As I began telling him about the judging at the finals he stopped me.

Barry you don't have to tell me about the judges, many rodeo fans have been calling here daily complaining about them. I hung up the

phone and began thinking about the next rodeo
I would be entering.

Chapter Thirty Six

The Rodeo Cowboys Association became the Professional Rodeo Cowboys Association (PRCA.)

It was now February and we were still pretty low on funds due to having a bad Final's. Margaret was in college at Auburn University and we were living in a trailer park her parents owned in Auburn, Alabama. I agreed to maintain the park in exchange for rent. It was only a few blocks from campus and Margaret would ride her bicycle to class.

Later in the month I drove out to San Antonio, Texas to judge their rodeo. Back in those days the judges had to arrive a day before the rodeo was to begin to draw all the contestants names who entered the rodeo and then we would draw the buckin' stock for each contestant. I was paid $100 dollars per day and was there for eleven days.

There were two go rounds in each event. Ivan Daines was a saddle bronc rider out of Innisfail, Alberta, Canada, and one of the top bronc riders in the country. He had qualified for the National Finals Rodeo six times, winning the average once. In his youth, Ivan competed in the boys steer riding at the esteemed Calgary Stampede, in Calgary, Alberta Canada.

During the San Antonio rodeo, Ivan received a reride in the second go round. The bronc he was riding stuck its nose into the ground causing him to flip and roll completely over Ivan. Neither the horse, which was Tucumcari and belonged to the Butler & Son Rodeo Company, nor Ivan had been injured. Ivan was glad to hear the rodeo announcer say he was awarded a reride.

When the performance was over, I talked to Ivan about his reride. Do you want Tucumcari back or would you rather have one drawn from the reride herd?

I would like to have him back, if I can, said Ivan.

You bet, you have that option.

He thanked me, then turned and walked off. The reride rule then read: If a contestant receives a reride, he can have the same animal back, or demand that one be drawn from the reride herd.

I returned to the office where the other judge, Curtis Hitt, and I had to draw the timed event cattle for the next performance that night. Billy Minick, who was one of the stock contractors, told Curtis and me we needed to draw Ivan another horse. I informed Billy that Ivan wanted the same horse back.

Ivan will not get Tucumcari back! I will not buck the horse again, Billy told me.

Then I explained the reride rule to Billy.

I don't care what the rule says! I am not bucking him again! Repeated Mr. Minick.

All the directors of the association were at this rodeo. After talking to them, each one said my interpretation of the rule was correct and Ivan could have the same horse and for me to hang in there for him. The next day before the matinee performance, Ivan came into the rodeo office to find out which performance he would be competing on Tucumcari.

You're not getting him back! The judges will draw one from the rerides spoke Billy.

At the time I was busy drawing timed event cattle for the performance that day and was unable to speak to Ivan. After the conclusion of this performance, I called Ivan at his room to ask if he still wanted Tucumcari.

Yes Barry, I would like to have him back.

According to the rules, you have the choice and you will get Tucumcari I explained.

Thank you Barry, It's good to finally have a judge who will stick up for the contestants.

Then I placed another call to the PRCA office and spoke with Hugh Chambliss.

Billy Minick is refusing to let Ivan have Tucumcari, claiming the horse could have been injured during the fall.

Hugh told me again I was right with my decision and Ivan should get the same horse back. Returning to the office, I told Billy to load Tucumcari for Ivan the next performance. At first Billy said he wasn't going to buck the horse again. Then he told me the horse belonged to Benny Beutler, of the Beutler and Son Rodeo Company and if Benny would agree to buck him, Ivan could have the horse back.

I immediately left the office to locate Benny. It took forty five minutes to find him. When I spoke his name, he turned around and said, Barry, I am not going to buck Tucumcari. I knew then Billy got to him before I had.

Back in the office after the performance, I was talking with Mike Cervi, who was the main stock contractor for the rodeo. Billy Minick walked over and said, Barry, Tucumcari could have hurt himself when he fell. I will not buck him again!

I told them if they would get a veterinarian out here to check the horse over and if the vet found anything wrong with the horse and gives me something in writing saying the horse shouldn't be used, then I will draw Ivan another horse. I also told them if the vet found the horse should not be used again, I would pay the vet bill. However, if the vet found nothing wrong with the horse, then they would have to pay the bill and buck the horse.

Mike and Billy refused the offer. Later during the rodeo, I saw the two men standing in front of the buckin' chutes talking and laughing. Standing close enough to hear what they were saying, neither one of them noticed I was there.

Mike Cervi said to Billy Minick, Oh, is that all it is, just a $50 fine?

Yes, replied Billy.

That's when I stepped in between the two of them. Billy is wrong! The fifty dollar fine is when an animal that's been drawn for a contestant is shipped out before the contestant gets to compete on the animal. Or if an animal is being housed away from the rodeo grounds, and wasn't brought to the arena the performance it was out, that's a fifty dollar fine, I then told the two of them, this situation was all together different. The horse is here but you are refusing

279

to load it for the contestant. If you don't load Tucumcari, it will be more than a $50 fine! With that said, I turned and walked away.

The motel where I was staying was ten miles from the grounds. It was now Sunday and the last day of the rodeo. I got up a little earlier that morning and drove to the arena. After locating the livestock pens with the bucking horses in them, I began searching for Tucumcari. Once I located him I climbed into the pen and walked the bronc around for a while, watching how he moved. If an animal is hurting, or lame, you can tell just by watching how they move. I determined that Tucumcari was as sound and looked as good as any horse in the pen.

About an hour before the last performance was to begin, I talked with Jerome Robinson. Telling him I needed help, since Billy Minick was still refusing to load Tucumcari for Ivan. Jerome followed me to the office and Billy was there.

Go ahead and buck the horse for Ivan this one time, Billy. All the directors have been talking about the problem and agreed to have a board meeting during the Astrodome rodeo in Houston next week.

The directors decided to change the reride rule to read: If a contestant receives a reride, he may have the same animal back, providing stock contractor is willing.

Jerome then said, just this once, let Ivan have Tucumcari.

No Jerome, it isn't fair to the stock contractor, insisted Mr. Minick. It was obvious to me Billy didn't care what the rules were; he was going to do things the way he wanted.

Jerome turned to me and said, draw Ivan another horse Barry.

I couldn't believe what Jerome just said. All week long he told me I was right. Now he has turned and sided with Billy Minick, telling a judge not to enforce the rule.

.What did you say, Jerome, I asked.

Draw Ivan another horse, he repeated.

Jerome, you are wrong, dead wrong! You and all the other directors told me I was right and to stick with it for Ivan. I have been fighting for him for several days, while Billy cussed me. Then I told Jerome, I am not drawing Ivan another horse. Even if I did he wouldn't accept it. Then I said to Jerome, Ivan should have his entry fees refunded.

During the last performance, I noticed Tucumcari was in the pen behind the chutes with the other broncs which were out that performance. During the bronc riding I spotted Ivan standing in the arena with his chaps and spurs on along with his bronc saddle, waiting for Tucumcari to be loaded. The horse was never loaded. Ivan had been cheated out of his second go round horse; even though he paid his $100.00 entry fee like all the other bronc riders who got to compete in both rounds.

Several years later, I heard Ivan had written and recorded a song about me eating grass, while grazing along the highway. I have never heard the song, if in fact he had recorded it. Five days later at Houston, the first person I seen upon entering the Astrodome was Hugh Chambliss, from the PRCA office.

Barry, Billy Minick was wrong. He and Mike Cervi will have to come before the board during the Hell Dorado Days Rodeo in Las Vegas, in May.

This made me feel better. I figured the directors would fine these two stock contractors big time. After all, they refused to follow the decision of a rodeo official. They also deliberately violated a rule, knowing full well what the rule was. I did not compete at the Las Vegas rodeo but was told the board had fined the two men a measly fifty dollars. I was mighty disappointed when I heard this.

When I was through competing at Houston, I returned home to judge the Montgomery, Alabama rodeo. There was a lot of timed event slack after the rodeo on Friday night. Margaret was sitting in the stands watching and waiting for the slack to end.

I was the field flagger and would not be able to leave until all the slack was completed. Margaret was having labor pains and got the alarm clock from the camper to time her labor pains. The slack ended around 2:30 a.m. and we were home by 4:00 a.m.

Margaret immediately called her doctor, to tell him how close her labor pains were. He told her to get to the hospital. I drove her there and sat with her until the time came to take her into the delivery room. She had our first born around noon Saturday.

I got to see them both for only a few minutes, as I had to be back in Montgomery for the Saturday matinee performance. There was another performance that night and I didn't make it home until around 1:00 a.m. Sunday. I had been up for two days with no sleep, so I went home and went to bed. When I saw Margaret later in the day, she was upset at me for not coming to see her before going home.

We named our daughter Sandy Kaye, after two good friends of mine, which were Sandy and his brother Kaye Kirby.

By the time Sandy was four months old, she had been in twenty five states.

Sandy and Dixie

Chapter Thirty Seven

During the month of July, my brother in law Cotton Young, along with Gary Dymmek, Freddie Gomez, and I left to compete in several rodeos. We drove to Morris Manitoba, Canada where Cotton, Gary, and Freddie were entered in the steer wrestling.

Cotton had a camper shell on the truck and we all slept in it each night. There were no window screens so we all had to sleep with our sleeping bags zipped all the way up and over our heads. It was too hot to close the windows and we sweat all night long because of those huge Canadian mosquitoes.

There was a place to shower on the fairgrounds but there wasn't any hot water. That water was so cold it would take my breath away.

After the Morris Stampede, we competed at the Hawley, Minnesota rodeo. One afternoon we drove into town for supper. After we had eaten and were back in the truck, I turned the key over to crank it and the carburetor back fired. Soon there was smoke coming out from under the hood. We all jumped out, and when the hood was raised we seen the carburetor burning. Running back into the restaurant I shouted give me some flour! With a small pot in hand I ran to the truck and poured it into the carbonator, smothering the flames.

It worked, the fire was out, but now the truck wouldn't run. The flour had messed up the carburetor. We called a mechanic and then got a room for the night. None of us won any money at those two rodeos.

Then we headed for Wyoming, Michigan. This rodeo was to be televised by CBS, Sports Spectacular. There was one long goround in each event. Then the top twelve contestants in each event would compete on the last day of the rodeo in the finals, or championship round. The championship round is the performance that is always televised. I was up during the Friday night performance.

After the rodeo we left and headed for Belle Vernon, Pennsylvania. We were to compete during the Saturday night performance. This was the last performance of this rodeo. I won first place after riding a real good spinning bull of the Rolling Rock Rodeo Company owned by Dave Dancy.

After receiving my prize money check, we loaded the horses and drove back to Wyoming, Michigan. I was placing among the top twelve when we left Friday night and was hoping to be among the top twelve so I would be able to compete in the finals.

We arrived Sunday morning and I went to the office to check the finals list. I had made the top twelve and would be going into the finals in sixth place. Then I went back to the camper where I slept several hours.

When I returned to the rodeo office, I was told I had drawn Fools Gold, of Jim Sutton's.

This was the Highlander bull I rode back in 1973 at Huron, South Dakota when I was cheated by the time keeper. I was glad to have drawn the bull at this rodeo. Even though I was going into the finals in sixth place, I knew I stood a very good chance to win the finals and the average if I could ride Fools Gold once more.

A local business was giving a $1,500 bonus in the bull riding. Earlier in the week, I asked rodeo secretary, Julie Sutton, how the bonus money was going to be awarded. She told me she had asked Jerome Robinson, who was still the PRCA bull riding director, how he thought it should be paid out. Usually these bonuses are awarded to the champion. The secretary told me, Jerome would call her back later in the week before the finals as to how it was to be awarded.

When the long go round was completed, Jerome called the secretary to see if he qualified for the finals. After being told he did not qualify, he told her to give $1,000 to the champion and $500 to the runner up. This is the first time I ever heard the runner up getting part of the bonus. I truly believe had Jerome made the finals, he would have told the secretary to award it all to the champ.

When I rode Fools Gold this time, he was not nearly as rank as when I rode him two years earlier. This trip he went further out from the chutes before going into a right hand spin.

When my score was announced, I knew I had won the Championship round. It wasn't long after that, I was named the average winner and Champion Bull Rider. Then I was interviewed in the arena by CBS, for their telecast at a later date.

About a month later, while at a rodeo in Georgia, a cowboy said, I thought you won the bull riding at the Wyoming, Michigan rodeo.

I did win it, I said.

Well it was on TV the other day, and you weren't on it.

I asked him which performance was shown.

It was the one Jerome Robinson competed in. He went on to say the Championship round in every event except the bull riding was televised. I knew then what the deal was.

Chapter Thirty Eight

A couple weeks later I was selected by the National Intercollegiate Rodeo Association (NIRA) to be one of the Judges for the NIRA finals, which was being held in Bozeman, Montana. I accepted the position and rode with my brother in law Rusty Young and his wife Sally to Bozeman. Rusty and Sally were on the Auburn University rodeo team and both had qualified for the NIRA finals. Rusty also was the NIRA Regional Director for the Ozark region.

College rodeo teams from across the US and Canada compete for points thru the year, for the right to compete at the NIRA Finals. This is where the winners are crowned, College World Champions in their respective events. The University of Tennessee at Martin boys team, won the All Around Championship title.

After the college finals were over, I caught a ride with a few college cowboys to a one performance rodeo in Western Iowa, which I was judging also. Bob Barns was putting on this rodeo. During the bull riding I had given Marty Melvin a reride.

Mr. Barns began yelling at me something fierce. He couldn't stand for a judge to award rerides. I tried to explain to Bob that the bull didn't buck and Marty was entitled to a reride. He continued verbally badgering me and said I would never judge another rodeo of his.

That's good Mr. Barnes; I don't want to work for anyone like you anyways! I gruffly told him. Once the reride was bucked, I stuck around just long enough to receive my check.

Later that night at the room, I had Margaret on the phone. She was wanting to rodeo and we were trying to decide where to meet up at. She was bringing the truck, horse, and daughter Sandy. I told her I would call her in the morning to let her know the time it would be that I was going to have a friend drive me out to Interstate 80, where I was going to start hitchhiking towards the Southeast. I was close to Omaha, Nebraska on the Iowa side and had a long way to hitchhike.

Come morning I spoke with Margaret, telling her to give me a day's head start. Then I told her I would call the next morning to let her know where I was and try to figure out where we could meet up at.

It had taken all day to go two hundred miles and I was still in Iowa. I was at a truck stop exit and stood there until nearly midnight. Finally giving up, I walked to the all night restaurant where I sat all night. Shortly after sunrise, I called Margaret telling her to drive to her Aunt Virginia Wood's home in Nashville, Tennessee and stay there until she hears from me.

Returning to the Interstate and while standing with my thumb out, a bird began chirping. Looking to my left, perched on a fence around forty feet from where I stood, sat a red wing blackbird. Just then it left the fence, flying directly towards me and began circling over head. While the bird was circling, it began trying to peck me. Wearing a felt hat, there was no way it could get to me but I still didn't like the idea of being attacked by a retarded bird.

When I began swatting at it, the bird flew back to the fence where it then began chirping loudly. Then I noticed a few other red wing blackbirds joining this bird on the fence. Now there were four birds watching me and all four of them were chirping loudly. I was getting a little spooked, and began having flashes of Alfred Hitchcock's movie, The Birds. Then all of a sudden, there was a whole herd of red wing black birds flying in, perching on the fence with the others. I decided it was time for me to move. Picking up my bags, I began walking. After a couple hundred feet or so, those birds never left the fence.

Sometime later two young men stopped to give me a lift. They were in a Chevy Impala convertible, with the top down, looking like hippies, while smoking weed. They were going to Florida and drove 90 mph the whole time I was with them.

I got the driver to stop twice so I could call my wife. We decided to meet at the Louisville, Kentucky State Fairgrounds. I arrived in Louisville two hours ahead of Margaret. After she arrived, I got behind the wheel and drove us back to Iowa for another rodeo.

Chapter Thirty Nine

We stayed close to home through most of spring in 1976, competing mainly throughout the southeast. By the first week of May, Margaret, Sandy, and I headed north to Minnesota. We were hauling Margaret's horse so she could compete in the barrel racing event.

By the middle of June we were almost broke and decided we would go stay with my mother in Michigan.

After a few days, I wanted to get back on the road rodeoing again. Plus I knew it was the only way I was going to be able to get any money. The only problem was I didn't have any to leave on.

Margaret and I talked about it and decided I would try and get a loan at the bank, which I was able to do and borrowed $250.00. The Fourth of July week was about to begin.

I rode the bus from Michigan to South Dakota, where I competed at the Belle Fourche rodeo the third of July, and Mobridge, South Dakota that night. On the fourth I competed at Killdeer and Dickinson, North Dakota. Then I caught a ride with some Minnesota cowboys who were going back to their homes. They dropped me off at the airport in Minneapolis, where I flew to Tampa, Florida on the fifth.

Curt met me at the airport and drove us to the Arcadia rodeo, where we both competed in the bull riding that afternoon. Then we went to Kissimmee, Florida for their rodeo that night.

When we got to Kissimmee, I was getting really worried, as I hadn't won any money and the Silver Spurs rodeo was my last chance to win any. I needed to return to Michigan and pay the loan off, get my family, and keep rodeoing.

As luck would have it, I won second at the Silver Spurs rodeo. My nephew, Frank Genest, who was competing in the bull riding at this rodeo, was leaving the next day for Michigan and I rode with him. I paid off the loan, loaded the horse and family, and we headed back to Minnesota for another rodeo.

I continued winning regularly throughout the rest of the summer. One night we were on our way to Burden Kansas. Sonny Linger was the stock contractor and he set the bull riding slack for 6:00 a.m. around 4:00, the truck gave out of gas. We were in the middle of nowhere, somewhere in Kansas. Steering the rig off the road, I left my family as I hitch hiked the rest of the way to Burden. It wasn't long when a carload of cowboys came along and gave me a ride. They, too, were on their way to the Burden rodeo.

By 6:00 a.m. the contest began. With more than 60 bulls to buck, it was close to 8:00 before the bull I had to ride was loaded. He wasn't much of a bucker, so I didn't come close to winning anything.

It wasn't long after I had ridden when Margaret arrived in our truck. A farmer had come along and stopped to see if she was broke down. When he learned of the situation, he returned to his farm for a can of gas.

During the first weekend in October, the two of us were competing in the Bonifay, Florida rodeo. When it was over, we returned home to Alabama.

The following June Cotton Young, his wife Martha, and I traveled to a rodeo in Jasper, Tennessee. The stock contractor was E.C. Hunt, from Huntsville, Alabama. Cotton entered the steer wrestling and me the bull riding.

The bull I had drawn was enormous and very strong. When he threw me off, I was against the chute gate. The bull's hip swung around hitting me hard in the back, breaking five ribs. This bull hit me with so much force my body bent the metal gate latch. Naturally, I fell to the ground in great agony.

I was hospitalized in Jasper, where I was in terrible pain for three to four days. The doctor told me my ribs were broken as bad as they could be, as there was a large gap between the breaks and they were the back ribs. On the fifth day Margaret arrived to take me home.

While signing the discharge papers, a hospital worker asked what I had in my chest. After telling her it was wire, she began telling me about the night I was brought in.

I was the radiologist. After taking that first x ray of your ribs and seeing the wire I thought to myself, that poor man must be lying on pieces of glass. Then she slid her hand under me to brush the glass off the table, but there wasn't anything there. That's when I realized it was inside you.

I thought what she said was funny, but it hurt too much to laugh. After being home one week, I began judging rodeos to pay the bills.

Two months later with the ribs healed, I was again straddling the backs of wild eyed, hookin' Braymers'. My first competition would be in Panama City, Florida.

Margaret's dad, Sonny Young, had his team of doggin' horses there and hauled her barrel horse for us. I would be making another all night drive to Lakeland, Florida for a matinee performance the next day. My family would be returning home with him.

It wasn't long after the rodeo I struck a lope for Lakeland. Around 2:00 a.m. east bound on Highway U.S. 98, 50, miles west of Perry, Florida, a west bound vehicle would not dim its lights. I tried several times to get the driver to dim but he wouldn't. I reckon I asked one too many times though, because as we were passing each other, I heard a gunshot. I immediately fell over onto the seat, while hanging onto the steering wheel and keeping my head just high enough to see over the dash.

A few years earlier, I was told to never stop at any bars in Perry, Florida. Now I understood why. When I got to Perry, I pulled into an all night cafe for a coffee. When I was out of the truck, I began looking for a bullet hole, but never did find one. I then decided the shooter must have shot into the air just to scare me. I got a coffee to go and continued driving a few more hours. Finally I had to pull off the road to sleep. I had the camper on the truck and decided I would get in the bed to sleep.

Once inside the camper, I never turned the light on. As I placed my left hand onto the counter top to boost myself up onto the bed, it felt as if it was covered with sand and gravel. I wondered how all that gravel could have gotten into the camper. As I turned on the light, I saw the screen on the television was broken. The gravel I thought I felt was the glass from the picture tube. At first I wondered how it could have broken. I thought that perhaps I left a bottle in front of the TV and it had fallen against the screen breaking it, but there was no bottle.

Then I remembered the gunshot and when I pulled the TV out to look behind it, I saw a hole in the bottom of the television. Then I looked at the window across from the TV. It was cracked. Checking further, I found the lead at the bottom of the window. The bullet hit the window frame, causing it to crack. I got out of the camper to find where the bullet entered the camper. By now it was daylight and I found the hole.

When that driver fired his pistol, the bullet entered the corner of the camper about twelve inches behind my head. I was pretty spooked by now and wide awake. It left no doubt, whoever done the shooting was aiming for me. I got back into the cab and drove to Lakeland. After arriving at the rodeo grounds, I laid down to sleep a few hours.

When the rodeo was over, I headed back to Opelika and had to pass thru Perry to get home. When I arrived in Perry I made a stop at the Florida Highway Patrol Station. Taking the lead with me I asked the officer if they had any reports of someone shooting at motorists. Then I showed him the lead and told him what happened. The lead flattened out from hitting the window frame and the officer told me it couldn't be traced.

All I can tell you is to drill a hole in it, put a chain thru it, and wear it around your neck for good luck.

With that bit of wisdom, I returned to the truck and continued my journey home. For a long time after the shooting, when meeting a vehicle with their bright lights on, I wouldn't ask them to dim.

Chapter Forty

Margaret was to begin law school in Birmingham, come September. We drove all over the surrounding area looking for a place to live for the next three years. We found a place in Shelby County, close to the town of Alabaster with sixteen acres and a mobile home lot. Then we bought a house trailer and rented the land to have the horses with us.

My daughter was now three years old and I wanted her to grow up knowing the Lord. We visited a few churches during the next few Sundays, and then decided up on Saluria Baptist, in Alabaster.

Then I took a truck driving job, competing in rodeos on weekends, for the next three years. Sometimes Margaret wasn't able to go on the weekends when she had to study for exams. One such weekend Sandy went with me to a rodeo in Fort Stewart, Georgia. It was Saturday night and after stepping off the bull I rode he turned on me, knocking me to the ground. The bull then ran a horn between my legs and was pushing me across the arena. This bull had only one horn and knew how to use it.

I was face down as he kept pushing and mashing me hard against the ground. My face was sliding across the sandy soil, which felt like someone rubbing sandpaper over it. The bull fighter finally got the bull's attention and it went after him. This gave me enough time to get up and run for safety. This is why the bull fighter is also known as the cowboy life saver.

My face was a bloody mess and much of the skin was peeled off it. One of the committee men knew my little girl was with me and while I was being attended to by medical personal; the rodeo committee man located Sandy and tried to get her to go with him. Sandy refused and told him she wouldn't go with a stranger. The rodeo clown overheard Sandy and said I will take you to your daddy. She knew the clown and went with him. Sandy was four or five years old at this time.

I had a really bad headache and my face was burning, since it was raw. Luckily there were two bull riders from Birmingham needing a ride home. One of them drove while I rode in the back seat with Sandy. She took good care of her daddy and was really worried about me. My face was a mess but at least I was able to compete in another rodeo the following weekend.

I quit the job I had and took a job hauling steel out of Birmingham for the O'Neal Steel Company, driving an eighteen wheeler.

Usually I spent no more than one night a week on the road. Once I made a run to Tampa, Florida on Thursday and had to spend the night. It was after dark before arriving back in Birmingham Friday. As soon as I was out of the semi, I ran to my truck and drove home to shower and change clothes. Then I left and drove back to Tampa in my pickup for a rodeo on Saturday.

I returned home after the Tampa rodeo, arriving Sunday morning. I slept a few hours then left out with another load of steel.

Another time when I got back to Birmingham on Friday after working all day, I jumped into my pick up and drove straight through to southwestern Missouri for a Saturday afternoon rodeo. As soon as the rodeo was over, I was back in the truck and drove to Birmingham, arriving late Sunday. Then I climbed into the semi and headed out with another load of steel.

One day I pulled out of Birmingham with the heaviest load of all and was badly over weight. My first stop was at a coalmine not far from Birmingham. I was on a dirt road and missed my turn into the mine. After continuing on a little further, the road made a sharp curve to the left and it was very narrow. Once around the curve there was a very steep hill I had to go up. When I was three fourths the way up, the rear wheels on the truck began spinning, and the tandem wheels were bouncing off the road. The truck was barely moving and I didn't think it was going to make it to the top of the hill.

I was getting very nervous and scared, and even thought of jumping out. I hung in there though and when we made it to the top, the road made another sharp curve to the right and back down the hill we went. I kept the transmission in low gear, and went slowly down the hill. At the bottom of this hill was another sharp curve to the left, and when I got around it, there was a long wooden bridge that looked very old. It didn't appear to be strong enough to hold a pickup, let alone a semi grossing more than 85,000 lbs.

Stopping the truck, I walked out onto the bridge to check it out. When I looked over the side to see what was holding it up, there were only long wooden poles. There wasn't one piece of iron in the bridge anywhere and it looked to be three hundred feet or more to the small creek below.

When I was back in the truck, I sat there looking at the bridge trying to decide whether to attempt crossing or not. There was no way to turn around and it would be impossible to back out. I then decided the only way to get the rig out was by helicopter or across the bridge.

Putting the truck into low gear, I crept across that bridge slowly as possible, figuring if I tried going fast it would cause too much vibration and the bridge would collapse.

As the truck eased across the wooden bridge, I was petrified, expecting it to crumble at anytime. Once across it, I went only a little ways and was out of the woods at a main state highway. Across the road was a church, where a man was mowing the lawn. As I pulled across the highway, he was looking directly at me. I stopped near him and asked how to get to the coalmine.

Did you come across the wooden bridge with that load? He asked. When I told him I did, he replied, there isn't any way that bridge could have held up that load. I was scared slap to death, I remarked. After thinking about it, I decided if I ever got in a predicament like that again, I would leave the truck and walk out regardless how far it was.

Eventually, I lost the job due to traffic violations. My father in law offered me a job working at his Farm and Ranch Supply store in Opelika, where I lived through the week and Margaret would come down on weekends. She was still in law school and stayed in Alabaster through the week.

One Monday after working all day at the feed store, I got into the semi and drove to Siler City, North Carolina for a load of dog food. It was around 6:00 a.m. when I arrived. After backing the trailer to the dock, I climbed into the sleeper for some shut eye. When the workers arrived at 7:00, they would begin loading the trailer. When the job was finished, they would wake me and I would make the drive back to Opelika.

Arriving home late Tuesday, I left two hours later for South Central Oklahoma, to pick up a horse Margaret and I purchased.

Shortly after daybreak Wednesday morning in Dallas, Texas, it was snowing and very cold. As I was driving on the LBJ freeway around the east side of the city, I noticed all the exit ramps on the south bound side were closed. Around forty miles Northwest of Dallas, it was still snowing and I could only drive thirty mph.

I began getting very sleepy and was having trouble staying awake. I grabbed the microphone to my cb, radio and asked if there was anyone on the highway going the same way. Then I said I was falling asleep and needed someone to talk to as it would help keep me awake.

A trucker came on the cb, and said he was going my way and we talked all the way into Oklahoma. I arrived at the Youree ranch owned by Dale and Florence around 1:00 p.m. to pick up the horse, Cruise Control. An hour later, I had the horse loaded and was on my way back to Alabama. Two hours later I was southbound on the LBJ around the east side of Dallas.

Approaching the I-20 exit, I noticed a car almost at the top of the ramp. Then I saw that the roadblock was open, so I figured the ramp had re opened. When I was nearly to the top of the ramp, which was a long steep grade, the rear wheels on the pick up began spinning. The weight of the load behind contributed to the problem. Then the back of the truck began sliding to the left towards the rail, which was perhaps three feet high at the most. I was thinking, if the truck slid into the rail, it would roll over it and I would fall to the highway below, which looked to be several hundred feet. I was really getting scared and my heart was beating rapidly.

I considered jumping out the driver's door but figured the truck would slide into me, knocking me over the rail or pin me against it. With that, I continued easing down on the accelerator and while the wheels were spinning, I turned the front wheels to the right. The truck kept moving forward at the same time it was sliding to the left. Finally, I reached the top of the ramp and the wheels quit spinning. There was a sharp curve to the left and then I crossed over the LBJ. Then there was a long steep ramp going down, which would put me onto I-20, east bound.

The truck was gaining speed so I shifted from second into third gear. By then I started down the ramp and with the clutch still pushed in, the truck was getting faster and faster from the weight of the horse and trailer pushing it.

My heart was beating rapidly again as I was looking through the windshield at the long steep grade covered with snow. I decided then if I left the truck in third gear it would be going way too fast. As I moved the gearshift back into second and began to release the clutch, it caused the rear wheels to begin spinning. Quickly pushing the clutch in, I shoved the gearshift into neutral and let 'er go.

I had a death grip on the steering wheel with both hands to prevent it from moving at all. The truck was wide open when we reached the bottom of the ramp. Luckily for me, it was a straight shot down this ramp or I would have never made it.

Interstate 20, was in much better shape, so I shifted into fourth and was on my way to Alabama. It's a good thing I had a strong heart, or I would have heart attacked twice on those ramps; once going up, and then back down.

Chapter Forty One

Late that night while in Louisiana, I pulled into a truck stop for coffee. Cruise Control had been on the trailer for a good ten hours, so I unloaded him and tied him to the rig. While drinking my second cup, a trucker came in and asked if that was my horse trailer outside. Thinking he must like the looks of my new horse, I told him it was.

Then he said, well, your horse is in the median of the Interstate. Jumping up, I ran to the truck and drove to the Interstate. Spotting Cruise, I stopped the truck and grabbed a bucket of feed and walked to him. After getting him back into the trailer, I never unloaded him again until arriving home around noon on Thursday.

Friday morning I left and drove to Baton Rouge, Louisiana to compete in their rodeo that night. By Saturday morning I was back in Opelika.

Margaret graduated law school in May, and then we moved to Hope Hull, Alabama five miles south of Montgomery. We found twenty acres with a mobile home lot, so we moved our trailer from Alabaster to Hope Hull.

Margaret took a job with Judge Wright, who was the Presiding Judge on the Civil Court of Appeals for Alabama. I was rodeoing close to home, mainly in the Southeast. One week in August, I entered six rodeos in as many days. I would compete first at a rodeo in Camdenton, Missouri on Tuesday night. Manhattan and Hill

City, Kansas the next two days. Then Deadwood, South Dakota Friday, and Hawley, Minnesota Saturday.

On Sunday I would be in Kankakee, Illinois and was back home in Alabama by Monday. In those seven days, I drove a little over 4,000 miles. I bucked off my bulls at Camdenton and Manhattan, but split first place with Charlie Sampson at the Hill City rodeo.

I was mad when I heard Charlie's score announced, as the judges marked Charlie's ride higher than what they scored mine. There was no way it was right. Charlie's bull comes to a complete stop before the whistle had blown.

Charlie became the first black cowboy to ever win a World Championship title in Pro Rodeo. The judges scored him high because of who he was.

After the performance, I went straight to one of the judges, introduced myself and told him I was a former NFR bull rider. I told the judge there was no way Charlie should have been scored more points than I. In fact, I told him, Charlie should have been offered a reride as his bull stopped before the eight second whistle blew. When I left Hill City, I was winning second.

An Alabama bull rider by the name of Joe Wimberley was at Hill City, and glad to see me when I arrived. Due to an injury from a previous rodeo, he was unable to compete and was trying to get home. Being broke, he had no way to get there. I told him he was welcome to ride with me and he wouldn't have to pay for any fuel.

I left my mailing address with the rodeo secretary, and then we headed up the trail for Deadwood, South Dakota. I rode my bull there Friday afternoon but didn't place. Then I drove onto Hawley, Minnesota for Saturday night, where I won first place.

The next day at the Kankakee rodeo I finished in second place, then returned home. A few days later I received a check in the mail from the Hill City rodeo. I tied for first place with Charlie. Talking to the judge paid off, as he raised my score.

Chapter Forty Two

A month later at the Jasper, Alabama rodeo, I drew a bull of E. C. Hunt's, his number I believe was 644, and he never had a qualified ride made on him. I rode him though, for a score of 85, points to win the bull riding by a large margin.

Lyle Sankey was at this rodeo and after I rode 644, Lyle came over and said, thanks Barry, you won me a steak dinner. He bet E.C. I would ride the bull.

The following weekend at another E.C. Hunt rodeo in Georgia, when the bulls were being loaded into the chutes, #644, refused to load. Finally, two cowboys on horseback each had a rope on the bull and had to literally pull him into the chutes. Another bull rider drew 644 and rode him as ole 644, never bucked a lick.

For the next few rodeos 644, would not go into the chutes on his own and never bucked again while E.C. owned him. Disgusted with the bull he was sold to a stock contractor in Mississippi, who produced amateur rodeos. The contestants at these rodeos don't ride as well as the pros. When a bull like 644 has gone un ridden for a long period of time and then gets rode, it breaks their heart and they quit buckin'

At the amateur rodeos the bull riders who drew 644 kept falling off him. This helped the bull to get his heart back and he began bucking once again.

By early October I was in Dallas, Texas judging the Texas State Fair Rodeo. There were ten performances with a lot of slack in the timed events, which would last until 4:00 or 5:00 a.m. After we finished all the slack and during the third performance after the steer wrestling event, I was standing in front of the chutes as many bulldoggers (steer wrestlers) were about to exit the arena. Before they walked out the gate, they stepped over and each one told me what a great job I was doing flagging the event. The last steer wrestler was Gary Green, who was an NFR steer wrestler from Louisiana and he said it was the best flagging he had ever seen. I thought it was mighty nice of those guys to take the time to tell me.

During the Circle D Ranch rodeo in Marianna, Florida, after stepping off a bull, he was on me immediately, knocking me to the ground. He then proceeded to hit me with his horns, while stepping all over me before the bullfighter could get him off. My ribs were badly bruised and it hurt just to walk.

Six days later I was thrown off a bull at the Arcadia, Florida rodeo. I hit the ground hard and was in a lot of pain, obviously the ribs hadn't healed. This was on Saturday afternoon and I was to compete during the Kissimmee, rodeo that night.

When we left Arcadia, Margaret had to drive as I could barely move. On our way to Kissimmee, I decided not to ride there and planned on turning the bull out I had drawn.

Then I got to thinking about the $150.00 entry fee I just lost at the Arcadia rodeo. I needed to win at Kissimmee to make up for the money lost.

In the next six days I had five Midwestern rodeos to compete in, with the first one in Madison, Wisconsin the next day.

Ten minutes before getting on the bull at Kissimmee, I began soaking my ribs with horse liniment, hoping it would ease away some of the pain. My ribs were really hurting as I pulled myself up the chute gate. When I sat down on the bull's back, he began to jump and thrash around inside the chute. This caused the ribs to hurt even more. I made a qualified ride on the bull and when I stepped off him, I hit the ground and couldn't move.

George Doaks, who was the bullfighter, could tell I was in a lot of pain and not able to get up from the ground. Scooping me up in his arms he literally carried me back to the chutes. I won second place and $910.00. It had been well worth all the pain and suffering. When I got to the truck Margaret said to me, George thinks you're in really bad shape and don't need to go to those other rodeos. I already decided I needed to go home to let my ribs heal.

At the Montgomery rodeo, I drew bull number #644, which was the same bull I rode and won the Jasper rodeo on just a couple years earlier. After the bull was sent to the amateur rodeos in Mississippi, he made a comeback and was buckin' hard again. The Harper/Morgan Rodeo Company out of Iowa, Louisiana, which is a PRCA stock contractor member, had purchased #644.

After wrapping the bull rope around my hand, I slid up close to the rope and called for the gate. The bull leaped out of the chute and bucked really hard for two jumps. He then went into a spin to the left, just as he did when I rode him at the Jasper rodeo. Only this time #644 threw me off away from my hand. When I hit the ground my hand was hung in the rope but I managed to stay on my feet.

Instead of trying to grab the tail of the bull rope and try to untie my hand like I should have, I began planting my feet and leaning away from my hand and pulling as hard as I could. My hand wouldn't come out of the rope.

The bullfighter was staying in front of the bull so it would stay after him instead of turning on me. Finally, the bull stepped on my left leg and the rope came loose from my riding hand as I fell to the ground in terrible pain. My left leg was broken and the tibia was sticking out of the leg. Ole 644 got even with me for riding him that first time.

I was taken to Baptist Hospital in Montgomery and Margaret rode in the ambulance with me. The pain was excruciating and I told her I didn't think I could take the pain anymore and was going to quit rodeoing. She repeated this to her brother Cotton, who told her I was from the old school and wouldn't quit.

At the hospital, x rays showed both bones in my leg were broken just below the knee and above the ankle and the doctor said I needed surgery. I told him I didn't have insurance and my wife could drive me to Veterans Hospital in

Birmingham. Leaving the room, he went to tell Margaret what I told him. He also told her there was a lot of dirt in the break and the bone sticking out of my leg was covered with dirt. It was imperative it be cleaned immediately.

Margaret told the doctor to knock me in the head and do the surgery. When the doctor returned telling what Margaret said, I told him to go ahead and operate. During surgery three screws were put into the leg.

When I came to, there was a cast all the way up to my hip. I was hospitalized about a week and then went home. The doctor told me not to put any weight on the leg at all and I was to wear this cast for six weeks. Then I would be put into a cast that would come to just below the knee.

Two weeks later while judging a rodeo at Stone Mountain, Georgia, I was nearly run over by a couple of buckin' horses for being unable to climb the fence to get out of the way. Realizing it was too hard and dangerous judging with a full length cast, this would be the only rodeo I would judge until receiving the shorter cast.

One day when Margaret returned home from work, she began yelling and cursing because the yard hadn't been mowed in weeks. Tired of listening to her, I grabbed the crutches and began mowing. Since I was told not to put any weight on the broken leg, I put the handle of the mower against my stomach and then hop on my good leg, pushing the mower one hop at a time.

The grass and weeds were tall and I could hardly push it at all. Within five minutes I quit and told Margaret she would just have to cuss me, I'm not able to do it.

Another time, Margaret began cussing because the oil in her car was way past due for a change. Again she kept cussing until I said, okay I'll change it. Hopping out to the car, which was a small Chevy Vega, I could barely reach the nut on the pan since the car was so low to the ground. I persevered and got the job done.

Six weeks after breaking my leg, I received the shorter cast. It felt so much lighter and I could maneuver around much faster but the doctor said he wasn't going to put a walking heel on the cast. He didn't want me putting any pressure what so ever on the leg. I asked if I could use the clutch in my truck. No! He replied, not even the clutch.

Shortly after arriving home, I called the PRCA office applying for several judging positions. The first one being in Missouri, then Iowa, Minnesota, back to Iowa, South Dakota, New York, and Pennsylvania. I received every job I applied for. Then I put the camper on the truck to live in while on the road. Since the doctor told me not to use the clutch with my broken leg, I bought a walking stick (cane) to use in place of my left leg.

At first it was hard trying to use the cane as a leg, since the truck had a four speed manual transmission. When first taking off, I would use my right leg to engage the clutch while holding the brake with the cane. Then as I began letting the clutch out once I had it in gear, I would quickly move the cane from the brake to the accelerator.

The first few times I attempted this, I ended up hitting the gas too hard while letting the clutch out too fast. This would cause the truck to lurch forward and stall out. When driving through a town and approaching a stop light, I would put the shifter into neutral and slow way down. Then I would drop it into second gear and hope the light would change before I had to come to a complete stop. I was able to do all this with one leg, without having to use the cane. It didn't take long though and I was using the cane as good as a leg.

During the Buffalo, Minnesota rodeo, stock contractor Bob Barnes told me I wouldn't be judging any more of his rodeos. He didn't like it when a judge gave a contestant a reride at any of his rodeos. George Messimer had been awarded a reride in the bareback riding. I informed him that the judges were hired by the PRCA and I had contracts to judge his next two rodeos.

I was to judge a one performance rodeo in Hampton, Iowa the next day, which was put on by Mr. Barnes. When I entered the rodeo office in Hampton, the secretary told me Hugh Chambliss at the PRCA office in Colorado Springs, Colorado left word for me to call him. It was late in the afternoon and I was unable to make contact with Hugh, so I judged the Hampton rodeo. The next morning as I was leaving town headed for Sioux City, Iowa I stopped and placed another call to the PRCA office. When I had Hugh on the phone he told me I would not be allowed to judge any more rodeos. The Sioux City rodeo had three performances and would pay pretty good to judge and it was the last rodeo I had to judge for this stock contractor. Then I would drive to Gerry, New York for six performances, then North Washington, Pennsylvania for five performances.

I reminded Hugh I had a broken leg and there was no other way for me to earn a living for my family. Hugh again said he could no longer allow me to judge. I was sixteen hundred miles from home with a broken leg trying to earn a living, but was forced to turn around and drive to Alabama.

By August the cast was removed from my leg. Since I wasn't allowed to use the leg at all, it was very small and weak. My right leg had a huge muscle on the calf as I had to do a lot of hopping on one leg judging those rodeos, as it was too hard getting around on crutches. It took over a year to rebuild my left leg to where it was strong enough to begin riding again.

Chapter Forty Three

The 29th of October my son Barry Lee Brown 2nd was born. There were already two Barrys' in the family, so I nicknamed him Bear when he was just a month old.

Bear competed in the chute doggin' event at junior rodeos for a year when he was eight years old. He quit after that, saying he didn't like it.

I began riding bulls again by June after being out three years due to the broken leg. My first rodeo to compete in was in Starkville, Mississippi. I rode a good spinning bull, to win 2nd place. I failed to win at the next few rodeos. Then at a rodeo in Tennessee I was thrown off and hung up to my bull rope. I was banged up pretty bad and was unable to compete for six weeks. During those six weeks I judged a few rodeos and then was back riding again.

I competed in just a few rodeos when I was thrown off and hung up again in my rope, this time being out of competition for eight weeks, but with no broken bones. There was however an injury to the elbow on my riding arm.

One of the rodeos I judged was in Hope, Arkansas, where World Champion Lane Frost was entered in the bull riding. It would be my last time to see him. Lane was killed by a bull during the 1989 Frontiers Day Rodeo in Cheyenne, Wyoming.

At a rodeo in Florida after making a qualified ride and stepping off, I was attempting to run when the bull hit me, knocking me down. Using his head he kept me pinned to the ground while mauling me. It wasn't long until the bullfighter got the bull's attention and it went after him and I made it to safety.

During the drive home Margaret began telling of how our son, Bear, who was only two years old, saw the bull hooking me. He crawled under the fence and started across the arena to rescue his daddy from the bull.

My next, and last, rodeo for the year would be at Biloxi, Mississippi where I took third place, paying $700.00. Little did I know this would be the last time I would ever win anything competing in rodeos.

Four months went by before entering my next contest, in Columbus, Georgia, 20 miles from the ranch.

At the age of 43, my mindset changed. Riding bulls was no longer my top priority. This became clearly evident after my poor performance on a nice easy to ride spinning bull. He was one bull riders refer to as a pup. Five seconds into the ride, I simply fell off. Embarrassed, I hung my head in shame as I exited the arena.

Next I competed at the Arcadia, Florida rodeo where I bucked off two jumps out of the chute. Returning home, I considered hanging up my rope. Quitting something I enjoyed doing for so many years was hard to do. After several days contemplating this, I decided to give it one more shot and went to the Silver Spurs Rodeo in Kissimmee. Again I fell off a real nice easy to ride bull around six seconds.

I decided then and there I wouldn't enter another rodeo until I went to the practice pen and got to where I could ride again. I never made it to the practice pen and never attempted to ride another bull. My bull riding career was over and I knew it. During the three years I was out with the broken leg, I had lost my craving for bulls. I was 43, years old now, and believe all the injuries I received over the years had finally taken their toll mentally, even though I was still in good physical shape.

When I sat on the back of a bull now, I was thinking about what might happen to me, like being stepped on, or the bull sticking a horn in me. Also, I now had three children. My daughter Dixie Ann, born in 1985, completed our family. I could no longer get riding on my mind without thinking I might get hurt or killed and not be with them.

Dixie tying a goat;

Chapter Forty Four

One day in March, my family and I were in the living room watching television. Bear was standing in the middle of the room not far from the fireplace. All of a sudden, both his arms came up and he was being jerked backwards. Then he was jerked over very hard, slamming him against the fireplace. Luckily he wasn't hurt bad or burned but it scared his mother and me to death. We couldn't figure out why it happened.

The next day it happened again and Bear was slammed over backwards hitting the floor hard with the back of his head. This happened two more times that day. By the third day instead of being jerked backwards they switched up and when Bear's arms came up, he was jerked forward and slammed down face first.

During dinner that day, while sitting in his high chair, he was jerked down with his face landing in his food. When Bear picked his head up from the plate, his face was covered with food.

The next day we took our son to Children's Hospital in Birmingham. Bear was diagnosed as having Cycle Motor Seizures. After many tests and brain scans we were given several different medications to administer to our son, along with a shot of steroids we were to inject into his thigh once a day, every day. These seizures continued for the next nine months.

Many times when Bear was having a seizure, I would carry him to the truck and head for the hospital. Within a few miles he would come out of it and then would sleep. I would turn the vehicle around and return home. Then I would make the 120 mile drive back to Children's Hospital where I would tell the doctor the medication wasn't helping at all.

More brain scans were taken and blood drawn. Then the doctor would change my son's medications, hoping it would help to control his seizures somewhat. We were told there was no cure for seizures and all they could hope for would be to find the right combination of medication to help control them.

After taking my son to the hospital for the fourth or fifth time, his doctor decided to do a spinal tap. We were told Bear would have to be hospitalized for two weeks and monitored around the clock. He would also have to be held from food for one or two days before the spinal tap. I stayed in the room with my son for those two weeks.

When the day came for the spinal tap, his mother was there but we were not allowed in the room where the procedure was performed. We waited in the hall as our son was taken into the room. When the spinal tap began, we could hear him screaming in pain and crying. It about drove the both of us crazy.

After two weeks we took our son home. He continued having seizures daily and had several every day.

One time we were at a rodeo in Mississippi and staying at a motel which had a swimming pool. One morning we all went to the pool, just as Bear stepped into the water he had a seizure, which jerked him forward. As soon as his face hit the water, I picked him up and we all ran to the room. While I was holding my son, Margaret called 911.

Before the ambulance arrived, Bear came out of the seizure and wanted to lie down and sleep. Laying him on the bed, we waited for the ambulance. By the time it arrived, Bear was sleeping. The medical personnel came into our room and after seeing him sleeping, they told us there was no need to transport him to the hospital. They went on to tell us that there wasn't anything a doctor could do or give him and we might as well save our money. We thanked them for coming and they left.

All this time, since the seizures began, our son was on a prayer list from Florida to Michigan. My sister Gloria's son, Glen Cowles, is a Baptist preacher in Lawrence, Michigan. His church was praying for our son, as well as my home church in Opelika, which was Providence Baptist. My mother's church was Friendship Bible Church in Keystone Heights, Florida and Ronnie's church, Windsor Baptist, in Windsor, Florida; all had Bear on their prayer list. My preacher, who was the Reverend Joe Sowel, aka Brother Rusty, held special prayer meetings just for my son.

The Youth Minister at my Church told me one Sunday that he wanted me to know he and his wife were on their knees every night before bed, praying for our son. There was no doubt in my mind, God would heal my son, I just did not know when.

By October, my family and I were attending a wedding in Melrose, Florida. Ronnie's son, Ronnie Junior, aka Crow Foot, was getting married. The wedding ceremony was held at Melrose Baptist Church. We put our two youngest children, Bear and Dixie, in the church nursery. During the wedding, a nursery worker ran into the church telling us our son was having a seizure. As we ran to the nursery, someone had called for an ambulance. When we got to our son, his eyes were rolled up to the back of his head and all we could see was the white of his eyes and he was shaking something awful.

The ambulance arrived and Margaret rode with Bear to Shands Hospital in Gainesville and I followed in the truck. The doctor at Shands told us he had what is called a grand mal seizure. Bear was now having other types of seizures, along with the cycle motor seizures. After leaving the hospital with our son, we returned to my mother's home in Keystone for the remainder of the weekend. Sunday afternoon we returned to Opelika.

Monday morning, we took Bear back to Childrens hospital. After telling the doctor about him having the grand mal seizure, more tests were taken. The doctor gave us other medications to try on Bear along with his steroid injections. Before leaving the hospital, his doctor informed us our son was going to have brain damage from all the seizures he was having.

Margaret and I cried as we drove home. It was now close to November and I stayed home with our children while Margaret practiced law.

One day while sitting in the living room, Bear went to the bathroom. In a few minutes Dixie, who was two, came to me saying something about her brother and pointing towards the bathroom. Rising from the chair, I hurried to check on my son. Bear was sitting on the commode slumped over, with both arms jerking. Lifting him up, I carried him to the bed. In a few minutes he came out of it and then he slept.

It was now December and Bear turned four years old the 29th of October. His seizures were increasing to where he was having several daily. About to go crazy with worry, I took him back to Childrens Hospital. I just knew there had to be something else they could do for him.

I was deeply saddened though, when Bear's doctor informed me there was nothing more available to give him.

Mr. Brown, your son has been given every medication available for him. There is a hospital in Maryland you could take him to. They will keep him thirty days where they will monitor him around the clock and even withhold food for a few days. They do this trying to figure out what medications will work best to control the seizures. There was a doctor in Auburn, who had taken his young daughter to the Maryland hospital and they had some success in controlling her seizures. If you want to try that, I will contact the Maryland hospital for an appointment.

I told him I would wait. I wanted my son to be home for Christmas.

The very next day, Bear went all day without having seizures. Then it was two days, then a whole week. We were jumping for joy and praising God. After our son went a week without seizures, I told Margaret, God healed our son. Then I told her I wasn't giving him any more medication or the steroid injections.

Margaret said she would continue giving the medication and his daily shots.

If you truly believe God healed our son, then he no longer needs medication. She was still afraid to withhold the medications but I never gave him another pill or shot. A month went by and Bear still didn't have any seizures. His mother finally stopped all medications too.

I have told this story many times and some would say, your son out grew the seizures. I would tell them there is no way he could have out grown them as they were increasing more and more every day. In fact, the day before they quit, he had the most seizures ever in one day. I then told them there is no way he could have out grown them and that God had healed my son.

It was perhaps a year or two later when I received a call from a woman in Auburn. She gave me her name then told me her baby daughter was having seizures. She went on to tell me she took her baby to the same doctor as my son had. The doctor told this mother she should call me as my son no longer was having seizures and she should find out what all I had done. He went on to tell her that he admired me for being so persistent about bringing my son back to the hospital so many times.

Then I told this mother my son was healed because of all the prayers. It wasn't anything I had done but that God healed my son. I went on to tell her to get her baby on a prayer chain.

My son has been seizure free for nineteen years now and is in college. He has earned his wings, becoming a private pilot.

Chapter Forty Five

I judged several rodeos the remainder of the year. One of them was the Ocala rodeo in September. There were three performances: Friday, Saturday night, and a matinee performance on Sunday. During the second performance in the bareback riding, two cowboys received rerides.

When the last horse out that performance had been bucked, I noticed the first bareback rider who received a reride was sitting on one of the broncs, about to nod his head for the gate. Running to the chute, I told the cowboy to hold up. We, meaning the judges, had to draw between him and the other cowboy to see which one got to draw at the reride horses first.

Leroy Mason was hired by Five Star Rodeo Company to be the arena director for this rodeo. When he heard my explanation of the rules, he began shouting, and cursing. Many spectators heard him using the F, word. Attempting to explain the reride procedure once more, rather than listen he continued ranting and raving.

Mike Gould, the other judge, told Leroy, Barry's right, we have to draw first.

Leroy angrily said, hurry up and draw then!

Pick a number Barry, spoke Mike. I refused, telling him the PRCA rule book states rerides must be drawn, so we have to draw them.

This judge kept on and on trying to get me to pick a number out of his head. I had seen him do this at other rodeos and the other judge would pick a number. It was all wrong doing it that way and I knew what this judge was trying to do. Back then the reride rule read, when two or more rerides are awarded in the same event, the same performance, judges must draw the names of the contestants to see, which contestant gets to draw at the reride animals first. It also states, all stock turned out, (contestant did not show up to compete), will be added to the reride draw, with the designated reride animal. There was one turn out this performance, which had to be put into the draw.

What Leroy did, was when the first reride was awarded, he had the designated reride horse loaded into the chute for the first reride awarded.

Finally the other judge gave in and we drew everything according to the rule book.

During the Sunday rodeo, there were two rerides awarded in the saddle bronc riding. It was just like Saturday night and Leroy had the first bronc rider getting on the designated reride horse. There were two or three horses turned out this performance and they had to be added to the reride draw before any rerides could be drawn.

Again, I had to run to the bucking chute to tell the Florida bronc rider, who was Clay Jowers, to hold up. I began explaining to Clay how the judges had to draw between him and the other bronc rider, to determine who got to draw at the reride horses first.

Yes I know Barry, but Leroy told me to get on this one, Clay responded.

Leroy began cussing again when the other judge said, pick a number Barry. Telling him I would not pick a number, they had to be drawn; Leroy accused me of delaying the rodeo.

I told him we could buck the rerides just before the bull riding or after the rodeo. This is the way it is done at most all rodeos.

No! I am going to buck them right now! Leroy exploded.

That's fine, but we have to draw them first, I repeated.

All the while, the other judge kept insisting I pick a number but we finally did draw them. Clay had to unsaddle the bronc Leroy had him getting on, as he had drawn a different bronc.

While the two contestants began saddling their broncs, we had the steer wrestling event, then the rerides were bucked. Clay's horse fouled him on the chute gate and he was knocked off the horse, receiving another reride. The other bronc rider bucked off.

As I was marking my judge's sheet, someone began shouting, reride, reride, hey judge, why don't you give him a reride too? Over and over it was being said and loud enough for all spectators to hear. Looking up I seen it was the flank man, Lucky Mansfield from Arcadia, Florida. He continued shouting as I walked to the chutes where he was standing, except Lucky was behind the chutes. Lucky, don't say any more. I don't want to turn you in, meaning, report him to the PRCA office.

Turn me in huh? I will give you something to turn me in for! Shouted Lucky.

About this time Leroy had me by an arm pulling me further out into the arena away from the chutes. While Leroy was talking, I kept an eye on Lucky as he entered the arena. He began running towards me and when he got close enough he drew his right arm back with a clinched fist. As he threw a punch, I turned my head and took the shot behind my left ear. I never fought back and never cussed them. I knew if I had, the PRCA would have held me responsible; I'm supposed to be a professional.

Just before the bull riding event, the other judge told me I better watch my back, as he overheard Lucky, and Leroy, talking about how they were going to whup me after the rodeo. About then I saw a cop standing next to the arena fence, with one of the committee men. Speaking to the officer, I told him what the other judge said. I asked if he would walk with me to my car after the rodeo; he said he would. Then I told the committee man Lucky was not allowed in the arena and was to be removed from the remainder of the rodeo. No, he is staying, the man spoke.

Then Leroy took a hold of both arms and began mashing his thumbs into them, shoving me backwards. Barry, why are you causing all this trouble at my rodeo?

To which I responded the problem is you don't know the rules. Now get your hands off me! I knew Leroy was trying to make me out to look like the trouble maker, which worked, as the cop told me not to be causing any more trouble. After the rodeo, the officer walked with me to the car and I drove back to Alabama.

The next day I sent a letter to the PRCA board of directors, explaining everything that took place at the rodeo, thinking the board would fine Lucky and Leroy and perhaps suspend their membership. I was told later by T.J. Walters, who worked in the PRCA office, that Lucky did not have a membership or labor card. Therefore he wasn't supposed to have been allowed to work at any PRCA rodeo. T.J. went on to tell me the board fined Five Star Rodeo Company $1,200 for hiring someone without a labor card. I hated to hear that, as Five Star owned by Troy Weekly, are good people. As far as I know, nothing was done about Leroy.

Chapter Forty Six

After the Ocala rodeo, I never received another judging assignment until April of 1988, even though I applied for dozens of rodeos to judge. When I had Jack Hannom on the telephone, who was the PRCA Judging Supervisor and whose job it is to assign judges for the rodeos, I asked him why I wasn't given any judging assignments.

He said I would no longer be allowed to Judge.

Why not? I asked. He told me I could have handled the Ocala situation differently. Then I asked how else I could have handled it.

You just could have, Jack responded. I was flabbergasted at his non answer. Jack was unable to give an intelligent answer.

Again I told him how I was cussed for two performances and never got loud nor did I cuss any of them. I also told him how I took the punch behind the ear and never fought back and seen to it the rule book was enforced. Even though I did everything right, I still got the blame.

Jack finally gave in and told me to reapply. Then he told me I wouldn't be allowed to judge any of the big rodeos. I didn't like it, but said okay.

Finally, seven months later I was allowed to judge the Ralph Morgan Ranch Rodeo in Meridian, Mississippi. The other judge at this rodeo was the same one I judged the Ocala rodeo with, Mike Gould. During the saddle bronc riding, a reride was awarded to one of the bronc riders. Mike immediately tried to have me pick a number.

I thought, oh boy, here we go again! Telling him we had to draw for the reride. He became incensed, claiming I was accusing him of cheating.

The bronc riding was over and the stock contractors, who were Ralph Morgan and James Harper, were at the roping chute waiting on us judges. It was time for the team roping event and we were at the opposite end of the arena.

The other judge was cursing and trying to get me to fight him. Whenever I tried to get around him, he side stepped blocking my path, angrily shouting out the F word where women and children could hear. Finally, he stepped out of the way but told how he was going to cut me from ear to ear, after the rodeo. This guy had a reputation for pulling a knife and cutting people.

Before the rodeo was over, I asked Gary Dymmek if he would stick around after the rodeo, as I may need some help. I told him what the other judge said about cutting my throat. Gary said he would. During the bull riding, Gary said he talked to Mike who promised to leave me alone.

When I returned home, I sent a letter to the board of directors about the situation at the Meridian rodeo. A few weeks later I received the outcome of the boards' decision.

Mike Gould will no longer be allowed to judge PRCA sanctioned rodeos.

Several months went by until being assigned another job. For the next fourteen years I only got to judge two or three rodeos each year. Finally, I had enough of Jack Hannom and never applied to judge another PRCA rodeo.

Before stopping completely, I attended a PRCA judging seminar during the Southeast Circuit Finals in Pensacola Florida. Judges must attend a clinic every two years to be eligible. The Supervisor usually is the instructor for these seminars. This time he wasn't able to make it but had one of the judges who was judging the circuit finals to teach at the seminar.

I couldn't believe what this so called Pro Judge was teaching at this seminar. He began talking about how the PRCA was coming out with a new rule, called the unintentional Rule. Then he gave an example of what unintentional would be. He told of a bareback rider who was disqualified for missing his horse out, meaning his spurs weren't over the break of the horse's shoulders and touching the horse its first jump out of the chute.

The instructor, who is supposed to be teaching the rules of the PRCA, went on to say that the bareback rider who was disqualified because he left a spur off, had done so unintentionally. Therefore, the judge should have given him a score, as it was unintentional. He then went so far as to say, no where in the book does it say you have to wear spurs.

I couldn't believe this guy could be so stupid saying such things. Unable to take it any longer I had to speak up.

The rule book certainly does say you must have spurs on to receive a marking score. It plainly states, in the bareback and saddle bronc riding, contestants must have spurs over the break of the horses shoulders and touching, when horse's front feet hit the ground the first jump out. Also, a contestant will be fined and disqualified for wearing SPURS that are too sharp.

Then the instructor said, you don't need to have spurs on to spur a horse. Barry, what would you mark someone without spurs on, if they were going through the spurring motion and making a whale of a ride?

I told him I wouldn't score the rider but would instead give him a goose egg (zero) for missing the horse out.

This so called judge then said to me, forget the mark out rule. Tell me what you would mark his spurring ride, without spurs.

I never heard of such idiocy. I sat there thinking about it and scratching my head. Everyone in attendance was waiting for my reply. Finally, I said, I have never heard of such a thing but if I had to mark him, it wouldn't be much.

Why not? He asked gruffly.

Because he isn't wearing spurs, therefore he isn't spurring the horse! I remarked.

Well Barry, I'll tell you what. If I'm ever at a rodeo you're judging and I forget to put both spurs on and you egg (disqualify) me, you and me are going to go at it buddy! Then I said to him, we sure will then, because I will egg you.

After returning home, I called the PRCA office and applied for fifty or more rodeos to judge. Ten months went by and I still didn't receive any assignments. I called Mr. Hannom to ask him why.

Jack told he heard how I went off the deep end at the seminar. Then I asked if he would allow me explain exactly what went on during the seminar and how his judge was coming up with amateur off the wall stuff.

Jack said, Amateur off the wall stuff! That's just like you, Barry. This guy is one of the best judges I have.

You don't have much for judges then, I replied.

Finally, he agreed to hear my side of the story. When I finished, Jack asked, did he really say such a thing?

He sure did, I remarked.

I suppose I should have a talk with him, said Jack.

You sure do.

The call didn't help any though, as I still only received one or two judging assignments per year while the other judge continued judging many of the top rodeos throughout the country.

Chapter Forty Seven

Sandy, my oldest child, was 14, when she became the Alabama Junior Rodeo Association, (AJRA) All Around Champion Cowgirl, competing in barrel racing, breakaway roping, goat tying, and pole bending. She won a nice saddle and buckle.

We bought 40, acres and I began building our ranch. It was just a big field with tall weeds, no fences, with three acres in woods, a well and septic tank. After building the fence, we moved our horses to their new home. I bought an old tractor and bush hog to mow all the weeds, plow the field, and planted it in Coastal Bermuda grass.

We continued living at the old place in a house trailer. I would make the twenty mile drive twice a day to feed and water the horses. Soon after planting the pasture, I began building the barn and arena. Several months later, we decided to buy another trailer and set it up on our ranch as we all were getting anxious to move onto our own place.

During the weekends we were hauling Sandy to high school rodeos and our other two children, Bear and Dixie, were competing in junior rodeos. June of 1991, Dixie, who wasn't quite six years old yet, competed in the Junior Rodeo Queen contest, which was for girls in kindergarten thru the eighth grade. Dixie won the Queen contest, and received a saddle, and buckle.

One of the duties for the Junior Rodeo Queen is to carry the American Flag at all junior rodeos during the Grand Entry and for the National Anthem.

Before moving furniture into the trailer, I had the carpet cleaned in all the rooms. This was done on a Friday afternoon and the next morning we began moving our things into our new home. Margaret had to use the bathroom and when she finished she told me there was something brown in the commode and it was stopped up.

I went to see what the problem was and while standing there looking at the brown thing, which at first I thought was a big turd, until it began moving. All of a sudden that turd turned into a huge snake. Its head was down in the drain of the commode and when it backed its self out, it swung around and up out of the water it came.

Jumping back, I hollered, Snake! Snake! Then it crawled out of the commode and onto the sink. By now I had a stick and went to beating it. Then I picked it up and threw it outside. Margaret brought my rifle to me and I shot it. Everyone ran outside and refused to go back in, until I assured them there were no more snakes.

I just about decided there weren't any when I spotted the end of a snake's tail sticking out from under the hot water heater in the same bathroom. Grabbing its tail, I snatched it out from under the tank. I beat it silly, then carried it outside and shot it.

There were no more snakes but Margaret and the children said they were not sleeping in the trailer. We had already moved all the beds except for the box springs, so they said they would sleep in the truck. I told them I wasn't sleeping in no truck. The five of us ended up sleeping on the same mattress on the floor.

One Friday during the summer we were getting ready to go to a rodeo in Wewahitchka, Florida. After loading the horses into the trailer, I pulled the truck up near the house. Bear and Dixie climbed into the back of the pick up, while I was sitting in the driver's seat. As Margaret reached her side of the truck the kids began screaming loudly.

I had just engaged the clutch and thought maybe the vehicle had rolled forward a little and had run over one of their feet. Leaping from the truck seat, I ran to the back of the pick up but the kids were sitting on the bed of the truck still screaming. Just then Margaret began screeching, Get in the truck! Get in the truck!

After leaping over the tail gate, with Margaret still screaming, I looked to see what she was yelling about.

Just after the kids were in the back of the truck, they saw a fox come out from the woods, running towards the pick up. That fox ran under the truck and took hold of Margaret's foot. She was wearing tennis shoes and the foxes teeth had gotten hung in the shoestring. When I looked to see what she was hollering about from the back of the truck, Margaret was trying to shake the thing loose. I picked up a bucket that

339

was in the truck and threw it at the fox, missing it. By this time Margaret had the truck door open and was hoping on one leg moving backwards, while trying to shake the fox loose. After she was part way in the truck, she slammed the door on her foot hitting the fox, and he turned her foot loose.

The fox then ran under the truck and was headed towards the house trailer. Our dog ran after it, catching it under the trailer and the fight was on. While they were going at it, I ran into the house for a rifle. By the time I got back out there, the fox had gotten loose from the dog and was gone.

We all got back into the truck and went rodeoing. Luckily the dog had its rabies shot.

Three days later we were back home and Margaret went to see her doctor. After telling him what had happened he informed her she needed to take the rabies shots. Then she asked him what would happen if she didn't take the shots and the fox was rabid?

Well hell, you die, replied doctor Thomas.

During the month of November my mother died. We had a funeral service for her at her church in Keystone Heights, Florida. Then her body was flown to Michigan for funeral services there, as our sister Marlene and her children were unable to come to Florida.

My family, as well as all my brothers and sisters all drove to Michigan for the funeral services in Owosso.

Chapter Forty Eight

By July 1995, we moved into our new home we had built, along with an in ground pool. A year later I asked Brother Lyle down in Florida to pick me up ten head of cross bred bull calves. Dixie began roping and I wanted calves for her to practice her roping on. I put in a roping chute and built four bucking chutes at the arena. When Lyle called to tell me he had the calves, I drove to Florida to pick them up. I was putting on high school and junior rodeos at the ranch, which we called [The Bar Five.] Parents from all across the state, and north Florida would bring their children to compete at our rodeos.

When the calves had grown and were too big to rope any longer, I decided to begin bucking them. Once I put the word out about having a buck out, would be young bull riders began coming every week to practice their bull riding. They had to pay five dollars for each bull they got on.

There were so many boys coming out to ride, I needed more bulls. When I would buy other bulls, I offered them for free to anyone that wanted to try them out for the first time. There were always plenty of hands willing to get on a bull for free.

My buck outs were on Wednesday nights, April thru October and Sunday afternoons, November thru March. I also put on a few bull riding schools each year, teaching those who thought they wanted to be bull riders, how to ride 'em. I also had several girls to show up wanting to ride.

Margaret received a call from Cotton one Sunday morning in September. It was around 3:00 a.m. His two sons Brian and Brent had been involved in a terrible automobile accident. They were returning home from a rodeo in Savannah, Georgia when a small sports car traveling at a high rate of speed slammed into the backend of their horse trailer.

It hit with such force, the back gate was knocked clean off the trailer. The blow caused the trailer to break loose from the hitch. The trailer immediately spun around so fast, it slung all three horses, (which were tied in) out of the trailer and onto the interstate. The truck also went spinning around and around.

Brian was at the wheel, while Brent was asleep on the back seat. Brent was knocked onto the floor when the car slammed into them. Thinking Brian had fallen asleep at the wheel; he jumped up, and reaching around Brian, grabbed the steering wheel as the truck was spinning around. His brother shouted, let go! That's when they noticed one of the horses up against the front fender going around with the truck.

When the pick up came to a stop, they were in the center of the medium on interstate 16, between Savannah, and Macon. Margaret's barrel racing horse Alibi was grazing in the medium. When Brent got to her she took off running. Brent, being worried his Aunt Margaret's horse might get hit, took after her.

343

Alibi would run a little ways, stop and begin grazing, but when Brent would get close she would run away from him. By the time he caught the mare they were a good mile from the truck. As he was leading the horse on foot, a man in a pick up truck offered him a ride. With Brent sitting on the tail gate, the lead rope in hand, the driver drove slowly back to where Brian and the truck were.

As Brent began walking towards Brian leading Alibi, he heard a gunshot, then another shot rang out, and another. One of the horses, which was part of a bull doggin' team (the hazing horse) had a severely broken leg, besides other serious injuries.

Brian was crying as he pulled the trigger each time but was unable to kill the horse. Brent grabbed the pistol from Brian's hand, placed the end of the barrel tightly against the horses head pulling the trigger one time, and the horse was dead.

The bull doggin' horse had many injuries to his legs, but was standing. Alibi had only a few small cuts and scrapes but nothing serious. She was the only horse insured.

The trailer was in the ditch off to the right of the road and was totaled. There was a big slide in camper mounted on the truck, which had the whole back end of it torn off. The bed and all their belongings were strewn all over the place. Brent told us he just about got into the camper to sleep on the way home, but then changed his mind. If he had, he would have been slung out with the mattress and likely killed.

Cotton and I took my truck and trailer to get the boys and two horses. After a two week's rest, Margaret was running barrels on Alibi. The doggin' horse had to be put down.

Margaret began telling me she wanted to ride a bull. When she said she was going to get on one during one of my buck outs, I told her she was crazy and she wasn't getting on any bulls.

After several weeks of having to listen to her about getting on a bull I gave in, and as I was heading out the door, I told her to get her spurs. Margaret was forty-five years old now, badly over weight, and had never been on a bull in her life. I knew she was trying to impress a young college bull rider, which she ended up falling in love with. Of course she denied it at the time.

The bull I loaded for her was a two year old brindle I called Brenda. This little bull barely weighed 800, pounds, didn't buck at all, and Margaret nearly rode him that night.

The following weekend was an all girl bull riding at Jeff Disharoom's ranch in Brooks, Georgia sanctioned by the Professional Womens' Rodeo Association (PWRA). There were two performances and only seven girls entered the contest. There were two go rounds and each girl would have to attempt to ride two bulls.

Cotton was the stock contractor for the men's bull riding and I furnished the bulls for the women.

Margaret was upset when she heard she would have to get on two head. She was more upset when she found out which bull she had drawn in the first go round. She knew the bull well, as I had been bucking it for two years. It was #100 and was a big stout Charbray. Margaret was really scared when getting on #100.

I was flanking the bull and didn't want her to get hurt, so I barely flanked him, leaving the rope loose around its flank, in hopes it wouldn't buck as hard as it usually did.

When the bull left the chute, he blew out harder and kicked higher than ever. Margaret was thrown off quick and hard. Before she hit the ground, #100 threw both its hind legs out at her, kicking her in the back with both hooves. She landed on both knees hard. Her right knee was swollen. Her left hand, which was her riding hand, was swollen and her back was bruised. By the next day she was sore all over. I told her not to get on her second bull. She told me she was going to switch and ride with her right hand.

Margaret had drawn Brenda for her second bull and fell off him third jump out. The bull stepped on the back of her left leg and she could barely walk out of the arena.

Two weeks went by and Margaret was feeling much better. There was to be a PWRA all women's' rodeo in Marietta, Georgia in two weeks. This would be the first ever all women's rodeo east of the Mississippi.

Margaret said she wanted to win the All Around Champion Cowgirl title at this rodeo by competing in the breakaway roping, pole bending, barrel race, and bull riding.

I told her she wasn't entering the bull riding unless she practiced first. I knew she stood less chance of getting hurt if she knew what she was doing. At first she did not want to practice but gave in after realizing I wouldn't let her compete in the most dangerous event if she didn't.

During my next buck out Wednesday night, Margaret got on Brenda. After the second or third jump, she opened her hand and came off the bull landing hard on her hip. I was standing behind the chutes, waiting for her to get up. Several of the riders ran to Margaret.

Mr. Barry, Ms. Margaret's hurt pretty bad one of them said.

When I got to her, she was trying to get up but was unable to do so. My two bullfighters, Brian McAwee and Jeremy DeLoach, helped her up and got her out of the arena. When she sat down on the bleachers, I could tell she was in a lot of pain. Then I told her I would bring the truck around and take her to the hospital. She told me the bull riders had come out to ride and I needed to let them.

When everyone's through riding, you can take me to the hospital she said. Around twenty minutes later Brian told me Margaret was in an awful lot of pain and I should take her on to the hospital. I stopped buckin' bulls then, to check on her. She admitted she needed to go, the pain had become unbearable. After helping her up from the bleachers, she was unable to walk. Brian and I were on each side as we helped her to the truck. Margaret kept saying she was going to faint.

When we reached the truck, I had Brian hold her up while I opened the back door to load her

347

in. I couldn't see how we were going to get her into the truck without hurting her more but just then her head went limp. Lifting her head up, all I saw was the white of her eyes. I knew then she fainted. I told everyone to hurry and get her into the truck before she came to. Once we got her loaded into the back seat, I took off for the hospital. My helpers told me they would take care of the bulls before they left. I thanked them and drove as fast as I could.

After x rays were taken, the doctor said Margaret's hip was dislocated and would need surgery in the morning. Margaret had the surgery and the doctor put two screws in her hip. A week later she was back in court trying cases from a wheel chair.

Two weeks later we were at the PWRA rodeo in Marietta. I furnished the bulls and was one of the judges, while Cotton furnished the stock for the other events. Margaret sat in a chair with a full length cast on her leg and could only watch.

It was May, and our son would turn sixteen in October. We decided to surprise him with an early birthday present and bought him a new Mercury Cougar before returning home.

Morgan running barrels in Paris, Texas

Chapter Forty Nine

One night while at the arena, about to begin bucking my bulls, Randy and Joann Esco introduced themselves and their twelve year old son Shane. They told me Shane had watched some bull ridings on television and told his parents he wanted to try it. Randy said they had been trying to find a place like mine for Shane to practice at. They lived ninety miles from the Bar Five but someone at the Montgomery Serum and Western Wear Store told them about my place and bull buck outs. They said they would like to watch the bulls buck that night, and wanted to know what all Shane would need to get started.

After telling them all they needed to know, I gave them the release form they would need to sign and have notarized.

After the buck out, they said they would be back the next week and then asked if I would be having a bull riding clinic anytime soon. I told them I could put one on that coming weekend. They paid for the clinic right then, which cost $250.00 for a two day school. I was now charging $10 a head or three for $25, at the buck outs.

That Saturday morning my bull riding clinic begun. There were a total of three students and Shane got on eighteen bulls in the two days. I could tell this kid liked it and wasn't afraid. Shane come to almost every buck out I had for the next three years. Every week his parents would make the 180, mile round trip so their son would get the practice he needed. I also put on four to five bull riding clinics each year and Shane attended every one of them for two years.

When Shane began his freshman year in high school, he joined the National High School Rodeo Association, (NHSRA) where he competed in high school rodeos throughout Alabama and North Florida.

In June each year the Alabama High School Rodeo Association holds their State High School Rodeo Finals in Montgomery. Shane was in the lead for the State Championship going into the finals, where he maintained his lead and was crowned the High School Bull Riding Champion of Alabama. Shane won his first championship title along with a saddle and buckle. A month later he competed in the National High School Rodeo Finals (NHSRF) in Gillette, Wyoming.

High School students from all across the United States and Canada compete at the NHSRF for a chance to become the National High School Champion in rodeo. In 2006, Shane was in the eleventh grade and again he won the Alabama High School Championship bull riding title.

The NHSRF were held in Springfield, Illinois where Shane received a serious injury and was hospitalized in Springfield and had to undergo surgery. He's about healed up now and can hardly wait to compete at his next High School rodeo

One evening as I entered the barn to feed, I noticed one of the horses had a severe wound over his left hip. Loading the horse into the trailer I took him to Auburn University

Veterinarian Clinic. After cleaning and sewing up the wound, the veterinarian handed me a bottle which contained ninety antibiotic pills. I was told to give the horse forty five pills twice a day. The vet told me I would need to give them for ten days. Then she said they didn't have enough pills to give me the amount I would need as she handed a prescription to me for eight hundred pills. The vet told me the pills were a people medicine and I could get the prescription filled at any drug store.

The next morning I gave my horse its first dosage of antibiotics, then went to a CVS pharmacy in Auburn. The veterinarian had put my horse's name on the prescription, which was Tee Oh. When I handed the pharmacist the prescription, she asked, are you Tee Oh?

Laughing, I said, no ma'am, that's my horse.

After filling the order, the pharmacist said, Mr. Brown these pills are very expensive. When I asked her how much they were she replied, $495.

Never mind, I don't want them, I responded. Then I drove back out to the Veterinarian Clinic. The vet who worked on my horse the night before was there. After telling her how much the pills were going to cost she replied, Barry, I can't believe that. We charge only $25.00 for 500 of those pills and we are making a profit, not much of a profit but still a profit. She then gave me some other antibiotics for the horse.

I realized right then just how bad the pharmaceutical companies are over charging for their medications. I believe that if a doctor prescribes it, the drug companies know the people will buy it regardless of the cost.

Later in the year, I sold one of my bulls to the Harper/Morgan Rodeo Company. I purchased the bull for $461, during the livestock sale at the stockyards in Roanoke, Alabama. I bucked this bull for two years before selling him for $4,000. He has a 78, brand on his left hip and a Bar 5 brand on his left side and his name is Texas Tea. This bull is now owned by another PRCA rodeo company in Mississippi and is still being bucked at rodeos today.

Margaret and I divorced in October after a twenty nine year marriage. We have three children and four grandsons. They all live in Alabama.

In November my pickup truck was stolen. Two days later I spotted my truck with a young man driving it. As he pulled into a parking lot, I pulled my Glock 45, on him and another man, and held them at gun point until the police arrived.

It was the talk of the town as many people saw me holding a gun on those two men. I was wearing my black Resistol hat with a black leather jacket and my Wranglers tucked in my Justin boots. I was told it looked just like a scene out of a western.

Photo by Jerry Gustafson

Phoenix, Arizona 1972,

Chapter Fifty

Three days later on a Wednesday night while bucking my bulls, David Smith, who was a nineteen year old bull rider from Montgomery, was killed in a freak bull riding accident and died in my arena that night.

When David was thrown off, he was lying face down on the ground. His bull rope was still around the bull, with the tail of the rope dragging on the ground. The bull, which I called Brown Gravy, was going away from David. Because David was face down, this caused his spurs to be sticking straight up. As the tail of David's rope was dragging past his feet, the tail popped up off the ground and moved over the top of one of his spurs. Then the rope dropped down over the spur and wrapped around it.

Brown Gravy continued moving away from the fallen rider. This caused the rope to tighten around the bull's middle and as it did, it also tightened around David's spur. Once the rope was tight it lifted him off the ground. Then David looked as if he had been shot out of a cannon, as his body looked to be traveling sixty miles an hour through the air.

David slammed into the back end of the bull, chest first, where he dropped to the ground and died. His chest had been shattered and the Coroner said his heart exploded. The Coroner also said if the injury to David's chest had happened while he was in the emergency room, there wouldn't have been anything anyone could have done to save him. It was David's rope that got him killed, not the bull.

A few days later Margaret told me the Grand Jury was investigating the accident and I might have to testify if they found any negligence on my part. Some of the parents in attendance that night had videotaped the accident and the Grand Jury had subpoenaed them to view.

I was never called to testify, as I was not found to have done anything negligible that caused David's death. Every bull rider knows that bull riding is a dangerous sport. He also knows he could be seriously injured or killed.

Because of the love of rodeo, and bull riding, we would rather take the risk than not rodeo. Rodeoing for a living, even though it meant going hungry at times, is the greatest life there is. Only those that have done it can understand what I am saying here. Even with all the injuries I have had, I would do it all over again if I could. Because of my age though, I had to join the over the hill gang.

Back when I was riding bulls, the tail of our ropes was tightly plaited. Today, bull riders use a rope that is loosely plaited. Over the past few years I have seen many bull riders being dragged by their ropes wrapping around one of their spurs. When this happens the spur rowel is getting hung in the plait of the rope. I have never seen this happen when a rope is tightly plaited, because the rope slips off the spur as it has nothing to grab hold of. David had just begun college at Auburn University two months prior. A year later I sold all my bulls and my ranch was ordered to be sold by a judge because of the divorce.

I couldn't stand the thought of living anywhere near Margaret, as she continued to cause many problems. I moved to Arkansas, where I met a beautiful young woman. Her name was Jennifer Sweeden, but it's now Jennifer Brown. We are living near De Queen, Arkansas with her fourteen year old daughter Chrystal Morgan. I am still involved with horses and bull ridings and have been judging a few PBR bull ridings and also competing in the sport of barrel racing.

When I first began rodeoing back in 1959, barrel racing was the women's event in rodeo. Men rode the buckin' horses and bulls. They also roped calves and dogged steers. These days barrel racing has become big business, with barrel racing horses selling for more than one hundred thousand dollars.

There are many men competing in barrel racing these days but not in rodeo, as it is still the women's event. There have been some men who have filed a lawsuit to allow them to compete in rodeo. So far, the court has ruled that men cannot enter the barrel racing event in rodeos, and I agree with the ruling. Rodeo wouldn't be the same if men were competing in the barrel racing event at rodeos.

Rodeo today is nothing like it was when I first began. It used to be that rodeo was a cowboy event/sport. Today, many of these modern day cowboys come from the city and have never lived on a ranch. Many of them don't have a clue as how to work or doctor cattle, and are in it for the money only, and have no desire to live the cowboy way of life.

I have heard some bull riders say they are scared when they set down onto a bull's back. These guys even said all bull riders are scared and those who say they aren't are lying.

Well, I am not a liar, nor was I ever scared riding bulls. I enjoyed riding 'em and I loved the challenge. Real cowboys want to prove to the horse or bull, it can't throw him off and many of the animals want to show the cowboy he can't ride them.

Due to the many bones I have broken, and the surgeries I had, I've been asked if I regret I ever rodeoed. Never once have I ever regretted rodeoing, and if I could, I would still be riding 'em. I do however regret all the drinking I did. My goals before I quit drinking in 1973, were to rodeo and drink.

As long as I was at a rodeo and had a bull to ride and a beer to drink, I was happy. I have no doubt if I hadn't drunk alcohol the way I did, I could have been a World Champion. Like the Scripture says, you reap what you sow.

Today, there are literally hundreds of rodeo bull riding, barrel racing, and roping associations across America, as well as a few all black rodeo associations. It is illegal however, to have an all white rodeo. Rodeos have changed a lot over the years. It used to be that the cowboys entry fees were the cheapest part of rodeoing. When I first began contesting in RCA/PRCA rodeos, entry fees ranged from $10 for the smaller rodeos, and up to $100 for the larger rodeos. Today, entry fees are upwards to five hundred dollars for one rodeo.

Travel and living expenses were the most costly for the cowboy. To cut back on travel expenses, he would get as many guys as his automobile had room for, to ride to the next rodeo. Everyone would chip in and split fuel costs. Usually when the owner of the vehicle had three or more riding with him, he didn't have to pay for any of the gas, as he was furnishing the vehicle.

Cowboys' rodeoing for a living would easily put a hundred thousand miles or more each year on their automobile, wearing a new vehicle out in a year or two. Many of the riding contestants didn't own a vehicle and had to get to the next rodeo however he could. Many times I had to hitchhike or ride the bus to make it to the next rodeo.

Rodeoing for a living, or trying to qualify for the National Finals, meant living in automobiles, motels, and many sleepless nights traveling from one rodeo to the next. These contestants were on the road eleven and a half months out of the year.

Today you hear bull riders talk about the adrenalin rush they get after riding a rank bull. My adrenalin rush came when I was behind the wheel headed for another rodeo, as well as after riding a rank one.

Many cowboys rodeo on weekends only, as they can't take all the miles it takes to rodeo for a living. Once when I was at the Wyoming,

Michigan rodeo, I tried to get Pat Porter, who was a good Michigan bull rider, to travel with me. Pat told me the way I rodeoed it would be like a job and he enjoyed riding in rodeos too much to make it be like work.

I didn't understand his logic. I loved competing in rodeos so much, it was all I wanted to do. The more rodeos I could get to the better.

Jennifer running barrels

The Modern Bull Rider

Many bull riders today are wearing helmets with a facemask, to protect their head. Back in my day a cowboy would have been laughed out of the arena and called chicken for wearing a helmet.

I don't approve of helmets being used. Cowboys are supposed to look like cowboys, not motorcycle riders. I have no problem with the protective vest most of the rough stock riders are wearing today. At least they have a western look to them.

I believe helmets should only be allowed for those contestants who have had a serious head injury and can produce a medical release. Bull riders, who wear a helmet solely because they are afraid of being kicked in the head or smacked in the face, should take up motorcycle riding instead. If he wants to compete in cowboy events then he should look the part.

I wonder if these helmet wearing bull riders wear their helmets when traveling in an automobile. This is far more dangerous than riding bulls.

But then, time changes everything.

Acknowledgements

Professional Rodeo Cowboys Association,
Colorado Springs, Co. (PRCA)

Pro Rodeo Sports News, Colorado Springs, Co.

Jerry Olson, Belle Fourche, South Dakota

(Author) Christy Fenton Jordan, British
Columbia, Canada

Mrs. Lorayne Brown Pate, Hendersonville, N.C.

Ronnie Brown Gainesville, Florida

(Author) Abe Morris, Denver, Colorado

Jennifer Brown, De Queen, AR.